CARPETBAGGERS, CAVALRY, AND THE KU KLUX KLAN

THE AMERICAN CRISIS SERIES
Books on the Civil War Era

Steven E. Woodworth, Professor of History,
Texas Christian University
Series Editor

CARPETBAGGERS, CAVALRY, AND THE KU KLUX KLAN

Exposing the Invisible Empire During Reconstruction

J. MICHAEL MARTINEZ

ROWMAN & LITTLEFIELD PUBLISHERS, INC.
Lanham • Boulder • New York • Toronto • Plymouth, UK

ROWMAN & LITTLEFIELD PUBLISHERS, INC.

Published in the United States of America
by Rowman & Littlefield Publishers, Inc.
A wholly owned subsidiary of The Rowman & Littlefield Publishing Group, Inc.
4501 Forbes Boulevard, Suite 200, Lanham, Maryland 20706
www.rowmanlittlefield.com

Estover Road
Plymouth PL6 7PY
United Kingdom

British Library Cataloging in Publication Information Available

Library of Congress Cataloging-in-Publication Data

Martinez, J. Michael (James Michael)
  Carpetbaggers, cavalry, and the Ku Klux Klan : exposing the invisible empire
during Reconstruction / J. Michael Martinez.
    p. cm. — (The American crisis series : books on the Civil War era)
  Includes bibliographical references and index.
  ISBN-13: 978-0-7425-5077-3 (cloth : alk. paper)
  ISBN-10: 0-7425-5077-X (cloth : alk. paper)
  ISBN-13: 978-0-7425-5078-0 (paper : alk. paper)
  ISBN-10: 0-7425-5078-8 (paper : alk. paper)
  1. Ku-Klux Klan (1866–1869) 2. Reconstruction (U.S. history, 1865–1877)
3. Southern States—Race relations—History—19th century. 4. Southern
States—History—1865–1877. 5. United States. Army.—Cavalry—History—
19th century. I. Title. II. Series.

E668.M37 2007
975'.041—dc22   2006034335

Printed in the United States of America

To my boyhood friends—especially Jeff Gallup, Darin Murphy, John Harris, and Mac McLean—who showed me a different side of South Carolina than the one depicted in these pages

They are the faction. O conspiracy,
Shamest thou to show thy dangerous brow by night,
When evils are most free? O, then, by day
Where wilt thou find a cavern dark enough
To mask thy monstrous visage? Seek none, conspiracy;
Hide it in smiles and affability:
For if thou put thy native semblance on,
Not Erebus itself were dim enough
To hide thee from prevention.

—William Shakespeare, *Julius Caesar*, Act II, Scene i

Missouri, the star-link of State now is free
Wherever the "Blue Caps" have been;
All glory and honor to Merrill shall be,
He's the Champion and pride of his men.

—"The Merrill Horse" or "The Guerillas Conquered"
Written and Composed by Polyhymnia
Dedicated to the Regiment of Merrill Horse,
St. Louis, Missouri

CONTENTS

PREFACE AND
ACKNOWLEDGMENTS

On June 21, 2005, as I sat down to write this preface, CNN Headline News blared from my office television set. Lost in thought, leafing through notes, books, and articles that littered my desk and credenza, I was oblivious to the news until I heard that a Mississippi jury had convicted Edgar Ray Killen, an eighty-year-old former leader of the Ku Klux Klan (KKK)—the so-called Invisible Empire—of manslaughter. According to the evidence, Killen masterminded the brutal murders of civil rights workers James Chaney, Andrew Goodman, and Mickey Schwerner in Philadelphia, Mississippi, forty-one years to the day before the jurors delivered their verdict. The manslaughter convictions struck me as a jury compromise. Either Killen ordered the killings, which was premeditated, first-degree murder, or he was not involved in the plot, and he should have been acquitted. In any case, at least the decision closed another sordid chapter in Southern history.

Startled by the coincidence of the Killen verdict announcement on the same day I started writing this book, I was mindful that the twentieth-century Ku Klux Klan of Edgar Ray Killen was not the Reconstruction-era Ku Klux Klan. The KKK has existed in many guises since the group formed in Pulaski, Tennessee, in 1866. The original Klan opposed social and political changes that occurred in former states of the Southern Confederacy during the period of Reconstruction following the American Civil War. Their targets included blacks, especially "freedmen" who had been emancipated from slavery, Northern "carpetbaggers" who came to the South to interfere in Southern affairs, and Southern Unionists derisively labeled "scalawags."

The original Ku Klux Klan died as an active organization before Reconstruction ended in the 1870s. It wasn't until 1915 that a new group emerged and expanded beyond the South to oppose blacks, Jews, Catholics, various ethnic immigrants, and other peoples who seemed to threaten traditional "American" values. Founded by a self-proclaimed Methodist minister, the twentieth-century Klan professed allegiance to radical Christian values in a manner that was absent from, or at least tangential to, the Reconstruction-era KKK. Unlike the original group, which was mostly a Southern phenomenon, the twentieth-century nativist Klan spread throughout the United States and reached the height of its power and prestige in the Midwest during the 1920s. The group enjoyed a brief surge of popularity in opposition to the Civil Rights Movement of the 1950s and 1960s, but since that time it has declined in power and prestige except among fringe elements of society. In the years following the rise of the modern KKK, many white supremacist groups, including the Mississippi Klan of Edgar Ray Killen, have adopted the original organization's name as well as some of its symbols and rituals, but generally they have existed as independent, autonomous units. In some cases, KKK dens and other white supremacist groups have even fought with each other.

Despite historical differences, doctrinal disputes, and internecine warfare, all groups using the name "Ku Klux Klan" are united by a common bond: fear. Fear convinces Klansmen that others, somehow different from them, have negatively affected their lives. Instead of looking ahead toward improving their condition as individuals, Klansmen look to the past and think of themselves collectively. They yearn for halcyon days when white men were masters of their domain and no one, least of all men and women of a different race or ethnicity, questioned their unbridled authority. Anything or anybody challenging the status quo threatens the established social order, and threats must be handled through extralegal means, if necessary. Consider Edgar Ray Killen. In his skewed view of the world, filtered through the lenses of the KKK, he was honoring God's will in snuffing out the lives of three young men who had contaminated his beloved Southland with their crazy ideas and newfangled ways. Klansmen fear the unknown future where uncertainty exists and the order of things undoubtedly will change.

The modern Klan will not appear in these pages except briefly in the epilogue when I discuss the revival of the KKK in 1915. Much has been written about the long history of the group, but the instant work is not an exhaustive account of the rise and fall of the organization. For readers interested in such works, I discuss Klan literature in the bibliographical essay following the text.

This work adds an in-depth analysis of the role of Major Lewis Merrill, the beleaguered career soldier who led the federal government's Reconstruction-era investigation into the South Carolina Ku Klux Klan. Merrill and the cavalrymen under his command did not eradicate the Klan by any stretch of the imagination, but they arguably did more than any other person or entity to expose the identity of the Invisible Empire as a group of hooded, brutish, homegrown terrorists. In compiling evidence for the Klan trials and restoring at least a temporary semblance of law and order to the Piedmont region of South Carolina, Merrill and his men demonstrated that the portrayal of the KKK as a chivalric organization was at best a myth, and at worst a lie.

It is difficult to imagine the successful prosecution of the defendants in the landmark South Carolina Ku Klux Klan trials of 1871–1872 without the evidence provided by Major Merrill's meticulously prepared dossier. As Allen W. Trelease documented in his classic 1971 book *White Terror: The Ku Klux Klan Conspiracy and Southern Reconstruction*, the Grant administration fought the Klan in many areas, and South Carolina was not the only state where prosecutions occurred. Be that as it may, Lewis Merrill's investigation and the KKK trials in South Carolina represented the apex of the federal government's efforts to curtail what some historians have labeled the "Counter Reconstruction." After Grant's attorney general, Amos T. Akerman, left the administration at the end of 1871 and the president was re-elected the following year, the federal government retreated from its commitment to protecting the freedmen. By 1877, when Rutherford B. Hayes became president following the contested 1876 election and promptly ordered federal troops to stop guarding the Louisiana and South Carolina statehouses, Reconstruction ended. Before the dawn of a new century, Jim Crow would begin his strange Southern odyssey. Thus, the story of carpetbaggers controlling South Carolina state government, the arrival of cavalrymen in that state's Piedmont region, and the unfolding drama of the Ku Klux Klan trials of 1871–1872 comprise a cautionary tale of the endless struggle between those persons who view American history as a journey toward inclusion and empowerment for all, and those who champion exclusivity and divisiveness culminating in power and aggrandizement for a select few.

Aside from the broad history of Reconstruction-era America, a more intimate story emerges. Lewis Merrill serves in many ways as a quintessential American symbol. A controversial figure—doggedly tenacious, heroically dedicated to his duty, and yet constantly short of funds and fearfully protective of his reputation—he symbolizes the two sides of a man often absent in the nostalgic portrait of historical figures found in history books. Despite his undeniable intelligence and energy, Merrill was a deeply flawed individual who never quite escaped the whiff of scandal. He could be petty and vindictive, overly concerned with his career, especially fond of financial remuneration, arrogant, condescending, and needlessly pedantic, but he also exhibited noble qualities—a passionate, almost fanatical, devotion to duty; a tireless, enviable worth ethic; and a strong commitment to protecting the civil and political rights of black men and women in an age not known for racial and ethnic tolerance.

Merrill's military career was filled with highs and lows. After performing competent, if largely unheralded, work during the Civil War, he was charged with corruption for accepting a bribe while acting as a judge advocate in a court martial proceeding in 1869. Although the charge was never proven, the episode tarnished his reputation and led to estrangement from his commanding officer, Lt. Col. George Armstrong Custer. Later, Southern legislators charged that Merrill had accepted bribes while on duty in South Carolina—a charge they knew to be false. The major had accepted more than $20,000 in reward money provided by the South Carolina General Assembly for rounding up leading Klansmen—and Merrill paid $5,000 of that money to a lobbyist who pushed the bill through the legislature—but the payment, aside from appearing opportunistic, was not technically illegal.

When he retired from active duty in 1886, Merrill's superiors recommended him for promotion to the permanent rank of lieutenant colonel. Congressman Newton Blanchard of Louisiana, still incensed at Merrill's "interference" with white citizens' rights in the Red River District of his state in 1874–1876, persuaded President Grover Cleveland to announce a new policy on officers' promotions. Under the new policy, an army officer could not be promoted to a higher rank when he retired on disability, as Merrill proposed to do. Thus, Merrill retained his rank as major (brevet colonel) when he left the service. He eventually won his promotion to lieutenant colonel, but a permanent general officer's rank was denied him.

He spent his twilight years fighting a rearguard battle to protect his good name while simultaneously fending off numerous creditors. Until his death in 1896, Merrill devoted his energies to reclaiming his health and spending time with his family, but he took no solace in the thanks of a grateful nation, for his services were largely forgotten. Today his efforts merit brief attention in larger works on the KKK and Reconstruction, but the man and his actions have been all but lost to history. This book seeks to rectify that oversight and clarify the record so that an intriguing and important figure of the Reconstruction era can be afforded his rightful due, while simultaneously not whitewashing Merrill's record or engaging in unreflective hero worship.

In writing a book about the Reconstruction-era KKK, I have been conscious that the subject is delicate and care must be taken to present information in a manner sensitive to modern readers. I sometimes hear from my students that I am "too focused on race" in teaching American history and government, an interesting comment since it usually comes from students of color. In my writing, as in my teaching, I try not to succumb to political correctness, but I recognize that I have an obligation to present the material in a way that does not demean readers and students. Thus, in these pages I have sought to present an accurate analysis that does not shy away from unpleasant parts of the record and never consciously distorts history, but also recognizes the sensibilities of the twenty-first century reader.

I have been fortunate to receive immense assistance in researching and writing this book although, as always, errors of fact or interpretation are mine. Series editor Steven E. Woodworth and peer reviewer David M. Chalmers provided excellent advice on writing and improving the manuscript. Jerry L. West, author of *The Reconstruction Ku Klux Klan in York County, South Carolina, 1865–1877*, corresponded with me frequently. He was kind enough to share his insight on sources and he even offered to read portions of the manuscript without remuneration—a rarity, indeed. Dr. William D. Richardson, a friend and mentor, taught me how to write a book proposal, and New York literary agent Geri Thoma provided sage advice (free of charge, no less) on how to perfect it so I could compete in a crowded marketplace. Stephen Davis and Rod Gragg kindly agreed to provide jacket quotes of the "I laughed, I cried, it became a part of me" variety. As he has with several of my earlier projects, John M. Coski of the Museum of the Confederacy in Richmond assisted me in innumerable ways, large and small, as I searched for information.

Beth Bilderback, visual materials archivist in the South Caroliniana Library in Columbia, South Carolina, assisted me in locating and reproducing the photograph of Daniel H. Chamberlain. Judy Bolton and Jessica Jones of the Special Collections Department in the Tulane Libraries in New Orleans, Mary Linn Wernet of the Archives & Research Center at Northwestern State University in Natchitoches, Louisiana, and Heather Moore in the U.S. Senate Historical Office in Washington, D.C., were instrumental in tracking down the photograph of Newton Blanchard. Teresa M. Burk and Kathy Shoemaker, archivists in the Special Collections & Archives Division of the Robert W. Woodruff Library at Emory University in Atlanta, helped me find rare books on the Ku Klux Klan and reproduced the photograph of William Joseph Simmons. Steven W. Engerrand, archives assistant director in the Georgia Archives in Atlanta, assisted me in acquiring the dramatic photograph of the Leo Frank lynching. Duryea Kemp of the Ohio Historical Society was kind enough to reproduce the Robert K. Scott photograph. Howard and Jean Merrill were helpful in tracking down information on their ancestor, Major Lewis Merrill. Heather W. Milne, manager of Photographic Services at the Museum of the Confederacy in Richmond, assisted me in acquiring the photograph of Nathan Bedford Forrest. Debby Pogue, archivist with the U.S. Military Academy at West Point, gathered material on Major Merrill's background. Nancy Sambets at the York County Historical Center in York, South Carolina, went above and beyond the call of duty in making photocopies of the *Yorkville Enquirer* and in reproducing the Yorkville photographs.

Friends and family were especially encouraging throughout the arduous process of research and writing. Gerd Eriksson of Kennesaw State University always bolstered my spirits and provided moral support when the going got rough. My uncle and fellow writer, William W. Mellette, has been generous with his advice and helpful comments throughout the years. My cousin and also a fellow writer, Walter Russell Mead, was supportive and encouraging with this work as well as with my previous works. His parents, Loren and Polly Mead, graciously opened up their home—which I refer to as the "Hotel Mead" owing to the many persons who partake of their unflagging hospitality—when I visited Washington, D.C., on research trips. Thanks also to my editor, Laura Roberts Gottlieb, who left the press between the time when the manuscript was acquired and when it was written. Fortunately for me, her assistant, Andrew Boney, stepped into her shoes and proved to be more than equal to the task of preparing the book for publication. In addition, I am indebted to many other dedicated professionals at Rowman & Littlefield, including Niels Aaboe, executive editor for political science and American history, Karen Ackermann, associate production editor, and Asa Johnson, editorial assistant.

Last, but not least, I extend thanks to my mother, Laura M. Martinez, and my wife, Paula R. Martinez. Their love, support, and understanding as I was ensconced in the library for many months allowed me to complete the project with minimal strife. What more can a fellow ask than the time and encouragement necessary to complete his work? Perhaps he can ask for a good story to tell. If so, I have been blessed in this regard as well.

Prologue

"JIM WILLIAMS ON HIS BIG MUSTER"

Southern folklore caricatured black folk as ignorant, servile simpletons, but James Rainey did not fit the stereotype. Never content to live as an indolent lackey, he was described as a "pretty independent negro" who "stood up for his rights." Born and reared in rural York County, South Carolina, he spent his youth as a slave struggling to survive on a plantation owned by Samuel Rainey along the York to Chester Road twenty miles from Yorkville, the terminus of the King's Mountain Railroad and thus the county's commercial hub. The young man earned a reputation for independence by escaping from the Rainey plantation when civil war erupted. Thereafter, he enlisted in the Union army. In the closing months of fighting, he served under General William T. Sherman, the Yankee commander hated by Southerners for cutting a swath of destruction through Georgia and the Carolinas in 1864–1865.

After the fall of the Southern Confederacy, Jim Rainey changed his offending surname to "Williams" and returned to York County. He was emboldened by his military experiences and saw the war, emancipation, and the protection of civil and political rights for former slaves as inextricably linked. During the ensuing six years, he protected the property and lives of freedmen as best he could by organizing a black militia unit—a "Union League" in the parlance of the day—and proclaiming himself its captain. It was difficult to know whether the unit represented a genuine threat to the peace, but rumor had it that Williams bragged he would "kill from the cradle to the grave." This bravado, real or imagined, evoked images of antebellum slave uprisings in which blacks slaughtered their white masters while the latter slept.

1

Like everyone else in South Carolina, Williams was all-too-familiar with a vigilante group patrolling the roads and forests of York County, a band of nightriders calling itself the Ku Klux Klan. If the KKK frightened Williams, he refused to show it. In fact, he goaded the Klan in a public speech at Rose's Hotel in Yorkville, vowing that if the group encountered his militia unit, few if any Klansmen would return to their homes. Coupled with his lack of deference to white community leaders, his reputation as a troublemaker training freedmen in military tactics, and his increasingly hostile public rhetoric, Williams had become a problem the white community could not ignore.[1]

A group of disaffected citizens resolved to confront this "pretty bad boy" and correct the problem. On the evening of March 6, 1871, approximately seventy white men assembled on horseback at the Briar Patch muster ground on Howell Mill Road five miles west of Yorkville. Forty-nine-year-old James Rufus Bratton, a prominent York County physician, was the acknowledged mob leader. After donning robes and crude disguises to obscure their faces and adorning their horses with clean white sheets, the men set out to visit Williams and his militiamen. On this night, they would demonstrate the fearsome power of the Ku Klux Klan.[2]

To outward appearances, Dr. Bratton was a professional man far removed from the rough and tumble world of vigilante justice. He was well educated, a property holder, a community leader, secure in his status as a man of means and respectability—or so it seemed. Appearances were deceiving. Beneath the public façade of respectability, Bratton seethed with resentment. He had left a lucrative medical practice to join the Confederate States Army in 1861. After serving for three years in the Richmond hospitals and advancing to the rank of surgeon, the doctor's health failed, and he finished out the war with the Twentieth Regiment of Virginia surgeons working near Milledgeville, Georgia. Upon returning home, he found his practice in ruins and his fortune decimated. To make ends meet, he took to the fields to plant cotton and raise much-needed capital. Unfortunately for Bratton and his family, he could not make a go of it.

He felt especially embittered at the "radical politics" of a freedman, Bob, who assisted him for a time. Bratton eventually sent Bob and his family packing. Wearing his public face, the good doctor professed horror and shame at the depredations of self-styled nightriders, but his neighbors harbored little doubt of Bratton's affinity for the group as well as his active participation in its nocturnal activities. J. Rufus Bratton wore many masks, not all of them fashioned from homespun fabric.[3]

The Klan was not an institution native to South Carolina, but it suited the Rufus Brattons of the South to use the organization as a means of terrorizing freedmen and ensuring white supremacy. The KKK had formed in Tennessee in 1866 and, like a cancer, had metastasized into virtually every state of the former Confederacy within a few years. In some places, the group was a joke, little more than a nineteenth-century version of a fraternity whose members enjoyed plentiful doses of sophomoric high jinks and homemade liquor. The Klan was a sinister presence in other areas, a paramilitary group intent on patrolling neighborhoods to keep freedmen quaking in fear, far away from two things near and dear to Southern hearts and minds—white women and ballot boxes. On this night and in this place, the South Carolina KKK would demonstrate its allegiance to the paramilitary school.[4]

Galloping along familiar country roads, the gang stopped at freedmen's homes to whip suspected militiamen as a chilling prelude to the night's main event. They grew increasingly intoxicated with the power wielded by a mob and, perhaps, the spirits poured from a bottle. Traipsing through the countryside past McConnellsville, the men hid in shadows until they approached a blind road leading to the Williams homestead. When they were three hundred yards away, Bratton ordered a dozen fellows to join him in reconnoitering the property. All was quiet. Satisfied that no outsiders would interfere with their scheme, the small group marched across the yard, bounded up the steps, and slammed their fists and rifle butts against the front door.[5]

Rose Williams, Jim's wife, answered. When the Klansmen demanded to know where Jim was, she said he was not there. They forced their way inside and encountered another freedman on the premises, but Jim Williams was nowhere to be found. According to M. S. Carroll, a Klansman who subsequently wrote of the event in his journal, the affair might have ended there had Bratton not seen through Rose Williams's ruse. "After a moment's reflection," Carroll recalled, "Dr. Bratton told someone to pull up some of the plank flooring. 'He might be under there,' he said. And sure enough, there was Jim crouched down under the floor."[6]

Gone was the freedman's braggadocio. In its place was naked fear, for Jim Williams knew what this band proposed to do. Even as he pleaded for mercy, the men fell upon him, jerking him up from the planking and hauling him outside. Someone, probably Bratton, placed a rope around his neck. The big man flailed his arms and legs, screaming and crying as if to raise an alarm. Behind him, Rose and the other black man also screamed, but to no avail.

The Klan would not be dissuaded from its work this night. If white Southerners were to reestablish home rule, black radicals would have to learn their place. The mob dragged Williams toward the horses. In Carroll's words, "someone spied a large tree with a limb running out 10 or 12 feet from the ground and suggested that that was the place to finish the job."[7]

They tied the rope around Williams's neck to the tree limb and forced him to climb onto another limb. There he stood, precariously perched on a ledge. Someone ordered Williams to jump, but he refused. Bob Caldwell, another Klansman who later recorded the night's activities, climbed up next to the captain and tried to push the frightened man. When Williams grabbed the limb with his hands, Caldwell used a knife to hack at the man's fingers until he released his grip, at which time he "died cursing, pleading and praying all in one breath." After Williams was dead, the Klansmen hung a sign around his neck that read "Jim Williams on his big muster."[8]

The night's activities had not ended. The mob visited several other homes, this time searching for weapons and members of Williams's militia. Carroll recalled that "we succeeded in getting 23 of the guns but never found a member of the company. They all had business away from home that night. I remember going to the house of Henry Haynes, whom I knew was a member, and when I knocked on the door his wife opened the door and thrust the rifle out and said, 'Here take it for Gawd's sake.'" These subsequent maneuvers were anticlimactic after the hanging. Even so, the Klansmen reassembled around midnight to enjoy a "bountiful lunch" and a measure of farewell camaraderie at Bratton's house.[9]

Fifty or more members of Williams's militia were on hand when the coroner arrived to remove the body at dawn. For two days, the militiamen swore oaths and threatened to kill all local white men, but they were without an effective leader. Their threats came to naught. In the meantime, the jury at the coroner's inquest returned a standard verdict of death by persons unknown despite widespread knowledge that Bratton's Klanmen were responsible.[10]

Federal troops had arrived in York County at the end of February to quell the escalating violence, and yet Jim Williams was killed with impunity. Despite some local citizens' insistence that the "legislature has been the prime cause of all the disturbances," federal officials observing events from Washington realized that the episodes would cease only when more troops patrolled county roads. They ordered additional soldiers to Yorkville at the end of March. On the twenty-sixth of that month, companies B, E, and K of Lt. Col. George Armstrong Custer's Seventh U.S. Cavalry arrived in Yorkville led by Major (Brevet Colonel) Lewis Merrill, a career army officer with extensive experience combating guerilla forces. More than any other individual of the Reconstruction era, Major Merrill methodically researched the facts and painstakingly probed behind the masks of the Ku Klux Klan to expose the Invisible Empire to the light of day.[11]

When he arrived in South Carolina after serving as a judge advocate in courts martial on the Great Plains, the major believed that rumors of the Klan were exaggerated. Neither he nor his subordinates imagined they would be in Yorkville for an extended time. In Merrill's view, after sufficient federal troops were on hand, the hooligans would tremble in fear and disband. During the two years he was stationed in the Palmetto State, however, he came to know the dark secrets lurking beneath the robes and hoods of the Ku Klux Klan, and he realized how naïve he had been to think that Southern white men would easily surrender to Northern troops a second time.[12]

NOTES

1. United States Circuit Court [4th Circuit], *Proceedings in the Ku Klux Klan Trials at Columbia, S.C., in the United States Circuit Court, November Term, 1871* (Columbia, SC: Republican Printing Company, State Printers, 1872), 389–92; Jerry L. West, *The Reconstruction Ku Klux Klan in York County, South Carolina, 1865–1877* (Jefferson, NC: McFarland & Company, Inc., 2002), 123–25.

2. Allen W. Trelease, *White Terror: The Ku Klux Klan Conspiracy and Southern Reconstruction* (Baton Rouge: Louisiana State University Press, 1971), 367–68; West, *The Reconstruction Ku Klux Klan,* 123–24; Lou Falkner Williams, *The Great South Carolina Ku Klux Klan Trials, 1871–1872* (Athens: University of Georgia Press, 1996), 76–77.

3. Fred Langdon, "The Kidnapping of Dr. Rufus Bratton," *Journal of Negro History* 10 (July 1925): 330–34; Trelease, *White Terror,* 367; West, *The Reconstruction Ku Klux Klan,* 123–24.

4. J. C. Lester and D. L. Wilson, *Ku Klux Klan: Its Origin, Growth, and Disbursement* (New York: Da Capo Press, 1973; originally published in Nashville, TN: Wheeler, Osborn & Duckworth Manufacturing Company, 1884), 47–61; J. A. Rogers, *The Ku Klux Spirit* (Baltimore, MD: Black Classic Press, 1980; originally published by Messenger Publishing Company, 1923), 14–21; Mr. and Mrs. W. B. Romine, *A Story of the Original Ku Klux Klan* (Pulaski, TN: The Pulaski Citizen, 1934), 3–17; Mrs. S. E. F. Rose, *The Ku Klux Klan or Invisible Empire* (New Orleans, LA: L. Graham Co., Ltd., 1914), 18–19; Herbert Shapiro, "The Ku Klux Klan During Reconstruction: The South Carolina Episode," *Journal of Negro History* 49 (January 1964): 34–55; Francis B. Simkins, "The Ku Klux Klan in South Carolina," *Journal of Negro History* 12 (October 1927): 606–47; J. C. A. Stagg, "The

Problem of Klan Violence: The South Carolina Up-Country, 1868–1871," *Journal of American Studies* 8 (December 1974): 303–18.

5. Trelease, *White Terror*, 367; West, *The Reconstruction Ku Klux Klan*, 123–24.

6. Quoted in West, *The Reconstruction Ku Klux Klan*, 124.

7. Trelease, *White Terror*, 367; quoted in West, *The Reconstruction Ku Klux Klan*, 124; Williams, *The Great South Carolina Ku Klux Klan Trials*, 76–77.

8. David Everitt, "1871 War on Terror," *American History* 38 (June 2003): 27–28; Eric Foner, *Reconstruction: America's Unfinished Revolution, 1863–1877* (New York: Francis Parkman Prize Edition, History Book Club, 2005; originally published by HarperCollins, 1988), 431; Kermit L. Hall, "Political Power and Constitutional Legitimacy: The South Carolina Ku Klux Klan Trials, 1871–1872," *Emory Law Journal* 33 (Fall 1984): 924–25; Trelease, *White Terror*, 367; United States Congress, *Report of the Joint Select Committee to Inquire into the Condition of Affairs in the Late Insurrectionary States*, 42 Cong., 2 Sess., No. 22 (1872), Vol. V, 1712–41, 1795–99; Williams, *The Great South Carolina Ku Klux Klan Trials*, 77.

9. Quoted in West, *The Reconstruction Ku Klux Klan*, 124. See also, Lacy K. Ford Jr., "One Southern Profile: Modernization and the Development of White Terror in York County, 1856–1876" (master's thesis, University of South Carolina, 1976), i–iii; United States Circuit Court [4th Circuit], *Proceedings in the Ku Klux Klan Trials*, 389–92; Williams, *The Great South Carolina Ku Klux Klan Trials*, 77.

10. Ford, "One Southern Profile," i–iii; Trelease, *White Terror*, 367–68; United States Congress, *Report of the Joint Select Committee*, Vol. III, 709–10; West, *The Reconstruction Ku Klux Klan*, 124; Williams, *The Great South Carolina Ku Klux Klan Trials*, 77.

11. "Arrival of a Cavalry Company," *Yorkville Enquirer*, Yorkville, SC (March 30, 1871); Hall, "Political Power and Constitutional Legitimacy," 925; United States Congress, *Report of the Joint Select Committee*, Vol. V, 1464; Trelease, *White Terror*, 369–70; Wyn Craig Wade, *The Fiery Cross: The Ku Klux Klan in America* (New York and Oxford: Oxford University Press, 1987), 93–94; "A Word to Congress," *Harper's Weekly* (April 8, 1871): 306.

12. George W. Cullum, *Biographical Register of the Officers and Graduates of the U.S. Military Academy at West Point, N.Y. From its Establishment, in 1802, to 1890 with the Early History of the United States Military Academy* (Boston and New York: Houghton, Mifflin and Company, and Cambridge, MA: The Riverside Press, 1891), 624–25; "Lewis Merrill Dead," *Yorkville Enquirer*, Yorkville, SC (March 4, 1896); United States Congress, *Report of the Joint Select Committee*, Vol. V, 1464–87; Wade, *The Fiery Cross*, 94–95; West, *The Reconstruction Ku Klux Klan*, 80–82; Williams, *The Great South Carolina Ku Klux Klan Trials*, 49; Richard Zuczek, *State of Rebellion: Reconstruction in South Carolina* (Columbia: University of South Carolina Press, 1996), 94–95.

1

"A BROTHERHOOD OF PROPERTY-HOLDERS, THE PEACEABLE, LAW-ABIDING CITIZENS OF THE STATE"

The Ku Klux Klan was born in Pulaski, the county seat of Giles County, Tennessee, a town of three thousand inhabitants adjacent to the L and N Railroad eighty miles south of Nashville near the Alabama border. "There, in 1866, the name Ku Klux first fell from human lips," cofounder John Lester and his literary partner, the Reverend David L. Wilson, recalled, although some accounts listed the date as December 1865. During antebellum times, Giles County was a large slave-holding region. After the Thirteenth Amendment abolished slavery, local residents were alarmed at the large number of freedmen roaming the countryside, so perhaps the birth of the Klan in this small community was no accident.

Despite its rural character, Pulaski was an important crossroads in Giles County; it lay at the intersection of the Nashville to Birmingham and Chattanooga to Memphis highways. Many displaced persons wandered the roads, which only reinforced the tenuous nature of postwar Southern life. A KKK apologist, Mrs. S. E. F. Rose, described Pulaski as "a town of importance, of culture and refinement" and "a town of churches, schools and colleges and not a community that would have produced desperadoes and cutthroats." Even after the Klan became infamous, Mrs. Rose bragged, "Pulaski always, in a way, remained headquarters for the Klan, as many of the officers lived there, and the town was proud of being the birthplace of this great organization."[1]

The "great organization" started modestly when six young men—former Confederate soldiers James R. Crowe, Calvin Jones, John B. Kennedy, John C. Lester, Frank O. McCord, and Richard B. Reed—lounged in the law office of Calvin Jones's father, Judge Thomas Jones. After the excitement of combat during the war, the young men were bored with "enforced inactivity." John Lester later mused that the "reaction which followed the excitement of army scenes and service was intense. There was nothing to relieve it." In the florid prose that characterized much of the writing of that era, these men "were returning to a land that once had known 'the glory which was Rome, and the grandeur which was Greece' but that was now a 'land which had known sorrow, a land which had broken the ashen crust and moistened it with her tears, a land scarred and riven by the plowshare of war, and billowed with the graves of her dead.'"

The Pulaski Six, as they were later called, resolved to have fun even when confronted with the ennui of Reconstruction. "Boys," someone suggested, "let us get up a club or society, of some description." Seeking "diversion and amusement," the fellows agreed to meet the next evening and found a new club.[2]

According to commentator Stanley Horn, the six young men were not thugs or budding nightriders, and they did not create the Klan to terrorize freedmen or circumvent federal Reconstruction policies. Their intent was apolitical, and their collective character was beyond reproach. "They were all men of the highest standing in their community, with unblemished records for good behavior," Horn contended. "Most of them were college graduates, and none of them at any time was ever accused of any offense against the law of even the mildest sort."

To some extent, Horn was correct; the founders were no mere ruffians. Each man had performed his military duty on behalf of the Confederate States of America and each was active in church and community affairs after the war. James R. Crowe had served as a major with the Fourth Alabama Volunteers and was wounded at First Manassas. John B. Kennedy had experienced the worst episodes of the war. Rising to the rank of captain, he was wounded three times and served a stint in the Camp Douglas Union Prison in Illinois. Jones, Lester, McCord, and Reed had served in the Tennessee infantry. After suffering the humiliation of defeat in wartime, each of the six burned with ambition to rise above his sordid postwar station in life, and at least two men succeeded. John Lester eventually became a lawyer and served in the Tennessee legislature while Frank McCord edited Pulaski's local newspaper, the *Citizen*.[3]

These "men of the highest standing" met a second time in Judge Jones's office, and they brought along several potential club members. During their second meeting, they appointed Calvin Jones and Richard Reed to a committee charged with selecting a name for their new club. As Jones and Reed explained during the third meeting, this time held at a private residence, the committeemen originally thought they would choose a phrase to highlight the group's purpose, but to no avail. Since the only purpose was social intercourse, a name did not immediately suggest itself.

Jones and Reed presented a list of recommendations to the full club, including the idea of using the word *Kukloi*, a derivation of the Greek word *kuklos*, referring to a band or circle of brotherhood. This idea sparked considerable interest. "At mention of this someone cried out: 'Call it Ku Klux,'" Lester and Wilson reported in their history of the group. "'Klan' at once suggested itself, and was added to complete the alliteration. So instead of adopting a name, as was the first intention, which had a definite meaning, they chose one which to the proposer of it, and to everyone else, was absolutely meaningless."[4]

The members were especially pleased at this inspired nonsense, for the name connoted a mysterious society and the alliteration suggested "bones rattling together." Other accounts reported that the name evoked the sound of cocking and discharging a firearm. The Memphis *Appeal* surmised that "Ku Klux Klan" was a Hebrew term that originally appeared in a Jewish work titled "A True and Authentic History of the Great Rebellion of the Hebrew Against the Ancient Egyptian King Pharaoh, B.C. 2000." According to this fanciful explanation, the term "Cu-Clux Clan" is translated into English as the "Straw Club," alluding to the Pharaohs' requirement that hod-carriers furnish their own straw, hence the saying "straws show which way the wind blows."

Another newspaper traced the Klan's roots to a secret society, the "Seven Confederate Knights," established by Southern inmates languishing in the Johnson Island Union Prison during the war. Perhaps the name referred to a well-known social fraternity of the time, the Kuklos Adelphion, or "old Kappa Alpha," founded at the University of North Carolina in 1812. The Richmond *Whig* supplied the most creative etymology in 1868 when it intimated that "Ku Klux Klan" derived from an "Oriental word" referring to opium smuggling in China.

Mr. and Mrs. William B. Romine, authors of a sympathetic Klan history, acknowledged that the name might derive from a Greek term for "circle" or "brotherhood," but they suggested another possibility. Admitting they were "without authentic information on the subject" because they had never thought to ask about it, the authors observed that many Pulaski residents had fought in the war with Mexico in the 1840s and had heard tales of the Mexican legend of Cukulcan, the god of light. In the Romines' version of the legend, Cukulcan constantly struggled against the vampire god of darkness and always triumphed. Well known to the fathers of the original Klansmen, this mythology appealed to young men who sometimes referred to themselves as "sons of light." The Klan was a champion of goodness and light struggling against the black forces of evil—carpetbaggers, scalawags, freedmen, and the dark legacy of Reconstruction. The Romines' explanation conveniently reflected the group's later claims to represent "manly virtues" such as a love of family and chivalry as well as the Klan's self-professed goal of protecting Southern womanhood from ravishment and miscegenation. The story also emphasized the importance of differences in skin color. White skin represented purity and virtue while black flesh was debased, sinful, and evil.[5]

However the name supposedly began, the club's origins were far more prosaic than apologists later suggested. The six young men simply chose a nonsensical name, a phrase they cobbled together from their limited knowledge of Greek and their pride in their Scottish ancestry, hence the reference to a "klan." The fellows delighted in the strange self-made mythology they had created. Conflicting reports on the origins of the group and its bizarre name only heightened the members' sense of exclusivity and self-importance.

The Pulaski Six's desire to create a club was hardly unique when considered in the context of the times. Americans always have enjoyed belonging to exclusive societies, clubs, and political parties. The Freemasons, the Mormons, the Order of the Star Spangled Banner, the Golden Circle, the Constitutional Union Guard, the Pale Faces, the American Party (commonly called the Know Nothings), various religious sects and cults, social and civics clubs, and other affiliations have been a ubiquitous feature of the American landscape since the founding period. After the Civil War, many new clubs sprang up, and in the Reconstruction-era South groups like the Ku Klux Klan, Knights of the White Camellia, and the White Brotherhood were especially popular. Later, rifle and saber clubs would serve as social and political outlets for disgruntled whites that felt alienated from the normal channels of political participation and free expression.[6]

By the summer of 1866, the Pulaski Ku Kluxers had created an organization in the rich American tradition of carving out "voluntary associations." All that remained was articulating an ennobling purpose, for "relieving boredom" was hardly an inspiring credo. To solve this dilemma, a rules committee convened to develop group rituals, mottoes, and insignia.

In the meantime, the fellows amused themselves by rummaging through a linen closet and adorning their bodies with sheets and pillowcases. They must have been quite a sight parading through the streets of Pulaski caterwauling and pretending to be spooks. Finding it all great fun, the young men improved upon their initial adventures by enhancing their costumes

Figure 1.1.   The original Ku Klux Klan robes featured elaborate, albeit nonsen-sical, symbols and designs.

with pointy hats, thick linen belts, colorful sashes, and long-flowing gowns sporting elaborate designs, many based on randomly drawn occult symbols such as half moons, stars, goblin faces, and animal shapes.

The rules committee eventually developed a hierarchy of offices and titles. As was the case with the Klan's original name and symbolism, the titles were nonsensical, their only purpose to sound eerie and mysterious. Thus, McCord, as the highest-ranking ex-Confederate officer, served as the KKK's first Grand Cyclops, or president. Kennedy, the next highest-ranking officer, was the Grand Magi, or vice president. Crowe was the Grand Turk, a kind of adjutant to the Grand Cyclops. Lester and Jones served as Night Hawks, charged with protecting the group from outside interference. For his part, Richard Reed was the Lictor, a position similar to a parliamentarian, designed to keep order at meetings.[7]

During its first year, the Klan was devoted solely to "farcical initiations." The founders discovered a vacant basement in a large house wrecked by a storm. There, they created their first Klan "den" for initiating new members. The initiation ceremony typically began when the group assembled in robes and the leader stood atop a nearby stump. With his long flowing gown covering the stump, he appeared ten feet tall. A sentinel in plain clothes would lead a prospective member to the scene and the Klansmen would recite a scripted greeting as if the sentinel had innocently stumbled upon the group while strolling in the forest with his friend.

"Who are ye that dare to intrude upon our sacred precepts?" the masked leader would call out in a booming voice. In response, the sentinel explained that no intrusion was intended. He and his friend had happened upon the scene by accident. The members exchanged pleasantries, after which the sentinel admitted that perhaps he and his friend would join the Klan. A shrill whistle sounded and other hooded Kluxers emerged from their hiding places, surrounding the sentinel and his candidate for membership.

The charade continued as the Klansmen blindfolded the unsuspecting fellow. They pretended to blindfold the sentinel, but of course, it was a trick. Leading the candidate into the den, they explained how the KKK operated and swore him to secrecy. Toward the conclusion of the initiation rite, someone asked, "What shall be done to the new brother whom we delight to honor?" A scripted conversation would ensue before someone suggested that the new member should be adorned in "royal apparel." Still blindfolded, the candidate learned he was being draped in royal robes with a sword around his waist and a crown on his head. He was made to recite a popular line from the Scotsman Robert Burns's poetry, which concluded:

O wad some power the giftee gie us
To see oursels as others see us.

When the blindfold was removed, the fellow found that he wore a donkey skin and a donkey head, props from *A Midsummer Night's Dream*, the Shakespearean comedy in which the unsuspecting Bottom is transformed into a jackass by the impish fairy Robin Goodfellow, the sprite also known as Puck. With this revelation, the Klansmen enjoyed a good laugh at the new member's expense. The initiate then was assigned a series of duties to prove his mettle to the group. Alternatively, he might be subjected to a series of humiliating "tests" to discern whether he was a suitable colleague.[8]

These kinds of fraternity pranks characterized the Pulaski den's activities in 1866 and 1867. While armed confrontations erupted in many Southern states as Presidential Reconstruction gave way to Radical Reconstruction controlled by Congress, the KKK remained an apolitical group of silly young men engaged in harmless games and shenanigans. Testifying during the KKK hearings in the 1870s, one young man from Alabama remembered seeing Klansmen emerge from the woods in the fall of 1866 wearing "rather a pretty and showy costume" decorated with tall hats and spangled stars. The group enjoyed a moonlight picnic punctuated with dancing and horseplay, which struck the observer as "a thing of amusement." As news of these costumed romps spread, young men in nearby Tennessee counties as well as in neighboring Alabama asked for permission to establish their own Klan dens. Within a year, the organization had spread across many parts of the South largely through word of mouth.[9]

It is difficult to pinpoint the exact moment when the group adopted a more sinister purpose than silly play-acting, but the transformation probably occurred in 1867. As the number of dens grew, control slipped away from the Pulaski Six. Never a highly centralized organization, the Klan took on the character of its local practitioners. In some areas, group leaders were satisfied to cavort about just as the founders had, enjoying the social aspects of their organization. It was fun to don sheets and pillowcases and pretend to be ghosts and goblins. Somewhere along the way, a few Klansmen chose to scare freedmen. The history of the antebellum South was filled with episodes of whites bullying blacks. It required little imagination for bored young men, ex-Confederate soldiers in many instances, to turn their attention to the source of much resentment and frustration.

The first recorded KKK visits to the homes of blacks occurred at night. Hidden beneath strange, elaborate costumes, the visitors spoke in "awfully sepulchral tones," often claiming to be a "spirit from another world" killed in service of the Southern Confederacy. According to Lester and Wilson, the freedmen's reactions delighted the Klansmen. As word circulated that the ghosts of dead Confederate soldiers roamed the countryside at night, "the feeling of negroes and of many of the white people, at the mention of the Ku Klux, was one of awe and terror."

Some blacks may have experienced awe and terror, but not because they were convinced that the ghosts of slain soldiers had invaded their homes. Instead, they feared the intentions of a group of masked white men parading around under cover of darkness. Already bands of armed thugs had appeared at inopportune times to interrupt blacks' church services, social outings, and political meetings. Self-styled "regulators" such as the Yellow Jackets and the Redcaps were well known in southern Tennessee even before the KKK appeared. With its spooky costumes, fancy, mysterious symbols, and strange hierarchy of offices, the Klan represented a potentially more ominous outlet for vigilantism than any predecessor group.[10]

The KKK might have died a natural death but for a series of occurrences, some planned and some fortuitous. The most significant planned occurrence took place in April 1867 when the Pulaski den held a secret meeting, dubbed a "general council," at the Maxwell House, a fancy hotel in Nashville, ostensibly to reorganize the various, and growing, Klan groups. The meeting coincided with a not-so-secret meeting to nominate Democratic candidates for the fall elections. Although the precise number of dens in existence at the time is unknown, most historians have concluded that the group was still fairly small. Nonetheless, the desire to hold a general council suggests that interest in the Klan was increasing; indeed, within a year it would emerge as one of the most important extralegal organizations in the Reconstruction-era South.

During the 1867 general council, the Pulaski Grand Cyclops unveiled a Prescript, essentially a constitution and a set of bylaws, for all Klan dens. Based on a military-style hierarchical structure, the Prescript identified rank-and-file Kluxers as "ghouls"—the military equivalent of enlisted soldiers—in keeping with the original "ghosts and goblins" theme developed by the group's founders. The document also outlined a confusing labyrinth of offices and duties above the ghouls. The Grand Cyclops was designated as the leader of a local den. He was assisted by two Night Hawks who served as his executive assistants. Each den also featured a Grand Magi (second in command) and a Grand Monk (third in command) as well as a Grand Turk (executive officer), a Grand Sentinel, a Grand Ensign, a Grand Scribe (secretary), and a Grand Exchequer (treasurer). According to the Prescript, officers of each den were elected semiannually by all members of the den.

Above the Grand Cyclops was a Grand Giant of the Province, essentially a county-level Klansman, assisted by four Goblins. The Grand Titan of the Dominion corresponded to a congressional district, and six Furies assisted him. The Grand Dragon of the Realm was analogous to a state governor, and he had eight Hydras at his disposal. The Grand Wizard of the Empire stood at the top of the hierarchy, assisted by ten Genii. The immediate subordinates elected each of the officers above the rank of Grand Cyclops to a two-year term. Thus, the Grand Cyclops elected Grand Giants, Grand Giants elected Grand Titans, Grand Titans elected Grand Dragons, and Grand Dragons elected the Grand Wizard. An exception was made for the first Grand Wizard, who was slated to serve a three-year term beginning on the first Monday in May 1867.[11]

The Prescript was the work of two former Confederate generals living in Pulaski—John C. Brown and George W. Gordon—both of whom became important KKK officers. Brown was politically well connected, and he was elected the redemption governor of Tennessee in 1870. A man of no small ambition, Brown eventually served as president of the Tennessee Coal and Iron Company, a position that made him one of the wealthiest and most influential men in the South.

George Gordon was an even more important figure in Klan history than Brown. Only thirty years old in 1867, he had been the youngest brigadier general in the Confederate army when the war ended. Brown helped to develop the Prescript, but Gordon actually wrote the document. Gordon's intuition that the KKK must adopt the style, organization, and tactics of a paramilitary group did more than anything else in that early period to ensure the continuation and longevity of the club. Without his skill and guidance behind the scenes before the April 1867 meeting, the Klan might have died out within a few years, remembered as little more than a curious footnote in Southern history.[12]

Although the name "Ku Klux Klan" was not mentioned prominently, the original Prescript, along with an amended Prescript that appeared in 1868, ensured a common grounding to the Klan. Members were required to swear an oath of secrecy on "the extreme penalty of the Law." According to the amendment, the organization was "an institution of Chivalry, Humanity, Mercy, and Patriotism." Its purpose was to "protect the weak, the innocent, and the defenseless, from the indignities, wrongs, and outrages of the lawless, the violent, and the brutal."

Although such a credo sounded noble, it held a specific meaning. Commentators such as the Romines pointed out that the Klan was designed to protect Southern whites from the actions of undesirable groups. "No more faithful or reliable servants were ever known than Southern negroes," they observed. "But as a free American citizen, serving in the army, voting, holding office, serving on juries, and getting drunk along with carpet baggers and scalawags, he became a very different individual." In their view, a carpetbagger was "a worthless, irresponsible fellow recently come into the South, who took an active interest in politics, could vote and hold office, but owned no real estate, and usually no more personal property than was carried about with him in his carpet bag." As for a scalawag, "he was very much the same kind of individual, only he was a home-grown product." These ne'er-do-wells bred social unrest by "stirring up trouble" and fostering resentment among black folk. Their actions went unchecked because they controlled the organs of state government protected by federal troops.[13]

While the Pulaski Klan was little more than a social club, the modified KKK promised to be something different. In a short time, it became an outlet for resisting Reconstruction through secret, armed disobedience. It is almost impossible to understand today how important such a purpose was to ex-Confederates still smarting from battlefield losses. To their way of thinking, if carpetbaggers and scalawags oppressed the citizenry, Southerners had to protect their way of life through extralegal means such as secret night riding. Appearing at a crucial moment in Southern history, the Prescript offered hope to whites disenchanted with Reconstruction.

Meanwhile, as the number of dens grew throughout 1867–1868, Klan regalia changed. Although some dens retained the elaborately designed costumes of the Pulaski Six, many groups adopted a plain white hood and gown. According to one source, white was chosen as the "emblem of purity." Moreover, "to render them startling and conspicuous, red, emblem of the blood which Klansmen were ready to shed in defense of the helpless, was chosen for the trimmings." Because the Prescript did not specify the requirements of an "official" KKK costume, the design was left to the imagination and resources of individual den officers. Some members preferred conical hats and fanciful symbolism while others adopted all-white gowns covering all but their feet. Many Klansmen even designed costumes for their horses. Over time, especially in the 1920s, after the KKK was reborn, plain white robes became the costume of choice probably because they were easier to fashion.[14]

Unlike Klan costumes, the group's banner was designated as an "official" flag, although individual dens often used their own banners in addition to, or in lieu of, the prescribed banner. According to the "direction" provided for the banner, it was to be an isosceles triangle, five feet long and three feet wide at the staff. The background was required to be yellow, laced

Figure 1.2. The most recognizable KKK robes consisted of a plain white sheet occasionally adorned with a simple cross. This design became the standard KKK uniform during the twentieth century.
Reprinted from the frontispiece to Mrs. S. E. F. Rose, *The Ku Klux Klan or Invisible Empire*

with red trim, and feature a flying dragon under a Latin phrase: *Quod semper, quod ubique, quod ab omnibus* ("What always, what everywhere, what by all [is held to be true].") The motto promised that the Klan would protect the noble virtues that every white Southerner knew to be eternal. In short, Klansmen viewed blacks as an inferior race that must be subjugated to protect whites from lawlessness, crime, and the despoliation of the white race.[15]

If the development of a Prescript along with goals, rituals, costumes, and mottoes were planned events, the appearance of legendary Confederate cavalryman Nathan Bedford Forrest as the Grand Wizard was a fortuitous occurrence. Accounts of Forrest's association with the Klan vary, but he seems to have joined the group not long after the April 1867 general council adjourned. John W. Morton, Forrest's former chief of artillery, had attended school in Pulaski and later became a Grand Cyclops in the Nashville den. Depending on who tells the tale, either Forrest came to Nashville seeking out Morton to question him about joining the Klan or else Morton traveled to Memphis to ask Forrest to serve as the Grand Wizard. In any case, Forrest accepted the position and, given his stature, led the group to prominence almost immediately.

General Forrest was a revered figure in the South, perhaps not as well regarded as Robert E. Lee or Stonewall Jackson, but nonetheless a symbol of the fiery, uncompromising brilliance cherished by many unreconstructed Confederates. Once described as "a vain, quick-tempered Tennessean, a successful businessman, slave trader and famed Confederate cavalry commander," the general was renowned for his utter fearlessness and audacity in battle. "That devil Forrest" was "the only Confederate cavalryman of whom Grant stood in much dread," a friend of the Union general remarked. Amassing a fortune trading in human bondage before the war, Forrest had laid it aside to serve in the Confederate States Army. Just as the ancient Roman general Cincinnatus had provided a model of simple virtue by abandoning his fields to render public service to his country at great personal sacrifice, so, too, had Forrest served his fledgling nation. Through four years of fighting, he was wounded many times, only to return home to find his nation humbled and his fortune squandered. His sole remaining asset at war's end was his reputation for military prowess and bold action, which led him into a postbellum career as a railroad executive and insurance man. During the war, he had been nicknamed a "wizard in the saddle" for his exploits, which may have suggested a natural fit as a KKK Grand Wizard.[16]

When he joined the Klan, Forrest brought prestige and legitimacy to the organization, at least in the eyes of many white Southerners. Forrest's

Figure 1.3. The KKK developed insignia and decorative banners to identify the group and promote its goals. The Latin motto, which quotes St. Augustine's definition of Catholic truth, reads: "What always, what everywhere, what by all [is held to be true]," referring to the Klan's supposition that the white race is superior to other races in accordance with the immutable laws of God and nature.

Reprinted from Mrs. S. E. F. Rose, *The Ku Klux Klan or Invisible Empire*

motivations for joining the group have been much debated and are not altogether clear even now. He seems to have been alarmed at the prolifera-
tion of black paramilitary groups such as the Union League, a political arm
of the Republican Party designed to shore up support for the party among
freedmen in the South. In Forrest's view, the Union League worked in concert with Reconstruction-era governments made up of Southern turn-
coats, Northern interlopers, and blacks of all social strata. Forrest saw the
Klan as a means for white Southerners, denied access to the normal instru-
ments of governmental control, to "defend" themselves and their honor. To
underscore his concerns, the KKK held a series of rallies and parades in
1867–1868 to drum up community support among whites, which greatly
increased the visibility of the hitherto "invisible empire."[17]

During the later Ku Klux Klan trials in the 1870s, the general was
called to testify as to his intentions and motivations when he served as the
first Grand Wizard, but his answers were vague and evasive. When asked if
the group had a political agenda when he assumed the helm, he said, "I
think it had not then; it had no political purpose." Instead, the club was an
outgrowth of white citizens organizing "so as to be ready in case they were
attacked." In Forrest's view, such preparations were necessary because "there
were a great many Northern men coming down here, forming Leagues all
over the country. The negroes were holding night meetings; were going
about; were becoming very insolent; and the Southern people all over the
State were very much alarmed." Testifying at the same time as General Forrest, his fellow Kluxer John B. Gordon, later a governor of Georgia, remarked, "the organization was simply this—nothing more and nothing less:
it was an organization, a brotherhood of property-holders, the peaceable,
law-abiding citizens of the State, for self-protection."[18]

Grand Wizard Forrest served as an inspiration for prospective Klan
members, but after the organization spread beyond Tennessee it evolved in
unforeseen ways. Assisted by published advertisements listing KKK activities and planned parades as well as favorable newspaper coverage, the group
garnered enormous publicity and assumed mythic status in the eyes of many
whites. The KKK was portrayed in the Southern press not as a group of
masked terrorists circumventing the law but as a quasi-public band of regulators enforcing the Southern code of honor. According to Mrs. S. E. F.
Rose, "ex-Confederates were denied the right of ballot, the right to testify
in the courts or the right to carry firearms. There were negro soldiers, legislators and magistrates, and as negroes held all the offices, the white men
were completely at their mercy." In light of this depressed condition, the
only recourse "to preserve some form of just government and have some

degree of freedom was to organize a compact secret body to do what openly they could not do."[19]

Whatever his original motives for joining, Forrest's association with the Klan was short-lived, although it started with much promise. He traveled extensively throughout the South during his tenure as the Grand Wizard from mid-1867 until early 1869, always stressing the "honorable" and "patriotic" purposes of the group, namely, retaining some measure of political power and control for white Southerners. He also was involved in efforts to influence the outcome of the 1868 elections, although the extent of his activities was never clear. In an August 28, 1868, interview for the Cincinnati *Commercial*, Forrest bragged that the KKK claimed 40,000 members in Tennessee alone and as many as 550,000 throughout the South. He probably exaggerated the numbers. Later, worried that he had said too much, the general disavowed the contents of the interview, arguing that the reporter had misquoted him. Nonetheless, Forrest's assertions provided a window into the growth of the Klan by the summer of 1868.[20]

Late in January 1869, the general reversed course and disassociated himself from the KKK, explaining that the "honorable and patriotic" club had been perverted by vigilantes more interested in terrorizing their enemies than in upholding the honor and traditions of the South. In "General Order Number One," the only directive ever issued by Imperial Headquarters, Forrest lambasted Klansmen who compromised public safety and security "to achieve personal benefit and private purposes, and to satiate private revenge by means of its masked features." At the conclusion of the order, Forrest directed the Grand Cyclops of each den to assemble his men and "require them to destroy in his presence every article of his mask and costume and at the same time [he] shall destroy his own." Persons who failed to comply with the directive were deemed "an enemy of the order."

Forrest's defenders point to General Order Number One as evidence of his realization that the Ku Klux Klan was a terrorist organization deserving of nothing so much as opprobrium. Such an interpretation is disingenuous. Through his actions and public statements, Forrest never rejected the need for a secret paramilitary group to patrol the byways of the community to terrorize freedmen and frighten them away from ballot boxes. His objection centered on the loss of control over dens that housed overzealous, reckless, unprincipled members. In military terms, Forrest agreed with the mission of the Klan; he simply objected to the lack of discipline among rank-and-file Kluxers and their poorly executed plan of attack.[21]

Subsequent Klan sympathizers acted as though Forrest's order effectively disbanded the Klan. It did no such thing. The Romines wistfully observed

Figure 1.4. More than any other single person, legendary Confederate General Nathan Bedford Forrest was responsible for the early success of the KKK after he became Grand Wizard in 1867. His subsequent efforts to curb the group's violent activities were ineffective.
Library of Congress, Copy Print Courtesy of The Museum of the Confederacy, Richmond, Virginia

that "so ended the organization which brought only relief to the desolated Southland in the dark days of reconstruction, immediately following that awful contest between the States, when brother's hand was lifted against brother." Mrs. S. E. F. Rose explained that she wrote her book so a "younger generation should know the true history of the Ku Klux Klan, and have the proper respect for this organization, which did so much for the South in her dark days." Lester and Wilson, the original KKK enthusiasts, wrote that the "Ku Klux Klan had no organized existence after March 1869," a little over a month after Forrest issued General Order Number One. "Thus lived, so died, this strange order. Its birth was an accident; its growth was a comedy; its death a tragedy."[22]

These apologists dated the Klan's demise from January 1869 so that subsequent abuses could be attributed to splinter groups, "false dens" that were not associated with the one true, "noble" Ku Klux Klan. Despite these transparent efforts to distinguish the Pulaski organization from "unauthorized" offshoots, the epitaph for the KKK was not written until much later than January 1869. The Pulaski Six and men like John C. Brown, George W. Gordon, John W. Morton, and Nathan Bedford Forrest sought to avoid responsibility for post-1869 Klan outrages, but they shouldered no small measure of blame for creating and structuring an organization devoted to promoting white supremacy through extralegal means. They unleashed forces they later could not control, but unleash them they did.

The post-January 1869 Klan grew without an overall plan or purpose. With the order from headquarters supposedly disbanding the KKK, the group's history became murky because the loss of even a semblance of centralized control meant that each den was free to act on its own authority. Some historians have suggested that after late 1868 the Klan was not fundamentally a political organization while others have contended that it was first and foremost a political group. The answer probably lies somewhere in between, depending on which Klan is examined. KKK dens continued to spring up in every Southern state despite General Order Number One. Sometimes these new groups adopted the name "Ku Klux Klan" although they did not receive permission from the Pulaski Six. Other groups adopted different names, including the Knights of the Rising Sun, Knights of the White Camellia, and Young Men's Democratic Clubs. Their only commonality was a desire to shield their faces beneath crude disguises as they patrolled neighborhoods and terrorized blacks.

As a decentralized, loosely structured series of groups, the dens sported different agendas and employed different methods. Some clubs were apolitical, purely social, and predominantly nonviolent. Others were active in opposing Republican-controlled Reconstruction governments through violence and intimidation. They targeted white Northern leaders, Southern sympathizers, and politically active blacks.[23]

By the time the 1868 elections occurred, the Klan was no longer a mysterious, invisible group. Membership was growing across the South. National publications such as *Harper's Weekly* began regularly reporting on the group's activities, arguing that the KKK was, in effect, a terrorist arm of the Democratic Party. "A rebel colonel from Georgia, at a meeting in New York, shouted that if 'Northern Democrats will take care of the bayonet, the Southern Democrats would be responsible for the result of the ballot in November,' meaning that the Ku-Klux Klan would take care of loyal voters," the magazine reported in July 1868. Indeed, from 1868 onward, apologists would face a difficult task in arguing that the Klan was merely a social club after many dens blatantly promoted the Democratic Party—through violent means, if necessary.

Elected president as a Republican in 1868, Ulysses S. Grant, the former Union general who accepted Robert E. Lee's surrender at Appomattox Courthouse, commented that the Klan was clearly a political group. In his view, the Klan was committed "by force and terror, to prevent all political action not in accord with the views of the members, to deprive colored citizens of the right to bear arms and of the right of a free ballot, to suppress the schools in which colored children were taught, and to reduce the colored people to a condition closely allied to that of slavery."[24]

Klan dens did not engage in concerted action, but they shared a common goal of electing Democrats to office at all levels of government. Despite their best efforts to intimidate would-be Republican voters, however, the Klan was unsuccessful in 1868. Republicans remained firmly in control in most Southern states. Consequently, the KKK escalated its campaign of violence against white Republicans and "uppity" blacks. Observing the increasing violence after 1868, federal Judge Hugh Lennox Bond, a man who would play a pivotal role in the subsequent Ku Klux Klan trials, wrote to his wife that he "never believed such a state of things existed in the U.S." Worried that he might be a target of violent retaliation by the Klan, Bond weighed his words carefully. "I will tell you all when I come home what I am afraid to pour out on paper."[25]

KKK dens sprang up in every Southern state, but South Carolina saw some of the worst abuses. Despite partisan writers' portrayal of the Klan as a band dedicated to reasserting community values and instilling a sense of honor among disenchanted whites, the group pursued political goals through violence from its first appearance in South Carolina in 1868. With the success of the state Republican Party and the failure of citizens to defeat the new state constitution that required adoption of the Fourteenth Amendment, the Klan was viewed by many South Carolinians as a legitimate form of political opposition to the ruling powers that be. If white Southerners could not find an outlet for their anger through the institutions of government, they would make their feelings known in other ways.

Acts of Klan violence in South Carolina became commonplace. On June 4, 1868, state senator Solomon Washington Dill was shot dead near his home. A few weeks later, legislator James Martin was shot and killed in front of the Abbeville County Courthouse. In October, Johnson Stuart, a Republican from Newberry, was shot dead on his way home from a political meeting. Lee Nance, Stuart's good friend and president of the local Union League, was murdered. Perhaps the most notorious act of terrorism sponsored by the Klan was the assassination of state legislator Benjamin F. Randolph, a black carpetbagger especially hated by the white establishment. While stepping off a train one day, Randolph was shot dead without warning. As the violence intensified, South Carolina Governor Robert K. Scott received a chilling telegram signed by William Lawton, a self-proclaimed "Republican Democrat," who warned: "By the 'Law of Success' the murder of your enemy is the righteous vindication of your 'Right to Rule.'"

Fearful that the violence could not be quelled, Governor Scott appealed to former Confederate General Wade Hampton, a prominent Democrat and later the state's redeemer governor, to speak out publicly against further violence. Although Hampton was not a friend to the freedmen, he feared federal intervention and so he agreed to denounce "general lawlessness." For a time, these efforts succeeded in curbing Klan violence, but outbreaks increased significantly after the 1870 elections ensured continued Republican rule. Finally unable to control the situation, Governor Scott contacted the Grant administration for assistance. In response, Grant used his powers under various Reconstruction-era statutes to intervene by sending troops into South Carolina.[26]

The rise and spread of the Ku Klux Klan beginning in the latter half of the 1860s was part of the larger story of American Reconstruction. As the nation struggled to overcome the cataclysm of civil war, citizens North and South were forced to come to terms with the abolition of slavery, military occupation of the South, and changes in social relations among the black and white races. That Southerners would resist the changes forced upon them by military reverses on the battlefield was hardly surprising. Their generals and political leaders were vanquished, but white Southerners would not relinquish their "way of life" without a fight. Thus, the story of Reconstruction is the story of how the Civil War continued through other means.[27]

NOTES

1. Paul H. Bergeron, Stephen V. Ash, and Jeanette Keith, *Tennesseans and Their History* (Knoxville: University of Tennessee Press, 1999), 158–80; Eyre Damer, *When the Ku Klux Rode* (Westport, CT: Negro Universities Press, 1970; originally published by the Neale Publishing Company, New York, 1912), 90–91; J. C. Lester and D. L. Wilson, *Ku Klux Klan: Its Origin, Growth, and Disbursement* (New York: Da Capo Press, 1973; originally published in Nashville, TN: Wheeler, Osborn & Duckworth Manufacturing Company, 1884), 51–56; Mrs. S. E. F. Rose, *The Ku Klux Klan or Invisible Empire* (New Orleans, LA: L. Graham Co., Ltd., 1914), 18–19; Allen W. Trelease, *White Terror: The Ku Klux Klan Conspiracy and Southern Reconstruction* (Baton Rouge: Louisiana State University Press, 1971), 8–11, 430–31; Wyn Craig Wade, *The Fiery Cross: The Ku Klux Klan in America* (New York and Oxford: Oxford University Press, 1987), 32.

2. Quoted in Mr. and Mrs. W. B. Romine, *A Story of the Original Ku Klux Klan* (Pulaski, TN: The Pulaski Citizen, 1934), 4. See also, Susan L. Davis, *Authentic History: Ku Klux Klan, 1865–1877* (New York: American Library Service, 1924), 16–21; Lester and Wilson, *Ku Klux Klan*, 51–56; W. T. Richardson, *Historic Pulaski: Birthplace of the Ku Klux Klan; Scene of Execution of Sam Davis* (Pulaski, TN: Author, 1913), 13–14; Wade, *The Fiery Cross*, 32–33.

3. David M. Chalmers, *Hooded Americanism: The History of the Ku Klux Klan*, 3d ed. (Durham, NC: Duke University Press, 1987), 8–9; Stanley F. Horn, *Invisible Empire: The Story of the Ku Klux Klan, 1866–1871* (Montclair, NJ: Patterson Smith, 1969), 9; Trelease, *White Terror*, 3–4; Wade, *The Fiery Cross*, 32.

4. Myra Lockett Avary, *Dixie After the War: An Exposition on the Social Conditions Existing in the South, During the Twelve Years Succeeding the Fall of Richmond* (New York: Doubleday, Page & Company, 1906), 268; Davis, *Authentic History*, 7–10; Horn, *Invisible Empire*, 9–10; V. C. Jones, "The Rise and Fall of the Ku Klux Klan," *Civil War Times Illustrated* 2 (February 1964): 13; Lester and Wilson, *Ku Klux Klan*, 51–56; Elaine Frantz Parsons, "Midnight Ramblers: Costume and Performance in the Reconstruction-Era Ku Klux Klan," *The Journal of American History* 92 (December 2005): 811–15; Richardson, *Historic Pulaski*, 11–16.

5. Horn, *Invisible Empire*, 7–13; Lester and Wilson, *Ku Klux Klan*, 56; J. Michael Martinez, "Traditionalist Perspectives on Confederate Symbols," in *Confederate Symbols in the Contemporary South*, J. Michael Martinez, William D. Richardson, and Ron McNinch-Su, eds. (Gainesville: University Press of Florida, 2000), 255; "One of the C7K," *Confederate Veteran* 25 (November 1917): 527; Richardson, *Historic Pu-*

laski, 16; Romine, *A Story of the Original Ku Klux Klan*, 6–7; Trelease, *White Terror*, 4; Wade, *The Fiery Cross*, 33; Allen Ward, "A Note on the Origin of the Ku Klux Klan," *Tennessee Historical Quarterly* 23 (June 1964): 182.

6. Eric Foner, *Reconstruction: America's Unfinished Revolution, 1863–1877* (New York: Francis Parkman Prize Edition, History Book Club, 2005; originally published by HarperCollins, 1988), 425; Edward John Harcourt, "Who Were the Pale Faces? New Perspectives on the Tennessee Ku Klux," *Civil War History* 51 (March 2005): 23–66; Parsons, "Midnight Ramblers," 813–15; Jasper Ridley, *The Freemasons: A History of the World's Most Powerful Secret Society* (New York: Arcade Publishing, 2001); Wade, *The Fiery Cross*, 39–40; Richard Zuczek, *State of Rebellion: Reconstruction in South Carolina* (Columbia, SC: University of South Carolina Press, 1996), 139–42.

7. Chalmers, *Hooded Americanism*, 8–9; Parsons, "Midnight Ramblers," 819–36; Richardson, *Historic Pulaski*, 17–20; Trelease, *White Terror*, 4–5; Wade, *The Fiery Cross*, 34.

8. Avary, *Dixie After the War*, 268; Jones, "The Rise and Fall of the Ku Klux Klan," 13–14; Lester and Wilson, *Ku Klux Klan*, 60–63; Richardson, *Historic Pulaski*, 19–24; J. A. Rogers, *The Ku Klux Spirit* (Baltimore, MD: Black Classic Press, 1980; originally published by Messenger Publishing Company, 1923), 15–16; Romine, *A Story of the Original Ku Klux Klan*, 7–9.

9. Avary, *Dixie After the War*, 269; Bergeron, Ash, and Keith, *Tennesseans and Their History*, 158–80; Walter L. Flemming, "Prescript of the Ku Klux Klan," *Publications of the Southern History Association* 7 (September 1903): 327; Jones, "The Rise and Fall of the Ku Klux Klan," 14; Trelease, *White Terror*, 8–11; Wade, *The Fiery Cross*, 34–35; D. L. Wilson, "The Ku Klux Klan: Its Growth and Disbandment," *Century Magazine* XXVIII (n.s. VI) (1884): 399; Charles Reagan Wilson, *Baptized in Blood: The Religion of the Lost Cause, 1865–1920* (Athens: University of Georgia of Georgia Press, 1980), 110–18. The question of whether the original Ku Klux Klan was as benign as many accounts claim has been called into question in recent years. See, for example, Harcourt, "Who Were the Pale Faces?" 29–35.

10. Thomas B. Alexander, "Ku-kluxism in Tennessee, 1865–1869," *Tennessee Historical Quarterly* 8 (1949): 198; Chalmers, *Hooded Americanism*, 2; Lester and Wilson, *Ku Klux Klan*, 73; Martinez, "Traditionalist Perspectives on Confederate Symbols," 255–56; Grady H. McWhiney and Francis B. Simkins, "The Ghostly Legend of the Ku Klux Klan," *Negro History Bulletin* 14 (February 1951): 109–12; Richardson, *Historic Pulaski*, 29; Romine, *A Story of the Original Ku Klux Klan*, 10–11; Rogers, *The Ku Klux Spirit*, 16–17; Wade, *The Fiery Cross*, 35–36.

11. Damer, *When the Ku Klux Rode*, 91–93; Horn, *Invisible Empire*, 32–33; Jones, "The Rise and Fall of the Ku Klux Klan," 15; Richardson, *Historic Pulaski*, 38–41; Romine, *A Story of the Original Ku Klux Klan*, 10–25; Rose, *The Ku Klux Klan*, 15–17, 37–42; Trelease, *White Terror*, 13–16; Wade, *The Fiery Cross*, 37–39.

12. Horn, *Invisible Empire*, 113; Enoch L. Mitchell, "The Role of General George Washington Gordon in the Ku-Klux Klan," *Western Tennessee Historical Society Papers* 1 (1947): 73–80; Trelease, *White Terror*, 13–14; Wade, *The Fiery Cross*, 38–39.

13. Parsons, "Midnight Ramblers," 815; Romine, *A Story of the Original Ku Klux Klan*, 17–25, quoted at 12; Trelease, *White Terror*, 14–19, Wade, *The Fiery Cross*, 37–40.

14. Gladys-Marie Fry, *Night Riders in Black Folk History* (Knoxville: University of Tennessee Press, 1975), 122–25; Horn, *Invisible Empire*, 58–66; Parsons, "Midnight Ramblers," 818–23; Romine, *A Story of the Original Ku Klux Klan*, 15; Rose, *The Ku Klux Klan*, 43–47; Albion W. Tourgee, *The Invisible Empire: Part I—A New, Illustrated, and Enlarged Edition of a Fool's Errand, By One of the Fools; The Famous Historical Romance of Life in the South Since the War; Part II—A Concise Review of Recent Events, Showing the Elements on Which the Tale is Based, with Many Thrilling Personal Narratives and Other Startling Facts and Considerations, Including an Account of the Rise, Extent, Purpose, Methods, and Deeds of the Mysterious Ku-Klux Klan; All Fully Authenticated* (New York: Fords, Howard & Hulbert, 1879), 131, 419–23; Trelease, *White Terror*, 18–19, 53–54; Wade, *The Fiery Cross*, 59–60.

15. Avary, *Dixie After the War*, 275; Parsons, "Midnight Ramblers," 819–36; Rose, *The Ku Klux Klan*, 39.

16. Avary, *Dixie After the War*, 275–76; Damer, *When the Ku Klux Rode*, 93–94; Davis, *Authentic History*, 81, 86–87; Shelby Foote, *The Civil War: A Narrative*, Vol. 2, *Fredericksburg to Meridian* (New York: Vintage Books, 1974), 65; Charles G. Jones, "Forrest: A Mixture of Genius and Guile," *Washington Times*, June 3, 1995, B3; J. Michael Martinez and Robert M. Harris, "Graves, Worms, and Epitaphs: Confederate Monuments in the Southern Landscape" in *Confederate Symbols in the Contemporary South*, J. Michael Martinez, William D. Richardson, and Ron McNinch-Su, eds. (Gainesville: University Press of Florida, 2000), 167; Andrew Lytle, *Bedford Forrest and His Critter Company* (New York: McDowell, Obolensky, 1960), 382–83; Martinez, "Traditionalist Perspectives on Confederate Symbols," 256–57; John Watson Morton, *The Artillery of Nathan Bedford Forrest's Cavalry* (Marietta, GA: R. Bemis Publishing, Ltd., 1995), 338, 343–45; Romine, *A Story of the Original Ku Klux Klan*, 17; Trelease, *White Terror*, 19–20; Wade, *The Fiery Cross*, 40–41; Henry C. Warmouth, *War, Politics and Reconstruction: Stormy Days in Louisiana* (New York: MacMillan, 1930), 70–71.

17. Davis, *Authentic History*, 89; Robert J. Kaczorowski, "Federal Enforcement of Civil Rights During the First Reconstruction," *Fordham Urban Law Journal* 23 (Fall 1995): 156–57; Parsons, "Midnight Ramblers," 830–36; Richardson, *Historic Pulaski*, 34–35; Trelease, *White Terror*, 21–27; Wade, *The Fiery Cross*, 43–44.

18. Quoted in Harvey Wish, ed., *Reconstruction in the South, 1865–1877: First-Hand Accounts of the American Southland After the Civil War, By Northerners and Southerners* (New York: Farrar, Strauss and Giroux, 1965), 156, 158. See also, Harcourt, "Who Were the Pale Faces?" 35; Jones, "The Rise and Fall of the Ku Klux Klan," 17; Wade, *The Fiery Cross*, 106.

19. Quoted in Rose, *The Ku Klux Klan*, 26. See also, Kaczorowski, "Federal Enforcement of Civil Rights During the First Reconstruction," 155–59; Richardson, *Historic Pulaski*, 41–49; Rogers, *The Ku Klux Spirit*, 29–31; Wade, *The Fiery Cross*, 57–59.

20. Richard Nelson Current, ed., *Reconstruction [1865–1877]* (Englewood Cliffs, NJ: Prentice-Hall, 1965), 92–94; Martinez, "Traditionalist Perspectives on Confederate Symbols," 256; James Ridgeway, *Blood in the Face: The Ku Klux Klan, Aryan Nations, Nazi Skinheads, and the Rise of a New White Culture*, 2d. ed. (New York: Thunder's Mouth Press, 1995), 51; Herbert Shapiro, "The Ku Klux Klan During Reconstruction: The South Carolina Episode," *Journal of Negro History* 49 (January 1964): 35; Tourgee, *The Invisible Empire*, 13–14; Wade, *The Fiery Cross*, 50–51.

21. Davis, *Authentic History*, 125–28; Lester and Wilson, *Ku Klux Klan*, 109–13; Martinez, "Traditionalist Perspectives on Confederate Symbols," 256–57; Romine, *A Story of the Original Ku Klux Klan*, 24–26; Rose, *The Ku Klux Klan*, 71–73; Trelease, *White Terror*, 173–74; Wade, *The Fiery Cross*, 58–60; Wish, ed., *Reconstruction in the South, 1865–1877*, 156–57.

22. Lester and Wilson, *Ku Klux Klan*, 131; Romine, *A Story of the Original Ku Klux Klan*, 26; Rose, *The Ku Klux Klan*, 74.

23. Lisa Cardyn, "Sexualized Racism/Gendered Violence: Outraging the Body Politic in the Reconstruction South," *Michigan Law Review* 100 (February 2002): 676–77, 680–83; Kaczorowski, "Federal Enforcement of Civil Rights During the First Reconstruction," 156–57; Trelease, *White Terror*, 28–30, 49–53; Wade, *The Fiery Cross*, 62–64.

24. Quoted in "The Lines Drawn," *Harper's Weekly* (July 18, 1868): 450; Wade, *The Fiery Cross*, 62. See also, Cardyn, "Sexualized Racism/Gendered Violence," 682–83; "The Democratic Hell-Broth," *Harper's Weekly* (October 31, 1868): 704; "Democratic Majority," *Harper's Weekly* (November 21, 1868): 747; "Domestic Intelligence," *Harper's Weekly* (October 10, 1868): 643; "Domestic Intelligence," *Harper's Weekly* (November 7, 1868): 707; Foner, *Reconstruction: America's Unfinished Revolution*, 425–26; Eric Foner and Olivia Mahoney, *America's Reconstruction: People and Politics After the Civil War* (New York: HarperPerennial, 1995), 119–25; Jones, "The Rise and Fall of the Ku Klux Klan," 16–17; Kaczorowski, "Federal Enforcement of Civil Rights During the First Reconstruction," 156–60; "Louisiana," *Harper's Weekly* (August 22, 1868): 531.

25. Quoted in Kaczorowski, "Federal Enforcement of Civil Rights During the First Reconstruction," 157. See also, Richard Paul Fuke, "Hugh Lennox Bond and Radical Republican Ideology," *Journal of Southern History* 45 (November 1979): 569–86.

26. Foner, *Reconstruction: America's Unfinished Revolution*, 548; Asa H. Gordon, *Sketches of Negro Life and History in South Carolina*, 2d. ed. (Columbia: University of South Carolina Press, 1929), 78–79; Shapiro, "The Ku Klux Klan During Reconstruction," 34–50; Francis B. Simkins, "The Ku Klux Klan in South Carolina," *Journal of Negro History* 12 (October 1927): 608; Francis Butler Simkins and Robert

Hilliard Woody, *South Carolina During Reconstruction* (Chapel Hill: The University of North Carolina Press, 1932), 457–58; J. C. A. Stagg, "The Problem of Klan Violence: The South Carolina Up-Country, 1868–1871," *Journal of American Studies* 8 (December 1974): 316; Trelease, *White Terror*, 116–17; Wade, *The Fiery Cross*, 73; Lou Falkner Williams, *The Great South Carolina Ku Klux Klan Trials, 1871–1872* (Athens: University of Georgia Press, 1996), 23–24; Richard Zuczek, *State of Rebellion: Reconstruction in South Carolina* (Columbia, SC: University of South Carolina Press, 1996), 55–61.

27. David H. Donald, *The Politics of Reconstruction, 1863–1867* (Baton Rouge: Louisiana State University Press, 1965), 1–17; Foner, *Reconstruction: America's Unfinished Revolution*, xix–xxvii; John Hope Franklin, *Reconstruction After the Civil War* (Chicago: The University of Chicago Press, 1961), 150–51; Jones, "The Rise and Fall of the Ku Klux Klan," 12–17; Martin E. Mantell, *Johnson, Grant, and the Politics of Reconstruction* (New York and London: Columbia University Press, 1973), 150–69; Richard Zuczek, "The Federal Government's Attack on the Ku Klux Klan: A Reassessment," *South Carolina Historical Magazine* 97 (January 1, 1996): 47–64.

2

"THE FOUNDATIONS MUST BE BROKEN UP AND RELAID, OR ALL OUR BLOOD AND TREASURE HAVE BEEN SPENT IN VAIN"

Reconstruction, the political process of bringing the seceding Southern states back into the Union, began before the Civil War ended. On December 8, 1863, sixteen months before Confederate General Robert E. Lee surrendered at Appomattox Courthouse, President Abraham Lincoln announced a plan to grant general amnesty to all but the highest-ranking Confederate civil and military leaders. As usual, the wily Lincoln combined current political expediency with unbridled optimism for the future. His short-term goal was to convince Southerners they would not be harshly punished if they threw down their arms and returned to the fold. In the long run, a reconstruction plan implied that the war would be won and a Union would exist to be reconstructed.

Lincoln's terms were simple. By affirming an oath to support the United States Constitution and agreeing to obey all federal laws, including those abolishing slavery, Southerners could rejoin the United States—not as it had been before secession, but as it stood when the war ended. Ex-Confederates would enjoy all property rights "except as to slaves." When the number of citizens taking the oath in a particular state equaled or exceeded 10 percent of the votes cast in the 1860 election, newly made loyalists could establish a state government.

As with many of Lincoln's wartime measures, the proposal was not a final decision, nor did the president expect the plan to be adopted without amendments. It was a starting point for crafting a policy. Moreover, Lincoln's terminology was telling. The Proclamation of Amnesty and Reconstruction did not offer to "reconstitute," "renew," "restore," or "resume" the old Union. It would "reconstruct" a new Union from the ashes of the old.

Ever the resourceful politician, Lincoln included something for almost everyone in his plan. Radical Republicans in Congress favored harsh reprisals against the traitorous South; they were pleased that the proposal unequivocally required ex-Confederates to recognize slavery as a defunct institution. Democrats and others sympathetic to the South realized that the plan was generous. Lincoln would not treat the seceding states as conquered provinces to be subjected to brutal military rule. Throughout the war, he had consistently argued that the states had not seceded from the Union; a disaffected minority of leaders had attempted to create a separate government. Once the war was won and the rebels were disarmed, the federal government need not punish the populace of the South for the actions of a few misguided leaders.

For all of the plan's ingenuity, critics argued that Lincoln conspicuously ignored the plight of blacks. In the words of abolitionist Wendell Phillips, the measure "frees the slaves and ignores the negro." Universal suffrage and equality before the law, essential features in a democratic regime, were absent. In his efforts to assuage the fears of Southerners, the president assumed that emancipation was all that the federal government need do for former slaves.

In his defense, Lincoln's paramount objective was to end the war as soon as possible. He already had issued the Emancipation Proclamation freeing slaves in the rebellious states. A harsh Reconstruction plan risked antagonizing whites on both sides of the Mason-Dixon line. If he could entice enough Southerners in border states and in areas under Union control to adopt his plan he could launch Reconstruction even before the rebels were brought to submission. The question of how the federal government would treat freedmen in the Southern states was a question best left for another time.

The plan's design may have been simple, but implementation presented numerous problems. As the Union army occupied parts of the Western theater, the administration adopted the plan, particularly in Louisiana, Arkansas, and Mississippi in 1864 and 1865. Results were mixed. Many elected officials in Lincoln's own party remained concerned that the "inverted pyramid" inherent in his plan undermined the sacrifices made by the Union army. If a small group of whites—the top of a pyramid—could seize control of state governments and exclude more numerous blacks and liberal Southerners from decision making—the base of the pyramid—the rule of a minority over a majority could lead to the return of slavery in everything but name. Lincoln was sympathetic to these concerns, but he never devoted his full energies to Reconstruction. Winning the war was his first priority.

When he proposed the 10 percent plan in 1863, victory on the battlefield—and in the 1864 presidential election—was far from certain.[1]

In the meantime, Radical Republicans in Congress exposed a rift in Reconstruction policy in July 1864 with the introduction of the Wade-Davis Bill, H.R. No. 244. Sponsored by Senator Benjamin F. Wade of Ohio and Congressman Henry Winter Davis of Maryland, the measure required a majority of a state's white males to pledge support for the U.S. Constitution before the state could be readmitted to the Union. After an "ironclad oath" had been administered to the requisite number of men, a state constitutional convention would be held. Leaders in the states proposed for readmission were required to guarantee equality before the law, although the bill fell short of calling for Negro suffrage. No one who had served as a high-ranking Confederate military or civilian leader was eligible to swear an oath or participate in a state convention.

Congress passed the bill before adjourning for the summer. Lincoln rightly viewed Wade-Davis as a rebuke from Radical Republicans—"they have never been friendly to me," he remarked—but he knew that vetoing the bill was politically risky, especially since he faced a difficult reelection bid in the fall. Despite warnings that he must not alienate influential members of Congress, the president needed time to assess the results of the 10 percent plan. After Congress adjourned, Lincoln employed the pocket veto, a rarely used presidential power at the time, which allowed him to ignore the bill, neither signing nor vetoing it. With Congress out of session, the bill died after 10 days.

Predictably, the sponsors were incensed. A month after the pocket veto, Senator Wade and Congressman Davis issued a public "manifesto" criticizing Lincoln's "dictatorial usurpation of power" and charging that "a more studied outrage on the legislative authority of the people has never been perpetrated." Their objections highlighted a long-running dispute between the legislative and executive branches. Article I of the U.S. Constitution grants authority to Congress to declare war, but Article II designates the president as the commander-in-chief. This division of responsibility serves as a check on the power of both branches; theoretically, they must share power and responsibility for conducting wartime activities. Unfortunately, dividing power in this way also creates ambiguity, resulting in conflicts between Congress and the president. During the Civil War, Congress created a Joint Committee on the Conduct of the War to oversee the Lincoln administration's actions, but the president always insisted that he, and not Congress, retained primary power and responsibility for suppressing a civil insurrection.[2]

Despite the harsh words of the Wade-Davis Manifesto, the dispute between Congress and the president was not necessarily permanent. Throughout his presidency, Lincoln demonstrated his willingness to forgive and forget in the interests of political expediency or to pursue a higher purpose. It would have been interesting to observe his reactions to the Radical Republicans' continued insistence on more stringent terms for the Southern states' readmission into the Union, but he did not live long enough to confront the issue directly. He died on April 15, 1865, just as the war ended.[3]

Lincoln's successor, Andrew Johnson, was a former Jacksonian Democrat who had served in the U.S. House of Representatives, the U.S. Senate, and as governor of Tennessee. Johnson has been blamed for the failure of Presidential Reconstruction, and to some extent this condemnation is justified. Unlike Lincoln, the Tennessean was not an adroit politician. He could be stubbornly defensive, rigid, petty, and impervious to the need for compromise. He was vain, temperamental, and impulsive, and frequently carried a grudge long past the point of sober judgment. Celebrated English author Charles Dickens once observed that Johnson's face showed great strength but lacked "genial sunlight." Never a friend to the freedmen, Johnson adopted his predecessor's leniency toward the South with little regard for the give and take necessary to shepherd legislation through Congress. In time, his inflexibility and confrontational approach empowered Radical Republicans to seize control of Reconstruction and impeach the president.

The condemnation of later historians was conspicuously absent at the beginning of Johnson's presidency. In the wake of Lincoln's assassination, the tough-talking Johnson seemed intent on prosecuting the war to a speedy end and bringing the rebels to heel. His fiery rhetoric included the sentiment that "traitors must be punished and impoverished." Hearing this and other similar comments, congressional Republicans took heart. The policies of this new, unproven leader occupying the Executive Mansion could be counted on to advance the Radicals' cause—or so they believed.[4]

Johnson surprised his early supporters when he issued a proclamation of amnesty on May 29, 1865. Except for the Confederate leadership, the president offered to pardon all Southerners for their roles in the rebellion. He also set about appointing provisional state governors who seemed far friendlier to the South than the Radical Republicans would have liked. As spring gave way to summer, it became increasingly clear that the new president's Reconstruction policy was closer to Lincoln's original 10 percent plan than it was to the Wade-Davis Bill.[5]

Figure 2.1. Andrew Johnson served as president during the early years of Reconstruction (1865–1869) as the Ku Klux Klan formed and grew in power.
Picture History

Congress was not in session when Johnson issued his amnesty proclamation, but the Radicals nonetheless began to plan their next moves. They believed that Johnson's proposal threatened to squander a once-in-a-lifetime "golden moment" to reshape race relations in the United States. Fundamental changes in society seldom occur in the absence of cataclysmic events such as a civil war. In the aftermath of that terrible conflict, the Union might yet profit by ensuring equal civil and political rights for all citizens. In the Radicals' view, if the federal government failed to ensure those rights in 1865, the window of opportunity would close and the bloodshed would have been for naught. Johnson either failed to see the tremendous opportunity he had been granted or he did not care. In any case, something had to be done to ameliorate the leniency of the president's proclamation.

When Congress finally reconvened in December 1865, a number of legislators, notably Senator Wade, Congressman Davis, Senator Charles Sumner of Massachusetts, and Congressman Thaddeus Stevens of Pennsylvania, quickly proposed legislation to undermine Johnson's permissive policies. The Radicals may have been true believers in the Negro cause, but they also had practical interests in ensuring that the Southern states did not reenter the Union too quickly. If Southern congressmen and senators joined forces with other Democrats, Republicans might lose control of the legislative process. To forestall this possibility, congressional Republicans pushed through a series of bills designed to strengthen punitive policies toward the South.[6]

Despite the Radicals' intent, the first two bills were relatively moderate. Sponsored by Senator Lyman Trumbull, chairman of the Judiciary Committee, the first measure extended the life of the Freedmen's Bureau, the federal agency designed to assist newly emancipated slaves in establishing themselves in the postbellum era. The bureau originally was slated to last a year, but as the time for the agency to sunset drew closer, it was clear that freedmen desperately needed assistance in securing clothing, housing, and education as well as in battling discrimination and violence. If the federal government left those chores to the states, it was doubtful whether blacks would ever rise above their modest station in life.

The second measure, the Civil Rights Bill of 1866, was designed to augment the Thirteenth Amendment, the constitutional provision that abolished slavery throughout the country in December 1865. Section two of the amendment declared, "Congress shall have power to enforce this article by appropriate legislation." A landmark piece of legislation, the bill recognized all persons born in the United States, with the notable exception of Native Americans, as national citizens entitled to the "full and equal benefit of all laws" without regard to race. U.S. district attorneys, U.S. marshals, and other federal officials could file suit in federal courts to ensure compliance. Before the war, it was unthinkable that blacks would be afforded any rights that a white man was bound to respect. Even after the guns had fallen silent between North and South, the bill's lofty goals, considered radical for their time, were not realized until well into the next century.[7]

If the Radicals were alarmed by President Johnson's amnesty proclamation, they were nothing short of astonished when he vetoed both the bill extending the Freedmen's Bureau and the Civil Rights Bill of 1866. In his veto message for the second bill, Johnson explained that the federal government could not constitutionally consolidate its power to protect any group, much less Negroes, from discrimination. In no uncertain terms, he voiced his opinion that "the distinction of race and color is by the bill made to operate in favor of the colored and against the white race." Citing fears of racial intermarriage and expressing his belief that blacks lack an adequate understanding of "the nature and character of our institutions," he echoed a widespread feeling in all sections of the country that Negroes simply were inherently inferior to whites. Johnson served notice that, unlike his predecessor, he was unable or unwilling to compromise or consider opinions aside from his own.

Even more shocking than the vetoes were comments he delivered to a group of six thousand Democrats that marched from a rally to the Executive Mansion to serenade the president. Delighted at the schism between Johnson and congressional Republicans, Democrats had rediscovered the virtues of a Tennessean who apparently had turned his back on his party and section only to show his true colors upon ascending to the presidency. Johnson seemed equally as delighted to find himself the toast of the Democratic Party. In a long-winded tirade delivered to the onlookers, the president compared the Radical Republicans to Judas Iscariot and himself to Jesus Christ. He also complained of the treachery evinced by the Radicals—"the Davises and Tombeses, the Slidells, and a long list of others."

"Give us the names," someone in the crowd called out.

The president happily obliged in one of the more misguided public statements of his troubled career. "I say Thaddeus Stevens of Pennsylvania, I say Charles Sumner of Massachusetts, I say Wendell Phillips of Massachusetts and others of the same stripe." They had betrayed the country and their president. Continuing the comparison of himself to Christ and his own possible martyrdom, Johnson told the crowd, "If my blood is to be shed because I vindicate the Union, let it be shed."[8]

With these virulent charges, the president ensured that his relationship with key members of Congress was irreparably damaged. Even former moderates such as Lyman Trumbull were embittered at what they viewed as the president's needlessly antagonistic behavior. Disgusted with Johnson's antics, Trumbull lamented the piteous condition of the poor black who would be "tyrannized over, abused and virtually reenslaved without some legislation for his protection." Moderate Republican Congressman Henry

Figure 2.2.   Thaddeus Stevens, a Pennsylvania Congressman, led the Radical Republicans' efforts to take control of Reconstruction as well as impeach President Johnson in 1868.
Picture History

L. Dawes of Massachusetts, previously a Johnson man, remarked to his wife that the president had deprived "every friend he has of the least ground upon which to stand and defend him."[9]

United in their outrage, the Radicals wasted no time in attacking Johnson and offering their own version of Reconstruction. The president faced several formidable opponents, some of the ablest legislators ever to serve in Congress. Three men especially stood out from the crowd. In the House, Thaddeus Stevens, chairman of the powerful Ways and Means

Committee and the acknowledged floor leader as well as one of the men Johnson singled out as a traitor, was a firebrand with a gift for sardonic oratory. He had been an abolitionist long before the war, and his longevity in Congress ensured that his eloquent rhetoric was matched by his inimitable grasp of parliamentary procedure and congressional maneuvering. Once described as "the Robespierre, Danton, and Marat" of the second American Revolution, he made no secret of his Reconstruction plans. Congress and the president must "revolutionize Southern institutions, habits, and manners. The foundations must be broken up and relaid, or all our blood and treasure have been spent in vain."

Stevens was in his seventies by the time Andrew Johnson stepped into the presidency, and his salad days were behind him. He had long struggled with physical infirmities dating from his birth. Time had been unkind, leaving this once imposing figure withered by the ravages of disease. Despite his ailments and advanced years, the Pennsylvania dynamo remained as uncompromising toward slavery and its vestiges as he had been in his youth. If anyone, including the president of the United States, stood in his way, he would not yield.[10]

Different in temperament from Stevens, Charles Sumner, chairman of the Senate Foreign Relations Committee, was the Pennsylvanian's equal in wearing moral righteousness like a sacred shroud. He could boast that he played a pivotal role in American history before, during, and after the war. Everyone was familiar with the vicious assault on the senator during the antebellum era. Known for his eloquent, learned speeches, in May 1856 the abolitionist Sumner rose on the Senate floor and delivered a long-winded harangue that lasted two days. Titled "Crimes Against Kansas," Sumner's rambling speech soared to rhetorical heights and fell to sophomoric lows, especially when he disparaged Senator Andrew P. Butler of South Carolina, a coauthor of the odious 1850 Fugitive Slave Act. Using sexual depravity as a metaphor, the New Englander depicted slavery as a "harlot" as well as Butler's "mistress." He also ridiculed Butler's mild paralysis of the lip by referring to the "incoherent phrases" and the "loose expectoration of his speech." The incendiary comments unleashed a torrent of angry words across the Senate aisle, but that was not the end of the matter.

Southerners had long held this Northern man in contempt; his blasphemous assault on Southern honor could not go unpunished. Three days after the speech ended, Butler's nephew, South Carolina Congressman Preston S. Brooks, charged into the Senate and cornered the senator at his desk.

"Mr. Sumner," he said as he brandished a gold-handled cane, "I have read your speech twice over carefully. It is a libel on South Carolina, and

Figure 2.3. As one of the Radical Republicans in the U.S. Senate, Charles Sumner led the effort to wrest control of Reconstruction policy making from the president. The Library of Congress

Mr. Butler, who is a relative of mine." With those words, Brooks struck Sumner on the head repeatedly, later bragging that he "gave him about thirty first rate stripes." Brooks ceased beating the unconscious man only when his cane snapped.

Reactions to the beating varied according to section. Northerners were outraged by the senseless violence while Southerners viewed the attack as comeuppance for Sumner's insults on Butler. The incident made heroes of Brooks in the South and Sumner in the North. It was a status that Sumner used to good advantage after a three-and-a-half-year recuperation. He never forgot what Southerners were capable of, which was perhaps one reason why he was determined to impose harsh Reconstruction measures on the former Confederacy.[11]

Benjamin F. Wade, a principal author of the Wade-Davis Bill as well as the manifesto chastising Lincoln after he vetoed the bill, was another influential Radical Republican. He began his career in the 1830s as a law partner of Joshua Giddings, a leading antebellum abolitionist. After his election to the U.S. Senate in 1851, Wade emerged as a fierce critic of slavery, arguing vehemently against proslavery measures such as the Fugitive Slave Act and the Kansas-Nebraska Act. Many of his public statements criticizing American capitalism were so strong and radical they echoed the arguments of European Socialists. In his view, an economic system "which degrades the poor man and elevates the rich, which makes the rich richer and the poor poorer, which drags the very soul out of a poor man for a pitiful existence is wrong."

Unhappy with Lincoln's tepid support for emancipation and black suffrage as well as his vacillating wartime leadership, Wade was the driving force behind the Joint Committee on the Conduct of the War, a relentless thorn in the president's side. He observed that Lincoln's perspective on slavery "could only come of one born of poor white trash and educated in a slave State." Later, he viewed Lincoln's assassination as an opportunity for more vigorous executive leadership. He had been an early supporter of the new president, declaring, "Mr. Johnson, I thank God that you are here. Lincoln had too much of the milk of human kindness to deal with these damned rebels. Now they will be dealt with according to their deserts." When the president's antipathy toward the freedmen became undeniable, Wade, feeling betrayed, was among Johnson's most vociferous critics.[12]

With these men arrayed against him, the president was assured of strife and contention in his dealings with Congress. Not surprisingly, the Radicals joined forces with moderates and overrode the president's veto of the Civil Rights Act as well as his veto of a second Freedmen's bill. Realizing

Figure 2.4.   Benjamin F. Wade of Ohio was another Radical Republican who opposed President Johnson's leniency toward the vanquished South.
The Library of Congress

that control of Reconstruction was passing out of the executive branch and into the hands of the legislative branch, the Republican-dominated Joint Committee on Reconstruction began debating methods for ensuring that the president would not interfere with congressional plans. Ultimately, the committee proposed a constitutional amendment to define national citizenship as "all persons born or naturalized in the United States," laying to rest the practice of counting former slaves as three-fifths of white citizens, as had been the case under the Constitution since its inception.

The amendment contained five sections. First, it forbade any state to abridge the rights of U.S. citizens or deny them "the equal protection of the laws" absent "due process of law." Section two declared that any state denying a person's right to vote, excepting untaxed Native Americans, persons convicted of a crime, or "participants in the Rebellion," would find its congressional representation reduced proportionally. Section three prohibited persons who "engaged in insurrection or rebellion" or who had "given aid or comfort to the enemies" of the Union from holding "any office, civil or military, under the United States, or under any State." The next section repudiated Confederate debt and affirmed "the validity of the public debt of the United States." In the closing section, the amendment directed that "Congress shall have power to enforce, by appropriate legislation, the provisions of this article."[13]

Article V states that the Constitution can be amended only after two-thirds of both houses of Congress agree to submit the proposed change to the states. Three-fourths of the states are required to ratify the amendment either through their state legislatures or in special conventions called to consider the amendment. Both houses of Congress provided the necessary two-thirds votes in June 1866, and the proposed Fourteenth Amendment was sent to the states for ratification.[14]

Officials in the Southern states denounced the amendment's punitive provisions. In barring pro-Confederate white leaders from holding elective office, the measure seemed contrary to Southern notions of a natural white aristocracy—a key ingredient in the argument that Southerners were descended from "civilized ancestry." North Carolina Governor Jonathan Worth expressed the opinion of many whites when he explained why Southerners would not vote to ratify the Fourteenth Amendment. "If we are to be degraded," he wrote, "we will retain some self-esteem by not making it self-abasement."

By now a pro-Southern president, Johnson made no secret of his disdain for the new amendment. He threw his weight behind a new National Union Party comprising conservative Republicans and Democrats anxious to prevent Radical Republicans from wresting control of Reconstruction from the president. Not content to stay above the fray, he also embarked on an eighteen-day train tour to publicize his opposition to any proposed legislation or constitutional amendments designed to lend assistance to any particular group of people, no matter how much the group had suffered. If he hoped to garner support for his Reconstruction policies, Johnson's efforts to "swing around the circle"—that is, to take his case to the people and circumvent dissident elements in Congress—were disastrous. Many crowds were hostile to the president, and Johnson acted anything but presidential. The New York *Tribune* labeled him an "irritated demagogue" after he exchanged epithets with hecklers, thereby appearing petty and mean-spirited.[15]

Although he was the most high profile opponent of full equality for freedmen, Johnson was by no means alone in harboring racist views. As

Figure 2.5. This 1868 Thomas Nast cartoon from *Harper's Weekly* depicts three forces in the Democratic Party—Irish immigrants, white Southerners, and Wall Street financiers—that subjugated blacks after the Civil War. The caption reads: "This is a white man's government."
The Library of Congress

Thomas Nast illustrated in *Harper's Weekly* in 1868, many forces, including Irish immigrants, white Southerners, and Wall Street financiers, had a vested interest in subjugating blacks. The president stood on solid ground; any effort to legislate in favor of former slaves was bound to meet determined, organized opposition.

In such a hostile climate, the Fourteenth Amendment failed to secure necessary support in three-fourths of the states owing to the Southern states' intransigence. Refusing to acknowledge defeat, the Radicals later led both houses of Congress in passing a simple resolution, in effect, adopting the amendment. In the meantime, Johnson was the primary target of their anger and resentment. In 1867, they launched a new series of bills that the president predictably vetoed and Congress, just as predictably, enacted over his veto.[16]

One of the more far-reaching measures passed into law was the first Reconstruction Act of 1867. If the South as it was then constituted would not ratify the Fourteenth Amendment, state governments in the South would have to be reconstituted. According to one commentator, "[o]n March 2, 1867, Congress passed the first Reconstruction Act over Johnson's veto and a new phase of reconstruction began." The act divided the eleven former states of the Southern Confederacy, except Tennessee, into five military districts under the command of a military officer charged with maintaining law and order and holding elections for constitutional conventions. When the new state constitutions had been developed, they could be submitted to Congress for approval. If approved—and if the Fourteenth Amendment was adopted—the state could be restored to the Union at the discretion of Congress.

Southerners bitterly denounced the act, seeing it as a license for despotic rule. It was bad enough that the Confederate States Army had fallen short on the battlefield, but when the Southland was forced to endure the indignities of an army of occupation, no end of vitriolic rhetoric was in sight. Although the small number of federal troops was hardly tantamount to tyrannical rule, the symbolism of Union soldiers patrolling the streets of Southern cities was enough to trigger violent reactions. President Johnson was heard to remark that Southerners "were to be trodden under foot 'to protect niggers.'" It is little wonder that groups such as the Ku Klux Klan flourished beginning in 1867.[17]

Once again in opposition to the president, Congress enacted a second Reconstruction Act on March 23, 1867. Aimed at increasing voter rolls without regard to race, the second measure directed district commanders to register eligible voters as a prelude to electing delegates to the state constitutional convention. The success of these efforts depended on the diligence of the commanders and compliance by the local population. In some places, district commanders embraced the status quo and turned a blind eye to illegalities. In other areas, they assumed an authoritarian manner befitting a victorious military conqueror. Whatever they did, the commanders were ensured of receiving criticism for acting in a fashion too lenient or too heavy-handed, depending on the political biases of the critic.[18]

Through these new laws, Radical Republicans sought to rewrite if not the history of the South, then certainly the future of the region. In extending political rights to blacks, they were subverting the social aristocracy that had been carefully constructed by white Southerners across many generations. Freedmen understood that radical change was afoot and responded accordingly. They organized Union Leagues as a mechanism for making their voices heard in political affairs and consolidating their power within the community. The Leagues organized voter registration drives, as did other black organizations. With assistance from Northerners who came South to teach school and help administer state governments—derisively labeled "carpetbaggers," an allusion to their supposed propensity to carry all they owned in cheap carpetbags—freedmen struggled to find a place in their new world. Southern Unionists who dared to lend a hand were deemed "scalawags," an epithet linked to the little town of Scalloway in the Shetland Islands, infamous for its poor quality, scrubby cattle.[19]

The third of the major bills enacted in March 1867 would prove to be the most contentious for President Johnson. Of dubious constitutionality, the Tenure of Office Act prohibited the president from removing from office any federal official who received Senate confirmation. Article II, Section 2, Clause 2 of the U.S. Constitution states that the president "shall nominate, and with the Advice and Consent of the Senate, shall appoint Ambassadors, other public Ministers and Consuls, Judges of the supreme Court, and all other officers of the United States, whose Appointments are not herein otherwise provided for, and which shall be established by Law." The Constitution is silent on whether Senate approval is required for removing officials from office. In most cases of constitutional and statutory construction, the most conservative, or cautious, interpretation is generally applied. Therefore, in this analysis, if the Founders had intended to require Senate approval before removing a federal official from office, they would have included the requirement in the Constitution, most likely in Article II somewhere near the requirement of Senate confirmation for appointments.

Johnson relied on this conservative interpretation in arguing that the Tenure of Office Act was unconstitutional. In his view, only a constitutional amendment could impose additional constraints on presidential appointments. It was clear to the president and his supporters that the act was designed to chill an executive who went against the political will of certain senators, a kind of *in terrorem* effect. Apart from the political context of the 1860s, Johnson and his cabinet worried that legislative control over executive powers set a dangerous precedent.[20]

The president originally vetoed the act but, predictably, Congress enacted the measure over his objections. Johnson tested the act later in 1867 by suspending Secretary of War Edwin M. Stanton, a holdover from the Lincoln administration and a favorite of the Radical Republicans. He had encouraged Stanton to resign, but when the secretary refused, the president felt compelled to act. Waiting until the summer congressional recess, on August 12 he suspended Stanton and asked General Ulysses S. Grant to administer the War Department until Congress reconvened. These machinations infuriated critics, but judging by Democratic gains in state elections during the fall of 1867, Johnson appeared to enjoy widespread public support. As a presidential aide memorably put it, "any party with an abolition head and a nigger tail will soon find itself with nothing left but the head and the tail."

Johnson's cronies need not have been so confident. When the August suspension came before the Senate for review, as required by the Tenure of Office Act, the Radicals persuaded their peers not to grant authorization to dismiss the secretary of war. The president's challenge had been checked, and the Senate awaited his response. It came a month later when, upping the ante and defying his detractors, Johnson violated the act by dismissing Stanton without Senate approval.

This bold challenge to the authority of the Radical Republicans was the final act in a battle that had been brewing for more than a year. The Radicals previously had accused the president of all manner of malfeasance—and some accusations, such as the rumor that he was a shadowy conspirator in Lincoln's assassination, were patently ridiculous—but heretofore nothing had warranted the preparation of articles of impeachment. With a blatant violation of statutory law, the president had provided his opponents with the grounds they desperately desired. He had failed to "play the part of Moses for the colored people," *The Nation* wryly observed, so he played the part "for the impeachers."[21]

Radical Republicans in the House of Representatives wasted no time in preparing eleven articles of impeachment, nine of which related to violation of the Tenure of Office Act. Article 10 condemned the president's "inflammatory and scandalous harangues" against Congress, and the last article summarized the accusations. Thus, "on Monday, February 24, 1868,

the House of Representatives of the Congress of the United States, resolved to impeach Andrew Johnson, President of the United States, of high
crimes and misdemeanors, of which, the Senate was apprised and arrange-
ments made for trial." The vote was 126 to 47 in favor of preparing articles
of impeachment for a trial in the U.S. Senate.

It was the first time in American history that Congress had successfully
marshaled sufficient forces to impeach a president. In the past, members of
Congress had called for proceedings against presidents, but the requirements
for impeachment and removal of a chief executive were daunting. Article
II, Section 4, of the Constitution states that a president, vice president, "and
all civil Officers of the United States, shall be removed from Office on Impeachment for, and Conviction of, Treason, Bribery, or other high crimes
and Misdemeanors." Under the constitutional scheme, the House of Representatives prepares the Articles of Impeachment and the Senate, presided
over by the Chief Justice of the U.S. Supreme Court, "shall have the sole
Power to try all Impeachments." Two-thirds of the members present must
agree to remove the president from office.[22]

From beginning to end, the impeachment was a bitterly partisan affair,
and the political motives of his opponents were pellucid. In the *New York
Tribune*, influential publisher Horace Greeley, who went on to become a
presidential candidate in 1872, labeled the embattled chief executive "an
aching tooth in the national jaw, a screeching infant in a crowded lecture
room." Not to be outdone, the Radicals denounced their nemesis as "an
ungrateful, despicable, besotted traitorous man—an incubus." Even men
like General William T. Sherman, who shared the president's views, agreed
that Johnson's behavior was disastrous. "He is like a General fighting without an army," the old soldier plaintively observed.[23]

Despite the sentiment allayed against Johnson, the impeachment was a
debacle. The seven congressmen who presented the case against Johnson
were so brazenly biased in their remarks they undermined the Radicals'
credibility. Even the most vehement Johnson critic could not fail to see the
charges as a pretext for opposing the president's Reconstruction policies.
With their overwrought rhetoric and sophomoric appeals on behalf of the
good of the country, the impeachment managers accomplished what Johnson himself had been unable to accomplish: they generated sympathy for
the president.

Benjamin F. Butler, the former Union general excoriated during the
war as "Beast Butler" for his rough handling of Confederates and impolitic
remarks about New Orleans womanhood in occupied Louisiana, presented
the articles to the Senate in a three-hour harangue. Now a congressman

from Massachusetts, the Beast knew he faced a formidable task. He had to fashion his opposition to Johnson's politics into an impeachable offense, no easy matter in light of the Constitution's stringent requirements. During his oral presentation, Butler spent much of his time presenting a lawyerly argument defining "an impeachable crime" as "one in its nature or consequences subversive of some fundamental or essential principle of government, or highly prejudicial to the public interest." In Butler's view, Johnson's deliberate violation of the Tenure of Office Act met this definition because it was "a violation of the Constitution, of law, of an official oath, or of duty." If that wasn't enough, an "impeachable crime" included the vague "abuse of discretionary powers from improper motives, or for any improper purpose." He did not say, but implied, that Congress would determine what constituted an abuse of discretionary powers or an improper purpose.

Although he was hardly a spellbinding orator, Butler whipped himself into a frenzy of histrionic words and gestures as his speech progressed. He lamented Johnson's ascension to the presidency "by murder most foul"—a hint at the president's complicity in the Lincoln assassination—and addressed Europeans directly, touting the virtues of an impeachment proceeding. "While your king, Oh, Monarchist, if he becomes a buffoon, or a jester, or a tyrant, can only be displaced through revolution, bloodshed, and civil war," in the United States other corrective measures existed to supplant violence and bloodshed.

Not satisfied to rely on words alone to convey his outrage at President Johnson, at the dramatic climax of his presentation Butler waved a shirt supposedly stained with the blood of an Ohio carpetbagger who had been murdered by Mississippi racists. Although it was direct evidence of nothing related to the case, he meant for the prop to illustrate the savagery routinely employed by Johnson's supporters. One commentator, David Miller DeWitt, characterized Butler as a man whose "reputation for sincerity was not high." As for his performance that day, DeWitt remarked that it "was enough of itself to shake the gravity of the whole procedure." In another passage, DeWitt labeled Butler's speech "a lawyer's plea tainted with a dash of the demagogue."[24]

The Beast's brand of demagoguery initially seemed to prevail during the eight-week trial before the Senate, but the tide inexorably turned in favor of Johnson's acquittal. It was one thing to denounce an incompetent executive from editorial pages in Republican newspapers; it was a far more difficult matter to set forth evidence of high crimes and misdemeanors inside the Senate chamber. Evidentiary questions were made worse for the Radicals by the chief justice. Presiding over the case with his customary imperial demeanor, Salmon P. Chase, himself a well-known perennial presidential aspirant, refused to allow the impeachment managers leeway in presenting their case. He held them to strict, legalistic interpretations, which, coupled with the president's appearance at a dinner party hosted by the chief justice at the outset of the trial, convinced the Radicals that Chase was their enemy.

Aside from legal problems with their presentation of the case, the seven congressmen found that passions had cooled and the anti-Johnson sentiment had subsided. The president was noticeably absent from public debate during the proceedings, which contributed to the perception that he was unjustly accused. He also took steps to ameliorate controversy. With an eye toward the trial, Johnson suggested that he would enforce the Reconstruction Acts passed by Congress despite his personal opposition. He also appointed a moderate, General John Schofield, to replace Stanton as secretary of war.[25]

Congressman John A. Bingham of Ohio served as the chief prosecutor of the case. Generally considered a moderate, the man known as the "Cicero of the Senate" for his impressive oratorical skills had not been among the zealous advocates of impeachment. When Speaker of the House Schuyler Colfax appointed him to the seven-man committee charged with preparing articles of impeachment, Bingham threw himself into the task with devotion. After initially objecting to serving on a committee that included his rival, Benjamin Butler, Bingham eventually played a prominent role in action on the floor, arguing that the president's major transgression was deliberately violating the Tenure of Office Act. According to the Cincinnati *Commercial*, he read the impeachment articles on the Senate floor with "a firm, measured voice which penetrated to the remotest parts of the chamber." Bingham also delivered the closing argument in the case in his role as chief impeachment manager for the House. According to David Miller DeWitt, Bingham "was well known as a clever and forcible speaker, overflowing with rhetorical phrases, patriotic appeals and the still warm rallying cries of war." On this momentous occasion, Bingham used his "store of uproarious invective" to condemn the president, regardless of the prosecutor's meager support for the proceedings.[26]

The House managers, despite their oratory, could not overcome inertia. As a further impediment to their cause, when public zeal for impeachment waned, some senators reluctantly concluded that although they despised the little man who occupied the big mansion, he was not guilty of impeachable offenses. Political opposition, no matter how aggravating, was not tantamount to engaging in criminal behavior. As Senator William P.

Fessenden of Maine put it, if Johnson "were impeached for general cussed-ness," he obviously would be found guilty and removed from office; how-ever, "that is not the question to be heard." Moreover, if they removed Johnson from office, he had no vice president to take his place. The presi-dency would pass to Benjamin Wade, president *pro tempore* of the Senate. A Radical Republican who possessed far more enemies than friends, Wade was as objectionable as Johnson to legislators outside the Radical camp. For senators not inflamed by a passionate hatred of Andrew Johnson, the prece-dent established by removing a sitting chief executive from office was a high price to pay, especially with Ben Wade waiting in the wings.

Fessenden was one of seven moderate Republican senators to change their votes in favor of the president. It was a crucial margin. The "Treach-erous Seven" were anathema to the Radicals, for they snatched defeat from the jaws of victory. Castigated with an almost religious fervor previously re-served for Johnson, these men weathered the storm as best they could al-though one senator, James W. Grimes of Iowa, suffered a mild stroke dur-ing the onslaught.

With Radicals at the helm, the trial dragged on through the spring. Johnson needed nineteen votes to win an acquittal, and the outcome was in doubt until the closing days. In the end, he received exactly the number of votes he needed to stay in office. On May 16, 1868, thirty-five senators voted for removal and nineteen against. Despite the Radicals' best efforts, the hated Andrew Johnson would serve out his term as president of the United States.[27]

Ironically, Johnson's impeachment damaged both Republicans in Con-gress and the president. The decline of the Radicals' political influence be-gan with the acquittal. They simply had exhausted their political capital. One Radical, Thaddeus Stevens, had exhausted his body as well. The grand old man of the Radical cause died on August 11, 1868, three months after the final impeachment vote. In a final act of political defiance, Stevens was laid to rest in the African American section of a Lancaster, Pennsylvania, cemetery.[28]

Following the messy trial and acquittal, public attention turned to the 1868 elections, which saw the rise of a war hero, Ulysses S. Grant, to the presidency. Although he was a Republican who did not share the Demo-cratic Party's hostility toward the freedmen, Grant was too slow and cautious for Radical tastes. He robbed them of their high moral ground, already weakened in the impeachment imbroglio, by undermining their arguments that Democratic policies would be improved with a Republican chief exec-utive. Although he had replaced the hated buffoon from Tennessee, the

Radicals contended that Grant was far too lumbering and methodical to enforce legislative initiatives designed to protect the rights of freedmen.

The new president was not afraid to implement vigorous financial and
foreign policy initiatives, but he delegated authority over Reconstruction to
cabinet members of varying abilities. As a moderate Republican, his actions
never matched the zeal of the Radicals to the freedmen's cause. In time, the
Radicals made a virtue of necessity and accepted the general, but he was
not the champion they had sought. The Ulysses S. Grant who occupied the
Executive Mansion displayed many of the same traits displayed by the
Ulysses S. Grant who led the Union army, but his new position required
caution. He worked in a theater of operations more confused, and confusing, than a battlefield where the line between victory and defeat was clear.

As for Andrew Johnson, he won the battle and lost the war. He had
secured an acquittal partly through deft maneuvering and partly through
luck and public weariness at the Radicals' partisan bickering, but his escape
found him incapacitated. Left standing, he was worse than a lame duck; he
was irrelevant. He had been exposed as a petty tyrant, politically tone deaf,
a man without a party. If he had hoped to be the Democratic Party stan-
dard-bearer in 1868, his hopes were dashed when party leaders chose former New York governor Horatio Seymour to face Grant in November.
Johnson lived until 1875—and he was even reelected to the U.S. Senate late
in his life—but history had no further use for this small man who found
Lincoln's shoes too big to fill and the executive mansion too exalted for his
plebeian sensibilities.[29]

Despite the damage sustained by the Radical Republicans and President Johnson, the real losers in the early Reconstruction era were blacks living in the former states of the Confederacy. They were promised that the
victorious Union army and a sympathetic federal government would support them as they moved from a world of human bondage to a world of
free labor. American society was to be refashioned so that the ideals of the
Declaration of Independence and the American creed could be realized in
their lifetimes. They were assured that amending the U.S. Constitution
would be a first step in abolishing the "pernicious institution" of slavery,
providing due process and equal protection of the laws, and securing the
franchise. The first promise—ending the legal institution of slavery—was
fulfilled, but the reality of Reconstruction exposed the hypocrisy of the remaining high-minded, empty rhetoric.[30]

Even when blacks wielded political power in Southern states where
Union troops prevented whites from fixing elections, they were viewed by
Northerners and Southerners alike as quarreling children unable to exercise

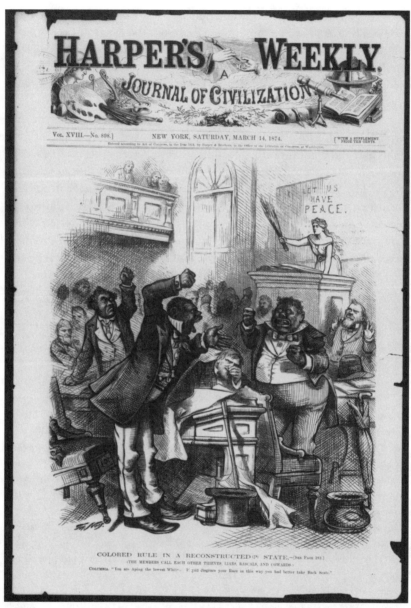

Figure 2.6. Even when blacks assumed political office in Reconstruction-era state governments, they were viewed as little more than quarreling children. The caption from this 1874 Thomas Nast cartoon reads: "Colored Rule in a Reconstructed (?) State," referring to South Carolina.
The Library of Congress

legitimate authority. This demeaning portrait was vividly illustrated by cartoonist Thomas Nast in a famous drawing from the March 14, 1874, issue of *Harper's Weekly*. As black legislators argue with each other, an emblematic figure in the background struggles to restore order. Grant's campaign pledge, "Let Us Have Peace," appears behind the frowning figure. The caption reads: "Colored Rule in a Reconstructed(?) State."

For their part, white Southerners developed their own inimitable interpretation of early Reconstruction. They viewed the passage of civil rights bills and constitutional amendments as well as the presence of federal troops on Southern soil as evidence that the North sought to eradicate their way of life. Believing they had no outlet for political expression through normal channels—controlled, as they seemed to be, by blacks, carpetbaggers, and scalawags with assistance from armed soldiers—disaffected whites acted in the only manner they thought feasible. A grassroots movement arose, a kind of counter-Reconstruction, aimed at opposing the rising tide of modernity and shifting social relations. The Ku Klux Klan was not the only component of this counter-Reconstruction movement, but under the Grant administration it would prove to be stubbornly persistent.[31]

NOTES

1. David Herbert Donald, *Lincoln* (New York: Simon & Schuster, 1995), 472–74; Eric Foner, *Reconstruction: America's Unfinished Revolution, 1863–1877* (New York: Francis Parkman Prize Edition, History Book Club, 2005; originally published by HarperCollins, 1988), 35–37; James M. McPherson, *Battle Cry of Freedom* (New York: Oxford University Press, 1988), 698–713; John C. Waugh, *Re-Electing Lincoln: The Battle for the 1864 Presidency* (New York: Crown, 1997), 68–71.

2. Herman Belz, *Reconstructing the Union: Theory and Practice During the Civil War* (Ithaca, NY: Cornell University Press, 1969), 214–16; Robert W. Burg, "Amnesty, Civil Rights, and the Meaning of Liberal Republicanism, 1862–1872," *Nineteenth Century American History* 4 (Fall 2003): 32–33; Donald, *Lincoln*, 510–12; William Best Hesseltine, *Lincoln's Plan of Reconstruction* (Tuscaloosa, AL: Confederate Publishing Company, 1960), 115–16; James M. McPherson, *Abraham Lincoln and the Second American Revolution* (New York and Oxford: Oxford University Press, 1991), 150–52; Waugh, *Re-Electing Lincoln*, 223–25, 259–63; T. Harry Williams, *Lincoln and the Radicals* (Madison: University of Wisconsin Press, 1941), 318–21.

3. Douglas H. Bryant, "Unorthodox and Paradox: Revisiting the Ratification of the Fourteenth Amendment," *Alabama Law Review* 53 (Winter 2002): 556; Burg, "Amnesty, Civil Rights, and the Meaning of Liberal Republicanism," 32–33; Don-

ald, *Lincoln*, 424–26; McPherson, *Abraham Lincoln and the Second American Revolution*, 138–43; McPherson, *Battle Cry of Freedom*, 712–13; Geoffrey Perret, *Lincoln's War: The Untold Story of America's Greatest President as Commander in Chief* (New York: Random House, 2004), 375–76; Ronald C. White Jr., *The Eloquent President: A Portrait of Lincoln Through His Words* (New York: Random House, 2005), 305.

4. Abel A. Bartley, "The Fourteenth Amendment: The Great Equalizer of the American People," *Akron Law Review* 36 (2003): 478–79; Howard K. Beale, *The Critical Year: A Study of Andrew Johnson and Reconstruction* (New York: Frederick Ungar, 1958; originally published by Harcourt, Brace and Company, New York, 1930), 10–19; Steven G. Calabresi and Christopher S. Yoo, "The Unitary Executive During the Second Half Century," *Harvard Journal of Law & Public Policy* 26 (Summer 2003): 737–39; Albert Castel, *The Presidency of Andrew Johnson* (Lawrence: University Press of Kansas, 1979), 2–6; Editorial, "For One Brief Moment, President Andrew Johnson was More Popular With Radical Republicans than Abraham Lincoln," *America's Civil War* 14 (May 2001): 6; Burton Folsom Jr., "Andrew Johnson and the Constitution," *Ideas on Liberty* 53 (September 2003): 32–33; Foner, *Reconstruction: America's Unfinished Revolution*, 176–78; Eric L. McKitrick, *Andrew Johnson and Reconstruction* (Chicago: University of Chicago Press, 1960), 85–89; Richard W. Murphy, *The Nation Reunited: War's Aftermath* (Alexandria, VA: Time-Life Books, 1987), 53; Hans L. Trefousse, *Impeachment of a President: Andrew Johnson, the Blacks, and Reconstruction* (New York: Fordham University Press, 1999), 67.

5. Beale, *The Critical Year*, 32–35; Bryant, "Unorthodox and Paradox," 556–57; Calabresi and Yoo, "The Unitary Executive During the Second Half Century," 739–41; Castel, *The Presidency of Andrew Johnson*, 26; Murphy, *The Nation Reunited*, 32.

6. Bryant, "Unorthodox and Paradox," 558–59; Burg, "Amnesty, Civil Rights, and the Meaning of Liberal Republicanism," 34–36; Editorial, "For One Brief Moment, President Andrew Johnson was More Popular With Radical Republicans than Abraham Lincoln," 6; Foner, *Reconstruction: America's Unfinished Revolution*, 221–27; Heather M. Hopkins, "Impeachment!" *Footsteps* 6 (September/October 2004): 34–35; Dr. Frederic Shriver Klein, "Personality Profile: 'Old Thad' Stevens," *Civil War Times Illustrated* 2 (February 1964): 23.

7. Bryant, "Unorthodox and Paradox," 558; Calabresi and Yoo, "The Unitary Executive During the Second Half Century," 741–43; Castel, *The Presidency of Andrew Johnson*, 67–70; Risa L. Goluboff, "The Thirteenth Amendment and the Lost Origins of Civil Rights," *Duke Law Journal* 50 (April 2001): 1637–38; Jacobus Tenbroek, *Equal Under Law* (New York: Collier-MacMillan, 1969), 201–33.

8. Burg, "Amnesty, Civil Rights, and the Meaning of Liberal Republicanism," 34; Calabresi and Yoo, "The Unitary Executive During the Second Half Century," 742; Castel, *The Presidency of Andrew Johnson*, 69; Folsom, "Andrew Johnson and the Constitution," 32; Foner, *Reconstruction: America's Unfinished Revolution*, 247–51; Robert Selph Henry, *The Story of Reconstruction* (New York: Konecky & Konecky,

1999), 160–62; McKitrick, *Andrew Johnson and Reconstruction*, 294; Donald G. Nieman, "Andrew Johnson, the Freedmen's Bureau, and the Problem of Equal Rights, 1865–1866," *Journal of Southern History* 44 (August 1978): 399–420; Murphy, *The Nation Reunited*, 39–40; Jeffrey K. Tulis, *The Rhetorical Presidency* (Princeton: Princeton University Press, 1987), 89.

9. Folsom, "Andrew Johnson and the Constitution," 32–33; Foner, *Reconstruction: America's Unfinished Revolution*, 242–51; Murphy, *The Nation Reunited*, 36–41; Trefousse, *Impeachment of a President*, 27.

10. Fawn M. Brodie, *Thaddeus Stevens: Scourge of the South* (New York: W.W. Norton, 1959), 231–32; David Miller DeWitt, *The Impeachment and Trial of Andrew Johnson, Seventeenth President of the United States: A History* (New York: The MacMillan Company, 1903), 24–27; Eric Foner, "Thaddeus Stevens, Confiscation, and Reconstruction," in *The Hofstadter Aegis: A Memorial*, eds. Stanley Elkins and Eric McKitrick (New York: Alfred A. Knopf, 1974), 154; Henry, *The Story of Reconstruction*, 48–49; Murphy, *The Nation Reunited*, 41; Klein, "Personality Profile: 'Old Thad' Stevens," 18–23.

11. DeWitt, *The Impeachment and Trial of Andrew Johnson*, 32–37; David Herbert Donald, *Charles Sumner and the Coming of the Civil War* (New York: Alfred A. Knopf, 1960), 278–347, especially 286; David Herbert Donald, *The Politics of Reconstruction, 1863–1867* (Baton Rouge: Louisiana State University Press, 1965), 7–8; Foner, *Reconstruction: America's Unfinished Revolution*, 239–40; Doris Kearns Goodwin, *Team of Rivals: The Political Genius of Abraham Lincoln* (New York: Simon & Schuster, 2005), 184–85; Henry, *The Story of Reconstruction*, 48; McKitrick, *Andrew Johnson and Reconstruction*, 268; Manisha Sinha, "The Caning of Charles Sumner: Slavery, Race, and Ideology in the Age of the Civil War," *Journal of the Early Republic* 23 (Summer 2003): 233–62; Kenneth M. Stampp, *America in 1857: A Nation on the Brink* (New York and Oxford: Oxford University Press, 1990), 11; Eric H. Walther, *The Shattering of the Union: America in the 1850s* (Wilmington, DE: SR Books, 2004), 96–100.

12. Beale, *The Critical Year*, 51–52; DeWitt, *The Impeachment and Trial of Andrew Johnson*, 6; Editorial, "For One Brief Moment, President Andrew Johnson was More Popular With Radical Republicans than Abraham Lincoln," 6; Foner, *Reconstruction: America's Unfinished Revolution*, 176–78; Henry, *The Story of Reconstruction*, 48; McKitrick, *Andrew Johnson and Reconstruction*, 85–89; Perret, *Lincoln's War*, 375–76; Jeffrey D. Wert, *The Sword of Lincoln: The Army of the Potomac* (New York: Simon & Schuster, 2005), 58–59.

13. Calabresi and Yoo, "The Unitary Executive During the Second Half Century," 745–46; Foner, *Reconstruction: America's Unfinished Revolution*, 251–61; Henry, *The Story of Reconstruction*, 164–65; Hopkins, "Impeachment!" 34–37; Murphy, *The Nation Reunited*, 54–56.

14. Bartley, "The Fourteenth Amendment," 473–74; Bryant, "Unorthodox and Paradox," 563–65; Calabresi and Yoo, "The Unitary Executive During the Second Half Century," 745–46; Foner, *Reconstruction: America's Unfinished Revolution*, 251–61.

15. Beale, *The Critical Year*, 13; Martin E. Mantell, *Johnson, Grant, and the Politics of Reconstruction* (New York and London: Columbia University Press, 1973), 94; McKitrick, *Andrew Johnson and Reconstruction*, 429; Tulis, *The Rhetorical Presidency*, 87–93.

16. Bartley, "The Fourteenth Amendment," 474; Bryant, "Unorthodox and Paradox," 564–65; Calabresi and Yoo, "The Unitary Executive During the Second Half Century," 745–46;

17. Michael Les Benedict, "From Our Archives: A New Look at the Impeachment of Andrew Johnson," *Political Science Quarterly* 113 (1998): 495–97, 502–3; Bryant, "Unorthodox and Paradox," 566–67; Calabresi and Yoo, "The Unitary Executive During the Second Half Century," 745–46; Michael D. Pierce, "Andrew Johnson and the South, 1865–1867," Ph.D. diss., North Texas State University, 1970, 251–52. Johnson is quoted in Foner, *Reconstruction: America's Unfinished Revolution*, 276.

18. Beale, *The Critical Year*, 43–47; Murphy, *The Nation Reunited*, 61–63; Pierce, "Andrew Johnson and the South, 1865–1867," 262–65.

19. Donald, *The Politics of Reconstruction, 1863–1867*, 8–11; Henry, *The Story of Reconstruction*, 76–78, 118–19; Murphy, *The Nation Reunited*, 63.

20. Benedict, "From Our Archives: A New Look at the Impeachment of Andrew Johnson," 509–10; Calabresi and Yoo, "The Unitary Executive During the Second Half Century," 746–50; DeWitt, *The Impeachment and Trial of Andrew Johnson*, 202–03; Folsom, "Andrew Johnson and the Constitution," 32–33; Hopkins, "Impeachment!" 34–37; Stephen W. Stathis, "Impeachment and Trial of President Andrew Johnson: A View From the Iowa Congressional Delegation," *Presidential Studies Quarterly* 24 (Winter 1994): 29–32; Trefousse, *Impeachment of a President*, 43–45.

21. Erving E. Beauregard, "The Chief Prosecutor of President Andrew Johnson," *The Midwest Quarterly* 31 (Spring 1990): 412–13; Benedict, "From Our Archives: A New Look at the Impeachment of Andrew Johnson," 505–10; Calabresi and Yoo, "The Unitary Executive During the Second Half Century," 750–52; Castel, *The Presidency of Andrew Johnson*, 139–42; DeWitt, *The Impeachment and Trial of Andrew Johnson*, 136–79, 339–47; Foner, *Reconstruction: America's Unfinished Revolution*, 334; Mantell, *Johnson, Grant, and the Politics of Reconstruction*, 36, 75; James E. Sefton, *Andrew Johnson and the Uses of Constitutional Power* (Boston: Addison-Wesley, 1980), 157–59; Trefousse, *Impeachment of a President*, 36, 78, 133.

22. Calabresi and Yoo, "The Unitary Executive During the Second Half Century," 755–56; Michael A. Genovese, *The Power of the American Presidency, 1789–2000* (New York and Oxford: Oxford University Press, 2001), 92–93; Henry, *The Story of Reconstruction*, 302–03; Norman C. Thomas, Joseph A. Pika, and Richard A. Watson, *The Politics of the Presidency*, 3d. ed. (Washington, D.C.: Congressional Quarterly Press, 1994), 256–58; Tulis, *The Rhetorical Presidency*, 90–91; United States Senate, *Proceedings in the Trial of Andrew Johnson* (Washington, D.C.: U.S. Government Printing Office, 1869), 1–6.

23. Foner, *Reconstruction: America's Unfinished Revolution*, 334; Genovese, *The Power of the American Presidency*, 93.

24. Beauregard, "The Chief Prosecutor of President Andrew Johnson," 415–16; DeWitt, *The Impeachment and Trial of Andrew Johnson*, 408–16, esp. 408; Henry, *The Story of Reconstruction*, 304–09; Murphy, *The Nation Reunited*, 72–73; Thomas, Pika, and Watson, *The Politics of the Presidency*, 257–58.

25. DeWitt, *The Impeachment and Trial of Andrew Johnson*, 388–90; Mantell, *Johnson, Grant, and the Politics of Reconstruction*, 95; Murphy, *The Nation Reunited*, 75.

26. Beauregard, "The Chief Prosecutor of President Andrew Johnson," 413–16, 418–19; Calabresi and Yoo, "The Unitary Executive During the Second Half Century," 755–56; DeWitt, *The Impeachment and Trial of Andrew Johnson*, 505–6; Folsom, "Andrew Johnson and the Constitution," 32–33; Foner, *Reconstruction: America's Unfinished Revolution*, 334–37; Murphy, *The Nation Reunited*, 72–75.

27. Beauregard, "The Chief Prosecutor of President Andrew Johnson," 419; Burg, "Amnesty, Civil Rights, and the Meaning of Liberal Republicanism," 37; Calabresi and Yoo, "The Unitary Executive During the Second Half Century," 756–58; Castel, *The Presidency of Andrew Johnson*, 192–93; DeWitt, *The Impeachment and Trial of Andrew Johnson*, 515–96; Editorial: "The Dissenting Senators," *Harper's Weekly* (June 6, 1868): 354; Folsom, "Andrew Johnson and the Constitution," 32–33; Foner, *Reconstruction: America's Unfinished Revolution*, 336–37; Genovese, *The Power of the American Presidency*, 93; Henry, *The Story of Reconstruction*, 308; Hopkins, "Impeachment!" 34–37; Mantell, *Johnson, Grant, and the Politics of Reconstruction*, 90–96; Klein, "Personality Profile: 'Old Thad' Stevens," 23; Murphy, *The Nation Reunited*, 75; Trefousse, *Impeachment of a President*, 130.

28. Bartley, "The Fourteenth Amendment," 478–79; DeWitt, *The Impeachment and Trial of Andrew Johnson*, 597–99; Foner, *Reconstruction: America's Unfinished Revolution*, 343–45; Henry, *The Story of Reconstruction*, 333–34; Klein, "Personality Profile: 'Old Thad' Stevens," 23.

29. Beale, *The Critical Year*, 10–50; Calabresi and Yoo, "The Unitary Executive During the Second Half Century," 759–66; Castel, *The Presidency of Andrew Johnson*, 392; DeWitt, *The Impeachment and Trial of Andrew Johnson*, 608–29; Hopkins, "Impeachment!" 34–37.

30. Foner, *Reconstruction: America's Unfinished Revolution*, 537–42; Julie Saville, *The Work of Reconstruction: From Slave to Wage Laborer in South Carolina, 1860–1870* (Cambridge: Cambridge University Press, 1994), 138–39, 182–91; Ralph Shlomowitz, "The Origins of Southern Sharecropping," *Agricultural History* 53 (July 1979): 557–75; Francis Butler Simkins and R. H. Woody, *South Carolina During Reconstruction* (Chapel Hill: The University of North Carolina Press, 1932), 457–62.

31. Calabresi and Yoo, "The Unitary Executive During the Second Half Century," 764–66; David H. Donald, *The Politics of Reconstruction, 1863–1867* (Baton Rouge: Louisiana State University Press, 1965), 1–17; Foner, *Reconstruction: America's Unfinished Revolution*, 412–25; John Hope Franklin, *Reconstruction After the Civil War* (Chicago: The University of Chicago Press, 1961), 150–69; Asa H. Gordon,

Sketches of Negro Life and History in South Carolina, 2d. ed. (Columbia: University of South Carolina Press, 1929), 78–79, 158–63; John Porter Hollis, *The Early Period of Reconstruction in South Carolina* (Baltimore, MD: The Johns Hopkins Press, 1905), 9–17; Thomas Holt, *Black Over White: Negro Political Leadership in South Carolina During Reconstruction* (Urbana: University of Illinois Press, 1977), 29–103; Mantell, *Johnson, Grant, and the Politics of Reconstruction*, 93–94; Shlomowitz, "The Origins of Southern Sharecropping," 557–75.

3

"THE WHOLE FABRIC OF RECONSTRUCTION . . . WILL TOPPLE AND FALL"

Ulysses S. Grant entered the presidency in March 1869 as revered as his predecessor was reviled. It was a high point in his life. The adulation of a grateful people, while it would outlive his tenure in office, would not survive the harsh judgment of history.

He had assumed many guises during his career: Grant the failed businessman of the antebellum years; Grant the hard drinking, daring military strategist of the early war years; and Grant the Butcher, tenaciously—or recklessly, as his detractors charged—pursuing a costly Overland Campaign in the closing days of the war. Most indelibly, in 1865 he had been transformed, phoenix-like, into Grant the triumphant, exalted Hero of Appomattox. He had been criticized savagely throughout his life, as he would be long after his death, but he emerged from the Civil War portrayed as a grand Union exemplar because he understood one inescapable fact. Whether the result of design, skill, luck, or a combination thereof, success is indispensable to securing the encomiums of public memory. History rewards victors and forgives them their foibles.[1]

A political novice who had voted only once in his life, Grant was a reluctant presidential aspirant. When it became clear that no one else could garner the widespread popular support enjoyed by this rags-to-riches figure, he allowed his name to be added to the list of candidates. The 1868 campaign was nasty, but he handily defeated former New York governor Horatio Seymour. Today the Grant administration is remembered as rife with scandal and corruption, one of the worst in American history. In his day, however, the former military leader was viewed as personally honest and upright, although he surrounded himself with men of low character and

Figure 3.1.   Ulysses S. Grant entered the presidency in 1869, replacing the hated Andrew Johnson and opening a new chapter in Reconstruction.
The Library of Congress

questionable motives. In light of his popularity at the time, it was no accident that Grant was the only man to serve eight consecutive years in the executive office between Andrew Jackson's presidency (1829–1837) and Woodrow Wilson's administration (1913–1921).

His reign started with great promise. Here was a new man in the Executive Mansion, a decisive man of action and daring, and he brought with him a new perspective on Reconstruction. "Let us have peace," he had extolled the nation during the campaign. For many citizens not directly immersed in the problems of Southern Reconstruction, the promise was becoming a reality. The horrors of war had receded as the country focused on new, exciting prospects. The Transcontinental Railroad was completed shortly after Grant's inauguration. Settlers were moving to the Great Plains; agricultural productivity was increasing; new industries, especially in steel and petroleum, were rising to prominence. After much bloodshed and sacrifice, the United States was on the road to a new and better age—or so it appeared as the long, tortured decade of the 1860s drew to a close.[2]

Grant consciously distinguished himself from Andrew Johnson by vowing that he would execute the laws without regard to his personal predilections, a far cry from the early Reconstruction years when the president continually interjected odious opinions with little concern for the political consequences. Grant was no pushover, however; he supported the concept of a vigorous, engaged chief executive. One of his first acts was to oppose the efforts of Jay Gould and Jim Fisk to corner the gold market on Black Friday, September 24, 1869. Anxious to preserve the powers of the presidency against congressional encroachment, Grant also strongly contested the Tenure of Office Act, a crucial first step in its eventual repeal.[3]

He was genuinely concerned for the plight of the freedmen, but his actions were compromised by intractable political realities and intransigent opponents, as is often the case when the political terrain is malleable and constantly shifting. While professing support for tough Reconstruction measures to ensure Southern compliance, Grant delegated implementation of his Reconstruction policies to his cabinet, which seemed to undermine the seriousness of the issue. Nonetheless, more than any other president of the post-Civil War era, he understood that former slaves would never enjoy the rights and privileges of citizenship, especially in the South, absent federal intervention and aggressive law enforcement. At crucial periods when federal initiatives reached an impasse, Grant intervened in the policy process and used presidential prestige to champion legislation protecting the freedmen.

As is true in any administration, Grant's cabinet featured an eclectic group of secretaries with varying levels of skill. Fortunately for the freedmen, Attorney General Amos T. Akerman, the cabinet officer who oversaw federal Reconstruction policy in 1870–1871, was one of the most accomplished cabinet officials to serve during the Grant years. Akerman was that rarity in any era, a dedicated public servant with a gift for using the mechanisms of government to achieve policy goals. That he failed to implement many of the administration's policies says more about the tenor of the times and the conflicted nature of the policy process in the early 1870s than it does about Akerman's abilities or willingness to fight for civil rights enforcement.

Having lived above and below the Mason-Dixon line, the attorney general brought an unusual perspective to Washington. He was, in a sense, a servant of two masters throughout his life. Born and reared in the North, he settled in Georgia after graduating from Dartmouth College. Before Fort Sumter capitulated, Akerman viewed secession as a mistake, but he would not turn his back on his adopted homeland once the guns had been fired. During the war, he remained loyal to the South, albeit he was filled with grave misgivings through four long years of bloodshed. Never a fierce ideologue, he refused to wallow in the bitterness and despair that engulfed so many Southern men of his generation after Appomattox. Instead, he recognized that he must obey the laws and policies of the victorious Union. Even more startling for that time and place, and despite his strong ties to Georgia, the attorney general did not share his kinsmen's disdain for the rights of black Americans. Elevated into a cabinet post, he devoted considerable time and energy to protecting the freedmen, which frequently placed Akerman at odds with Southerners protesting congressional passage of the Fifteenth Amendment to the U.S. Constitution.[4]

In February 1869, shortly before Grant's inauguration, Congress approved the Fifteenth Amendment to extend the franchise to all males of legal age, including freedmen. A year later, the required three-quarters of the states ratified the measure. For Democrats, the amendment was yet another example of the autocratic, Republican-dominated federal government imposing its will on the vanquished Southland. They viewed this development as the "most revolutionary measure" ever devised by Congress, loathsome because it specifically adopted "the colored race as its special wards and favorites."

Despite Southerners' fears of sweeping changes soon to be triggered by the Fifteenth Amendment, Republicans contended that the amendment was too weak to secure voting rights for newly emancipated slaves. It failed to define citizenship, and it did not guarantee blacks the right to hold public office. States were not prohibited from designing literacy tests, collecting poll taxes, or instituting property ownership requirements that precluded blacks from political participation. To ensure that poor, mostly illiterate whites were not trapped by the same impediments, many Southern states implemented an ingenious grandfather clause: Any person whose grandfather had been eligible to vote did not have to meet the new, stringent voting requirements. Since few, if any, freedmen were grandfathered in

Figure 3.2.   Amos T. Akerman, President Grant's attorney general, recognized that the federal government must intervene in state affairs to protect the rights of the freedmen.
The Library of Congress

through legal loopholes, they were disenfranchised while whites of the same social stratum could participate in a political system that increasingly marginalized blacks.[5]

In the meantime, Republican leaders had heard talk of a new group, the Ku Klux Klan, that was dedicated to blocking implementation of the Fifteenth Amendment, but even the most avid Republican wondered whether reports of KKK atrocities were true. Lurid tales of whippings, beatings, lynchings, shootings, rapes, and torture were sensationalistic and outrageous; for many citizens, they simply strained credulity. Playing on the general state of disbelief and anxious to curtail GOP political gains, Democrats contended that stories of the Klan riding the roads at night as masked vigilantes were myths conjured up as a convenient pretext for continued federal military control of Southern state governments. Reflecting the typical Democratic view, the *Daily Phoenix* of Columbia, South Carolina, dismissed tales of nightriders terrorizing blacks as little more than "ghosts, hobgoblins, jack-o'-the-lanterns"—imagery knowingly or unknowingly reminiscent of the Klan's jejune origins.[6]

Despite lingering skepticism about Klan activities, the Republican-controlled Congress enacted two bills to ensure that the Fifteenth Amendment would be enforced if Southerners resisted. Without effective enforcement, in the words of Senator John Pool of North Carolina, the "whole fabric of Reconstruction, with all the principles connected with it, amounts to nothing at all, and in the end it will topple and fall." The first measure, the Enforcement Act of 1870, was a "criminal code upon the subject of elections." Election officials were prohibited from discriminating against voters on the basis of race. The statute also allowed the president to appoint election supervisors who could file election fraud cases in federal court when intimidation and bribery were used to prevent citizens from exercising their Fifteenth Amendment rights. The second act strengthened federal enforcement powers in urban areas, especially in those Northern cities where Democratic political machines manipulated the franchise.[7]

When he became attorney general in June 1870, Akerman used the authority granted through these legislative initiatives as well as the resources of the newly created Department of Justice to investigate the stories filtering into his office. Even if some of the tales were fanciful or exaggerated, he did not doubt that shadowy Southern groups resisted federal civil rights legislation or that Northerners were anxious to move beyond ugly reminders of the war, essentially ignoring evidence of Southern intransigence. "The Northern mind being active, and full of what is called progress, runs away from the past," he mused. "Even such atrocities as Ku-Kluxery do not hold their attention." Akerman was determined to use the power of the federal government to curb state abuses "while the national spirit is still warm with the glow of the late war" or risk the likelihood that "the state rights' spirit may grow troublesome again."

Working closely with his solicitor general, Benjamin Helm Bristow, this reconstructed Confederate investigated reports of Klan activities, most notably in South Carolina. Not satisfied to rely on second-hand reports, the attorney general personally visited several Southern states. His fact-finding trip was instructive. He conferred with Governor Robert K. Scott, South Carolina Attorney General Daniel H. Chamberlain, United States District Attorney David T. Corbin, and military officers charged with securing the peace in the Military District of South Carolina. Sifting through the evidence, reviewing testimony from eyewitnesses, and observing the general demeanor of local citizens, Akerman concluded that the stories he had heard were mostly true. In his opinion, "from the beginning of the world until now," no community or nation-state "nominally civilized, has been so fully under the domination of systematic and organized depravity."

Armed with the results of his investigation, the attorney general could draw only one reasonable conclusion: "These combinations amount to war." Reconstruction, at least as it was practiced in South Carolina, was a continuation of the Civil War. The soldiers' guns may have fallen silent after reverses at Appomattox Courthouse and Durham Station, but the struggle for state rights persisted in the hearts and minds of many Southerners. Their fight was now underground, a guerilla campaign directed against freedmen in rural areas scattered throughout the former Confederate states.

In Akerman's view, admonitions to obey the law and threats of legal prosecution absent a credible show of armed force were useless—probably worse than useless. They sent a message that the federal government was a paper tiger full of bluff and bluster, appearing to be tough but not genuinely serious about protecting the rights of all citizens. Lincoln's promise of "malice toward none, charity for all" also proved to be ineffective. Klansmen viewed kindness and generosity as timidity evincing a lack of resolve. If domestic terrorists were to be rooted from the American landscape, the federal government must "terrify evil doers" and "command their respect by the exercise of its powers." The only effective means of combating recalcitrant Southerners would be to arrest and prosecute high-profile Klan leaders in one or two key states to show the community the consequences of opposing federal laws through violence and intimidation. Federal troops must be afforded an active role in law enforcement; the days of providing assistance to civil authorities—many of whom were Klan participants or sympathizers—were over. If Klan leaders were brought to justice, the group's followers would acquiesce in short order.[8]

Aside from the symbolic value of prosecuting high-ranking Klan leaders, Akerman had little choice but to focus on high-profile participants. His office was inundated with requests for assistance from federal prosecutors, state investigators, military officers in Southern states, and clerks preparing federal cases against states and citizens on trial for violating civil rights laws. One beleaguered federal investigator pleaded in a letter, "Attorney General, it is too bad to let us fight this thing against all the public opinion single handed as we are. We need force enough to inspire respect and command order." Akerman agreed, but he had few resources at his command. His standard reply to requests for assistance was contradictory; he urged his subordinates to enforce the law vigorously, but he also reminded them that "the strictest economy is necessary." An iron fist must be used, but it must be used judiciously lest the criminal justice system be overwhelmed.[9]

Based on Akerman's direction that the justice department pick and choose places to prosecute the Klan, South Carolina was the leading candidate for increased federal intervention. Robert K. Scott, a carpetbagger from Ohio and former assistant commissioner of the Freedmen's Bureau, was elected governor of that state in 1868. After he won reelection in 1870, Governor Scott grew increasingly alarmed at the rising tide of violence, especially in the Piedmont region. He sent word to President Grant that something must be done to curb the "general reign of terror and lawlessness." With many state and local institutions populated by Klansmen or their sympathizers, the Grant administration was obliged to intervene. "If the State is powerless the duty clearly devolves upon the National Government" to act in the best interests of all citizens, black and white, the governor observed.[10]

In response to numerous requests for federal assistance, including Governor Scott's pleas, the justice department began investigating Klan abuses and preparing cases for court even before the attorney general's trip through the South. For its part, Congress had already provided the president with additional authority to fight the KKK. Congressman Benjamin F. "Beast" Butler, the Radical Republican who had argued so passionately and futilely in Andrew Johnson's impeachment trial, drafted an anti-Klan bill for consideration. By all accounts, it was a punitive measure. State officials suspected of securing their offices through suspicious means could be removed from their posts. Federal juries comprising persons in collusion with the Klan, or at least sympathetic to their ideals, could be altered so that a pool more favorable to the federal position could be constituted. These features undoubtedly would have strengthened the president's authority, but moderate congressmen expressed reservations about adopting such extreme measures.

Realizing that many members of Congress refused to believe tales of the Klan's activities, the president appeared at the Capitol to argue for anti-Klan legislation. As he later summarized the situation in his message to Congress, "[a] condition of affairs now exists in some of the States of the Union rendering life and property insecure." Only federal intervention could ensure that "these evils" would be rectified. As Grant saw it, the problem was that "the power of the Executive of the United States, acting within the limits of existing laws . . . is not clear." Thus, he urged the passage of "such legislation as in the judgment of Congress shall effectually secure life, liberty, and property and the enforcement of law in all parts of the United States."

With Grant's prestige behind the legislation, Congress was not long in responding, although several Democrats in the House of Representatives tried to prevent passage of an anti-Klan bill. One congressman from Grant's home state of Ohio even questioned the wisdom of allowing the president, "a mere military chieftain, unlearned in the civil policy of the Government," discretion to use troops to fight domestic terrorism. "Beast" Butler, with his well-known penchant for high drama intact, again waved the bloody shirt to good effect. After reading a poignant letter from a member of the American Missionary Association who had scribbled a few lines to his wife before the Alabama Klan lynched him, Butler challenged his colleagues. "Let each member of the House read that letter," he said, "then let him vote against a bill to repress such outrages, if he dare, and then reckon with the people of his country and afterward with his God."

The Republicans easily secured the necessary votes to ensure the bill's passage. Drafted by Ohio Congressman Samuel Shellabarger, the final measure was ready for the president's review in April 1871. On April 20, largely at Akerman's urging, Grant signed the third Enforcement Bill—the Ku Klux Klan Act of 1871, commonly called simply the "Force Bill" or the "Ku Klux Klan Bill"—which made it a federal offense for any persons to conspire to deny a citizen of the United States the right to participate in political life, own property, vote, or serve on a jury. It was illegal for persons "to conspire together, or go in disguise upon the public highway, or upon the premises of another for the purpose . . . of depriving any person or class of persons of the equal privileges or immunities of the laws." The new statute was not as far-reaching as it might have been; it fell short of authorizing the imposition of martial law or trying defendants before a military tribunal. Nonetheless, the president was empowered to intervene into state affairs if, in his view, it was necessary to keep the peace.[11]

Probably the most controversial section of the new law was the provision allowing the president to suspend the writ of habeas corpus at his own discretion. A well-established feature of Anglo-American jurisprudence, "habeas corpus"—literally, "you have the body"—is shorthand for "habeas corpus ad subjiciendum," a writ directed to a person or authority that detains an individual. The writ, or court order, commands that the detainee

Figure 3.3.   On April 20, 1871, President Grant signed the Ku Klux Klan Force Bill. The new law empowered the federal government to investigate KKK abuses in Southern states and prosecute responsible parties. This drawing of Grant signing the bill appeared in *Frank Leslie's Illustrated Newspaper* **on May 13, 1871.**
The Library of Congress

be produced, in person, before a judge, but it is not designed to delve into the guilt or innocence of a detainee. It merely questions whether he or she was lawfully detained.

The "great writ of liberty" was considered so important to the common law tradition that partisans on both sides of the aisle questioned whether Klan atrocities, no matter how egregious, warranted interference with civil liberties to such an extent. Allowing a president to suspend the writ without congressional approval during wartime or when facing an insurrection, as Lincoln had done, was justified as a necessary measure to preserve law and order in the Union, but granting such broad authority to a president in peacetime was an altogether different matter. After much debate, Congress agreed to allow for the suspension of habeas corpus in situations where the Ku Klux Klan could not be constrained through other means, but the measure remained controversial even among members of the president's party.[12]

With support for the new measure largely split along party lines—Republicans falling in line behind the president and Democrats vehemently denouncing the law—enforcement remained a difficult question. On May 3, Grant issued a proclamation urging citizens in states where Klan activity was reputed to be rampant to obey the new law on penalty of increased federal intervention. Far from assuming an angry or defiant tone, Grant's statement sounded conciliatory and plaintive. Moreover, the proclamation added no additional law enforcement mechanisms. Perhaps the president expected that tough talk would scare Klansmen into complying with the law. More likely, he realized that the administration could do little to fight KKK activities absent specific information on the structure, strategy, and tactics of the Invisible Empire.[13]

The relatively ineffectual nature of the new law and the accompanying proclamation did not prevent Democrats from fanning the flames of discontent among whites suspicious of federal power. Arguing that stories of the KKK were wildly exaggerated, Democratic Party faithful circulated rumors that President Grant and his cabinet were power hungry and intent on using the Force Bill as a pretext for encroaching on the sovereignty of the states. Legislators already were wary of protecting black rights; to many moderates and conservatives, the statute seemed to be the first step toward creating a military dictatorship. Congressman James Madison Leach of North Carolina typified the Southern reaction when he called the statute "an outrage upon the Constitution, an outrage upon liberty and free government, an outrage upon the good name and noble State and a law-loving people."[14]

For all of the outrage and demagoguery afoot in 1871, the Democrats raised a valid issue. Most tales of the Ku Klux Klan were circulated through word of mouth, repeating wild rumors unsupported by verified facts. If federal intervention were to be legitimized, more information and data were needed. To assuage concerns that the cure of increased federal authority was worse than the disease of lawless Klan activity, on the same day that Grant signed the Force Bill the Forty-second Congress created the Joint Select Committee to Inquire into the Affairs of the Late Insurrectionary States. Established to investigate conditions of the freedmen in the Reconstruction-era South, the committee eventually published the most comprehensive contemporaneous data and information about conditions in the former states of the Confederacy. When it appeared in February 1872, the final report was 632 pages long and included a twelve-volume appendix containing eyewitness testimony and findings of fact. Coupled with Akerman's investigations, the committee's efforts were the first steps on the long road of dragging the Invisible Empire into the light of day.

Comprising seven senators and fourteen representatives, the committee was charged with investigating tales of Southern depredations and issuing recommendations when the full Congress reconvened in December. Senator John Scott of Pennsylvania, selected for his knowledge of Klan activities after he had investigated similar complaints in North Carolina, served as the committee chair. He had spent January and February 1871 examining fifty-two witnesses, including numerous Klan victims and half a dozen Klansmen, a laborious undertaking that convinced him of the dangers posed by the group.

The new committee commenced hearings in Washington, D.C., in May 1871 and continued, apart from a month-long recess, until September. To observe conditions firsthand, a subcommittee of three members visited South Carolina in June and July, and other committee members traveled to North Carolina, Georgia, Florida, Tennessee, Alabama, and Mississippi. During these sessions, prominent Klansmen and former Klansmen, including Nathan Bedford Forrest and John B. Gordon, were hauled before the members of Congress and compelled to testify. Victims told their stories plainly and more or less honestly, but suspected Klan leaders, not surprisingly, were less forthcoming. They lied, told half-truths, or claimed to have forgotten key events and activities.[15]

Even as Congress pursued the KKK, other departments of the federal government sprang into action. General Alfred H. Terry, commander of the Department of the South under General Henry Halleck's Division of the South, was determined to craft a military solution to what he deemed to be a military problem. A Yale-educated lawyer in civilian life, Terry had fought throughout the Civil War, distinguishing himself at the Second Battle of Fort Fisher and proving that previous military training need not be a prerequisite for exercising effective military command.

Beginning in December 1869, he was stationed in and around Atlanta, Georgia. He had seen the pervasive influence of the Klan in local communities, and he knew that nothing short of federal intervention would restore law and order. As he observed in a June 1871 letter, echoing Akerman's assessment, the Grant administration must focus its limited resources on one state and vigorously prosecute the group as an example of what lay in store for Kluxers and their sympathizers. The "insurrectionary movement" could be eradicated "if in a single state it could be suppressed, and in that State *exemplary* punishment meted out to some of the most prominent criminals."[16]

General Terry and civilian administration officials had received numerous letters from Governor Scott in 1870 and 1871. The South Carolina governor wrote to complain about deteriorating circumstances. In a typical missive he sent to President Grant, Scott explained that the Klan was so

Figure 3.4.   The attorney general turned to General Alfred Terry, commander of the Department of the South, pictured here, to send federal troops into South Carolina to quell KKK violence.
The National Archives

powerful in some areas that the group's activities "render the power of the State and its officers unequal to the task of protecting life and property." Surrounded by Klan sympathizers and possessing few military resources, the governor felt impotent, absent federal intervention, to respond.

Scott's pleas were filled with hyperbole, but he also had ample reason for alarm. In January, after several dozen black militiamen had been arrested and charged with murdering a whiskey peddler and Confederate veteran, Mat Stevens, in Unionville, South Carolina, more than forty masked marauders stormed the jail with axes in hand. After hacking their way through the front door, the nightriders herded five prisoners from their cells and whisked them from town. All five men were shot, and two died. To protect the remaining defendants, the judge of the trial court in Columbia ordered the sheriff to remove the prisoners to the capital city for their own safety. Before the sheriff could comply, the Klan turned up again. This time, hundreds of armed men sealed off the town, surrounded the jail, and demanded that more prisoners be released into their custody. The deputy was a brave man with an admirable sense of duty. He initially refused to comply with the demand, but he relented when the Klansmen produced his wife and held a gun to her head. The mob eventually removed ten additional prisoners. In time, eight of their bodies were recovered, but two men were neither seen nor heard from again.[17]

The savagery did not begin or end with the Unionville incident. Klan violence had been steadily increasing since the summer of 1870, and by late 1870 and early 1871 it reached a crescendo. In York County, another Klan stronghold in South Carolina, one incident especially stood out for the level of violence and sheer audacity it revealed. In December 1870, Kluxers turned their attention to Thomas Black, also known as Thomas Roundtree. Incensed that this "bad Negro" had been threatening to kill whites, the group resolved to administer its own brand of vigilante justice. William C. Black, a prominent Klansman, landowner, and former legislator, assembled at least fifty masked men and adorned them in full KKK regalia. In a scene eerily similar to the subsequent murder of militiaman Jim Williams, around midnight on the night of December 2, the Klansmen surrounded Roundtree's house on horseback and called him outside. Hurling epithets and firing untold rounds into the house, their purpose was plain.

Roundtree was hiding in a loft inside the house, but when the gunfire grew too intense, he climbed out a window and threw himself on the ground. Panicked, he tried to flee on foot, but the mob shot him down before he had traveled more than thirty steps. One of the assailants dismounted, grabbed Roundtree, and slit his throat with a knife. A simple murder would not satisfy their bloodlust; the mob mutilated Roundtree's body. In a rage, they shot it more than thirty times and sank it in a river.

Tom Roundtree's widow, Harriett, later identified several of the men, and they were arrested. Southern justice prevented a successful prosecution, however, for William C. Black stepped forward to provide an alibi for the defendants. He even arranged for their defense. Fearful for her safety, Harriett left her home for the protection of federal troops that soon would arrive in South Carolina. All across the state, but especially in the Piedmont region, scenes of violence resulting in few, if any, legal consequences were replayed many times.[18]

Faced with mounting horror stories and the governor's pleas for federal assistance, General Terry replied, "Have you the power to proclaim martial law? If you have, I will enforce it with my whole command if necessary." The governor hesitated to take such a bold step; despite his entreaties, he was fearful of the community reaction and worried about his precarious position in state government. It was no matter; General Terry had heard enough. He and Attorney General Akerman agreed that if the federal government were going to intervene to halt the growth of the Ku

Klux Klan, South Carolina was the logical place. As the general later explained to his subordinate, Major Lewis Merrill, "when you get to South Carolina, you will find that the half has not been told to you."[19]

In March 1871, six months before Attorney General Akerman visited South Carolina, General William T. Sherman announced that federal troops would be sent to restore law and order in the Palmetto State. Five companies of the Eighteenth Infantry already had been sent, but the army was reorganizing its command and three additional companies would soon arrive. The additional companies originally were part of the Seventh United States Cavalry that had been fighting Arapaho, Cheyenne, Comanche, and Sioux Indians on the Western Plains. Companies B, E, and K were dispatched to the state late in March.[20]

The Seventh was an inspired choice to fight a band of guerillas in the South Carolina Piedmont. The regiment was formed as the United States resumed the march westward that had been sidelined by the Civil War. In 1866, Congress authorized the creation of four additional cavalry units. Major (Brevet Major General) John W. Davidson of the Second U.S. Cavalry was ordered to select "from the subalterns of the Second U.S. Cavalry a suitable number of officers to assist in the organization." Davidson never assumed command of the regiment, but he performed the work necessary to bring the Seventh to life. He was replaced by Colonel (Brevet Major General) Andrew J. Smith. Smith, in turn, served for only five months before he was replaced by a far more illustrious character, Lieutenant Colonel (Brevet Major General) George Armstrong Custer.

Custer's date with destiny at the Little Bighorn was nine years in the future when he assumed command of the Seventh U.S. Cavalry on February 26, 1867, but already he was well known as an enigma. On one hand, he had compiled an impressive military record, fearlessly fighting in every major battle of the Eastern Theatre of the Civil War. When he was promoted to the rank of brevet major general on June 29, 1863, Custer became the youngest officer ever to hold that rank in the U.S. Army. His zeal, or recklessness, depending on one's point of view, was legendary, as was his ruthlessness toward the enemy, especially when that enemy was Indian. On the other hand, the impetuous young man was relieved of command and court-martialed for his brutal pursuit of Sioux and Cheyenne warriors on the Plains. It was hardly surprising that the former "goat" of his West Point Class—thirty-fourth out of thirty-four graduates in the class of 1861—should be ignominiously stripped of his command. His relatively light punishment, a one-year suspension, was probably a reflection of the high regard his superiors held for his Civil War record.[21]

During Custer's tenure, the Seventh spent most of its early years fighting Indians in Kansas, Montana, and the Dakota territories. Mounted troops were needed to enforce order in far-flung corners of the territories; consequently, finding a suitable company and dispatching cavalrymen to battle the Klan was no simple matter. Through administrative reorganization, Washington finally sent companies from the Department of Missouri to undertake garrison duty in the Piedmont region of South Carolina. What the companies lacked in numbers—no more than one thousand federal troops came to the Palmetto State at any time in the 1870s—they compensated for by virtue of their physical presence. No group, including the Klan, relished a confrontation with well-trained, armed, professional soldiers led by capable officers with an indefatigable sense of duty.

The commander of the arriving companies, Major (Brevet Colonel) Lewis Merrill, had long experience fighting guerilla bands. Thirty-six years old in 1871, he had spent his adult life—more than fifteen years since he had graduated from the U.S. Military Academy at West Point—in military service. He was tall, with an imposing physique and a regal manner that impressed his supporters as a commanding presence while detractors spoke of arrogance and a propensity for self-aggrandizement. His physical appearance was softened by the presence of wire-rimmed glasses, which led one reporter to describe him as having "the head, face, and spectacles of a German professor, and the frame of an athlete." Although he had been embroiled in a recent scandal with charges of bribery lodged against him—never substantiated—he was well known for his logical, inquisitive mind and his unrivaled tenacity. He "was probably the superior not only of the other field officers, but also of most of his own contemporaries in the Seventh," one commentator concluded. Nonetheless, his "excruciating precision and verbosity of expression" could be off-putting, symptoms of "a style which tended to be unctuously didactic." He was not an attorney, but he hailed from a family of attorneys and, having served as judge advocate in numerous courts martial, was well-versed in the language and logic of the law.

Merrill initially viewed his duties in the Piedmont with no small measure of skepticism. He arrived during a period of tranquility, although "the people, both black and white, of [York] county, were still very much excited." His orders were clear. "My duty here was to aid the civil authorities of both the State and the United States, should they call upon me for assistance," he later testified. "I was instructed by my commanding officer to exercise all the moral influence possible to bring about a better state of things here, and in any case to protect individuals against mob violence or illegal arrest, should they seek the shelter of my camp."[22]

With orders to assist local authorities only when requested to do so, Merrill could not assume an active role in law enforcement. Required to stand by until needed, he was pleased to find a lull in the violence. As soon as he was in command, the major met with several prominent community leaders, including J. Rufus Bratton, John F. Lindsey, and Isaac D. Witherspoon. The group was anxious to prevent federal scrutiny into local affairs, and with little wonder. Bratton was the Klan leader who led the mob in the attack on the freedman Jim Williams earlier in the month. As the major would later testify, most white leaders in York County either participated in the Klan or were sympathetic to its aims. "In short," Merrill would have occasion to reflect, "the conspiracy may be stated to have practically included the whole white community within the ages when active participation in public affairs was possible."[23]

Of all the incidents confronting Merrill after he arrived in York County, the first episode left the most lasting impression. It involved a strange freedman named Elias Hill. Born into bondage, Hill suffered a malady, perhaps muscular dystrophy, at the age of seven, rendering an arm and a leg useless. Around that same time, about 1840, Hill's father purchased his and his wife's freedom for the princely sum of $150. Unable to use a crippled boy for labor, the master agreed to free young Elias as part of the transaction. Elias thus grew to adulthood as a free man. Unfortunately, his disease progressed, leaving his legs the size of a man's wrists, his arms withered, and his jaw deformed.

Viewed as a harmless, good-natured freak of nature, Elias became a kind of mascot for white schoolchildren in York County. They taught him to read and write, although their motivations were open to interpretation. They may have taken an interest in the sad little boy with few prospects for future advancement or they may have reveled in his misfortune, in which case their charity was an excuse to keep their pet close at hand for maximum merriment. In any case, no one objected to allowing this pitiful wretch to hang around the school.

Whites never recognized Elias Hill's native intelligence and extraordinary drive. What he lacked in physical prowess he more than compensated for in intellectual ability. By 1871, when he was fifty years old, he had emerged as a strong, charismatic force in the black community of York County. President of the local Union League and an ordained Baptist minister, Hill exercised the kind of clout that threatened anxious white leaders. He held regular political meetings in his cabin, and his eloquent preaching from the pulpit reverberated throughout the community. If anyone in the county was "uppity" and likely to inspire freedmen to forget their place, it was this wizened little man with the malformed limbs and silver tongue.

On the evening of May 5, masked nightriders appeared on Hill's land. His brother and sister-in-law lived in a cabin next door to his house, and it was there that the Klansmen initiated their search. Hill heard them slapping the woman as they demanded to know his whereabouts. Moments later, the masked terrorists burst into his home, pulled him from his bed, dragged him by his withered arms and legs into the yard, and hurled him to the ground. Beating him on his deformed limbs with a horsewhip, the Klansmen screamed obscenities as they charged him with inciting a riot, ravishing white women, and denouncing the KKK from his church. Hill vehemently denied the accusations. When they saw that Hill was not cowed by threats to heave him into the river, the marauders left, admonishing him, "Don't you pray against the Ku-Klux."

Whatever defiance he had displayed in the past, Elias Hill knew he was living on borrowed time. The Klan had killed freedmen in the past, and he harbored few doubts that he would be their next victim. With help from Congressman Alexander S. Wallace and the American Colonization Society, Hill and 135 other local blacks moved from South Carolina to Liberia, West Africa, in October 1871. Before he left, he testified before a congressional committee that emigration was the only sensible solution. "We do not believe it is possible, from the past history and present aspect of affairs, for our people to live in this country peaceably and educate and elevate their children to any degree which they desire," he said.[24]

Merrill had entertained doubts about Klan outrages in South Carolina, but the Hill case and other events that followed on its heels convinced him that he must act. Eight days after Elias Hill was whipped, the major told a group of fifteen or twenty prominent citizens in a booming voice and with a confident air that the U.S. government would not tolerate further abuses. Anyone who participated in KKK activities or aided and abetted its members could expect to suffer the full consequences of the law. If later actions failed to match his tough words and stirring rhetoric, at least he put York County citizens on notice that the KKK would no longer own the night.

With Merrill's permission and encouragement, the more conservative community leaders circulated a letter asking citizens to renounce violence and act in a lawful manner. The text eventually appeared in the local newspaper, the *Yorkville Enquirer*, on May 25. The group expressed its desire for "preservation of the public peace" to prevent "a spirit of general insubordination" from overwhelming the county. "As members of the community whose common interest is imperiled, we pledge our individual efforts and influence to prevent further acts of violence, and will aid and support the civil authorities in bringing offenders to justice."

Whether the publication of this letter was a good faith effort to curtail additional Klan activity or a not-so-subtle act of chicanery to hoodwink federal troops into assuming that stories of the KKK were greatly exaggerated is a matter of debate. Some question also exists whether groups of freedmen donned sheets and robbed a store to frame the Klan for another violent episode around this time. Whatever the precipitating event or motives of the perpetrators, it did not take long for the Klan to test Merrill's resolve. Within a few weeks of his arrival, the group struck again, shattering the calm and triggering a new wave of violence.[25]

NOTES

1. Steven G. Calabresi and Christopher S. Yoo, "The Unitary Executive During the Second Half-Century," *Harvard Journal of Law & Public Policy* 26 (Summer 2003): 759–60; Gary W. Gallagher, "The American Ulysses: Rehabilitating U. S. Grant," *The Virginia Quarterly Review* 81 (Summer 2005): 234–41; Brian J. Murphy, "Ulysses S. Grant's Yazoo River Bender," *America's Civil War* 17 (January 2005): 30–36; Henry M. W. Russell, "The *Memoirs* of Ulysses S. Grant: The Rhetoric of Judgment," *The Virginia Quarterly Review* 66 (Spring 1990): 189–209; Brooks D. Simpson, "Grant the Boss," *Civil War Times Illustrated* 43 (April 2004): 50–61; Jeffrey D. Wert, "All-Out War," *Civil War Times Illustrated* 43 (April 2004): 34–40.

2. Calabresi and Yoo, "The Unitary Executive During the Second Half-Century," 759; Michael A. Genovese, *The Power of the American Presidency, 1789–2000* (New York and Oxford: Oxford University Press, 2001), 58–63, 94–96, 117–21; Robert Selph Henry, *The Story of Reconstruction* (New York: Konecky & Konecky, 1999), 330–47; Joseph Nathan Kane, *Facts About the Presidents* (New York: Ace Books, 1976), 87–100, 196–211, 292–307; Geoffrey Perret, *Ulysses S. Grant: Soldier and President* (New York: Random House, 1997), 433.

3. Calabresi and Yoo, "The Unitary Executive During the Second Half-Century," 759–62; Eric Foner, *Reconstruction: America's Unfinished Revolution, 1863–1877* (New York: Francis Parkman Prize Edition, History Book Club, 2005; originally published by HarperCollins, 1988), 444–46; Gallagher, "The American Ulysses: Rehabilitating U. S. Grant," 240–41; Henry, *The Story of Reconstruction*, 362–63; Jean Edward Smith, *Grant* (New York: Simon & Schuster, 2001), 481–90.

4. Henry, *The Story of Reconstruction*, 284–85; William S. McFeely, *Grant: A Biography* (New York: Norton, 1981), 367–74; Smith, *Grant*, 542; Allen W. Trelease, *White Terror: The Ku Klux Klan Conspiracy and Southern Reconstruction* (Baton Rouge: Louisiana State University Press, 1971), 402–03; Wyn Craig Wade, *The Fiery Cross: The Ku Klux Klan in America* (New York and Oxford: Oxford University Press,

1987), 87–88; Jerry L. West, *The Reconstruction Ku Klux Klan in York County, South Carolina, 1865–1877* (Jefferson, NC: McFarland & Company, Inc., 2002), 86, 90–91; Lou Falkner Williams, *The Great South Carolina Ku Klux Klan Trials, 1871–1872* (Athens: University of Georgia Press, 1996), 44–46.

5. Foner, *Reconstruction: America's Unfinished Revolution*, 446–49; William Gillette, *Retreat From Reconstruction, 1869–1879* (Baton Rouge: Louisiana State University Press, 1919), 17–19; Everette Swinney, *Suppressing the Ku Klux Klan: The Enforcement of the Reconstruction Amendments, 1870–1877* (New York: Garland, 1987), 22–23; Wade, *The Fiery Cross*, 82–84.

6. David Everitt, "1871 War on Terror," *American History* 38 (June 2003): 26–28; Foner, *Reconstruction: America's Unfinished Revolution*, 425–33; Edward John Harcourt, "Who Were the Pale Faces? New Perspectives on the Tennessee Ku Klux," *Civil War History* 51 (March 2005): 23–66; Robert J. Kaczorowski, "Federal Enforcement of Civil Rights During the First Reconstruction," *Fordham Urban Law Journal* 23 (Fall 1995): 156–60; Wade, *The Fiery Cross*, 82–84.

7. Foner, *Reconstruction: America's Unfinished Revolution*, 454–59; John Hope Franklin, *Reconstruction After the Civil War* (Chicago: The University of Chicago Press, 1961), 161; Henry, *The Story of Reconstruction*, 397–98; Kaczorowski, "Federal Enforcement of Civil Rights During the First Reconstruction," 157–59; Richard W. Murphy, *The Nation Reunited: War's Aftermath* (Alexandria, VA: Time-Life Books, 1987), 98–99; Trelease, *White Terror*, 385–87; Wade, *The Fiery Cross*, 82–84.

8. Calabresi and Yoo, "The Unitary Executive During the Second Half-Century," 765–66; Everitt, "1871 War on Terror," 27–28; Foner, *Reconstruction: America's Unfinished Revolution*, 454; Kermit L. Hall, "Political Power and Constitutional Legitimacy: The South Carolina Ku Klux Klan Trials, 1871–1872," *Emory Law Journal* 33 (Fall 1984): 925–26; Kaczorowski, "Federal Enforcement of Civil Rights During the First Reconstruction," 157–60; Murphy, *The Nation Reunited*, 97–98.

9. Quoted in Kaczorowski, "Federal Enforcement of Civil Rights During the First Reconstruction," 163. See also, Calabresi and Yoo, "The Unitary Executive During the Second Half-Century," 765–66; Everitt, "1871 War on Terror," 27; Foner, *Reconstruction: America's Unfinished Revolution*, 457; Hall, "Political Power and Constitutional Legitimacy," 928–30; Trelease, *White Terror*, 402–03.

10. Everitt, "1871 War on Terror," 27; Trelease, *White Terror*, 387–88; Wade, *The Fiery Cross*, 88; West, *The Reconstruction Ku Klux Klan in York County, South Carolina*, 68; Richard Zuczek, *State of Rebellion: Reconstruction in South Carolina* (Columbia: University of South Carolina Press, 1996), 88–93.

11. Everitt, "1871 War on Terror," 31; Hall, "Political Power and Constitutional Legitimacy," 929–30; Henry, *The Story of Reconstruction*, 449; V. C. Jones, "The Rise and Fall of the Ku Klux Klan," *Civil War Times Illustrated* 2 (February 1964): 16–17; Kaczorowski, "Federal Enforcement of Civil Rights During the First Reconstruction," 158–160; Smith, *Grant*, 544–46; Trelease, *White Terror*, 386–91, 402–5; Wade, *The Fiery Cross*, 90–93; Williams, *The Great South Carolina Ku Klux Klan Trials*, 44–45.

12. Everitt, "1871 War on Terror," 31; Hall, "Political Power and Constitutional Legitimacy," 931–32; Trelease, *White Terror*, 388–90; Wade, *The Fiery Cross*, 90–92; Williams, *The Great South Carolina Ku Klux Klan Trials*, 42–43; Zuczek, *State of Rebellion*, 96–97.

13. Henry, *The Story of Reconstruction*, 449; Trelease, *White Terror*, 391; Zuczek, *State of Rebellion*, 97.

14. Quoted in Trelease, *White Terror*, 390. See also, Everitt, "1871 War on Terror," 30–31; Wade, *The Fiery Cross*, 90–93; Williams, *The Great South Carolina Ku Klux Klan Trials*, 42–44.

15. Swinney, *Suppressing the Ku Klux Klan: The Enforcement of the Reconstruction Amendments, 1870–1877*, 156–75; Jones, "The Rise and Fall of the Ku Klux Klan," 17; Trelease, *White Terror*, 392–93; Williams, *The Great South Carolina Ku Klux Klan Trials*, 43; Zuczek, *State of Rebellion*, 96–97.

16. Quoted in Zuczek, *State of Rebellion*, 97. See also, Henry, *The Story of Reconstruction*, 394–96; Carl W. Marino, "General Alfred Howe Terry, Soldier From Connecticut," Ph.D. diss., New York University, 1968; "Obituary: Alfred Howe Terry," *Army and Navy Journal* XXVII (December 20, 1890): 285; Swinney, *Suppressing the Ku Klux Klan*, 156–75; Trelease, *White Terror*, 233–38, 370, 402–03; Ezra J. Warner, *Generals in Blue* (Baton Rouge: Louisiana State University Press, 1964), 497–98.

17. Everitt, "1871 War on Terror," 27; Trelease, *White Terror*, 356–58; United States Congress, *Report of the Joint Select Committee to Inquire into the Condition of Affairs in the Late Insurrectionary States*, 42 Cong., 2 Sess., No. 22 (1872), Vol. III, 64–68, 74–75, 80, 98; Zuczek, *State of Rebellion*, 90–92.

18. Everitt, "1871 War on Terror," 27; Trelease, *White Terror*, 363–64; United States Congress, *Report of the Joint Select Committee*, Vol. V, 210–11, 702, 718, 1472; West, *The Reconstruction Ku Klux Klan in York County, South Carolina*, 61–62.

19. James E. Sefton, *The United States Army and Reconstruction, 1865–1877* (Westport, CT: Greenwood Press, 1967), 224–225; Trelease, *White Terror*, 402–03; Wade, *The Fiery Cross*, 94; West, *The Reconstruction Ku Klux Klan in York County, South Carolina*, 79–80; Zuczek, *State of Rebellion*, 90–93.

20. Everitt, "1871 War on Terror," 28, 30; "Just A-Rolling Along the Way; Log of the Green Chevrolet As It Voyages Over More of York County, *Yorkville Enquirer*, Yorkville, SC (June 3, 1932); "Lewis Merrill Dead," *Yorkville Enquirer*, Yorkville, SC (March 4, 1896); "Merrill Assumes Post," *Yorkville Enquirer*, Yorkville, SC (March 16, 1871); Sefton, *The United States Army and Reconstruction, 1865–1877*, 224–25; Trelease, *White Terror*, 369–71; United States Circuit Court [4th Circuit], *Proceedings in the Ku Klux Klan Trials at Columbia, S.C., in the United States Circuit Court, November Term, 1871* (Columbia, SC: Republican Printing Company, State Printers, 1872), 743–48; Wade, *The Fiery Cross*, 93–94; West, *The Reconstruction Ku Klux Klan in York County, South Carolina*, 80–81; Williams, *The Great South Carolina Ku Klux Klan Trials*, 38–39; Zuczek, *State of Rebellion*, 93–95.

21. Stephen E. Ambrose, *Crazy Horse and Custer: The Parallel Lives of Two American Warriors* (New York: Anchor Books, 1996), 99–117, 257–71, 278–89, 312–23;

Walter L. McVey, "When My Grandfather Rode With Custer," *Wild West* 15 (October 2002): 38–44, 69–70; Clyde A. Milner II, "National Initiatives," in *The Oxford History of the American West*, Clyde A. Milner II, Carol A. O'Connor, and Martha A. Sandweiss, eds. (New York and Oxford: Oxford University Press, 1994), 182; Sefton, *The United States Army and Reconstruction, 1865–1877*, 224–25.

22. Quoted in United States Congress, *Report of the Joint Select Committee*, Vol. V, 1464. See also, "Arrival of a Cavalry Company," *Yorkville Enquirer*, Yorkville, SC (March 30, 1871); Samuel Baird, *With Merrill's Cavalry: The Civil War Experiences of Samuel Baird, 2nd Missouri Cavalry, U.S.A.*, with Notes and an Introduction by Charles Annegan (San Marcos, CA: The Book Habit, 1981), 5; George W. Cullum, *Biographical Register of the Officers and Graduates of the U.S. Military Academy at West Point, N.Y. From its Establishment, in 1802, to 1890 with the Early History of the United States Military Academy* (Boston and New York: Houghton, Mifflin and Company, and Cambridge, MA: The Riverside Press, 1891), 624–25; Everitt, "1871 War on Terror," 28, 30–32; Stanley F. Horn, *Invisible Empire: The Story of the Ku Klux Klan, 1866–1871* (Montclair, NJ: Patterson Smith, 1969), 234–35, 368; Barry C. Johnson, *Custer, Reno, Merrill and the Lauffer Case: Some Warfare in "The Fighting Seventh"* (London: The Pilot Printing & Publicity Service on Behalf of the English Westerners' Society, 1971), 1–2; "Lewis Merrill Dead," *Yorkville Enquirer*, Yorkville, SC (March 4, 1896); Sefton, *The United States Army and Reconstruction, 1865–1877*, 224–25; Trelease, *White Terror*, 369–70; Wade, *The Fiery Cross*, 93–95; West, *The Reconstruction Ku Klux Klan in York County, South Carolina*, 80–81; Williams, *The Great South Carolina Ku Klux Klan Trials*, 38–39, 44–45; Zuczek, *State of Rebellion*, 94–95.

23. Quoted in United States Congress, *Report of the Joint Select Committee*, Vol. III, 1603. See also, Trelease, *White Terror*, 369–70; United States Circuit Court [4th Circuit], *Proceedings in the Ku Klux Klan Trials at Columbia, S.C., in the United States Circuit Court, November Term, 1871*, 743–48; Wade, *The Fiery Cross*, 93–95; West, *The Reconstruction Ku Klux Klan in York County, South Carolina*, 80–81; Williams, *The Great South Carolina Ku Klux Klan Trials*, 38–39, 44–45; Richard Zuczek, "The Federal Government's Attack on the Ku Klux Klan: A Reassessment," *South Carolina Historical Magazine* 97 (January 1, 1996): 47–64; Zuczek, *State of Rebellion*, 94–95.

24. Quoted in Wade, *The Fiery Cross*, 75. See also, Hans L. Trefousse, *Reconstruction: America's First Effort at Racial Democracy* (New York: Van Nostrand Reinhold Company, 1971), 137–46; Trelease, *White Terror*, 371–72; United States Circuit Court [4th Circuit], *Proceedings in the Ku Klux Klan Trials at Columbia, S.C., in the United States Circuit Court, November Term, 1871*, 221–24; United States Congress, *Report of the Joint Select Committee*, Vol. V, 1406–15, 1477; West, *The Reconstruction Ku Klux Klan in York County, South Carolina*, 83–84.

25. Quoted in "To the Citizens of York County," *Yorkville Enquirer*, Yorkville, SC (May 25, 1871). See also, Trelease, *White Terror*, 372–73; Wade, *The Fiery Cross*, 95–96; West, *The Reconstruction Ku Klux Klan in York County, South Carolina*, 84.

4

"IT WAS TO BE HIS LIFE-LONG COMPLAINT THAT HIS SERVICES WERE NEVER PROPERLY RECOGNIZED OR REWARDED"

Lewis Merrill was born in New Berlin, Pennsylvania, on October 28, 1834. By tradition, the men in his family served with distinction in one of two careers: the military or the law. His grandfather, Jesse, and great-grandfather, Samuel, were soldiers in the Revolutionary War. Brothers Charles, George, and Jesse served in uniform during the American Civil War. In addition to their military service, Charles and Jesse were trained as lawyers.

James, father of the group, was a prominent attorney and long-time colleague of Republican firebrand Thaddeus Stevens. The elder Merrill participated in the state constitutional convention of 1838 and helped draft provisions that incorporated notions of equity into Pennsylvania law. Echoing Stevens's progressive views on race, throughout his career James Merrill argued passionately in favor of extending the franchise to blacks. His influence on young Lewis's life and career was considerable, although the fifty-one-year-old James died only a few days after Lewis's seventh birthday.

Lewis Merrill was said to have inherited his father's keen legal mind, but he eschewed a career practicing law to pursue the second family vocation. Enrolled at the U.S. Military Academy at West Point at the age of sixteen, he was graduated twentieth in a class of thirty-four on July 1, 1855. He assumed the rank of (brevet) second lieutenant of the United States Dragoons upon graduation, and won a permanent promotion as second lieutenant on December 13 of that year.

Lieutenant Merrill's assignment to the dragoons was fortuitous; it introduced him to military operations in the territories, a region where clear lines of battle did not exist and an officer learned to exercise sound judgment in resolving conflicts with little oversight or direction. First organized in 1833, dragoons were frontier soldiers who provided armed escorts for settlers and merchants traveling out West, especially along the Santa Fe and Oregon Trails. In the period between the end of the Mexican War and the beginning of the Civil War, commissioned army officers often found themselves stationed in the United States Dragoons or in other units assigned to remote outposts with little to do except provide routine escorts or assume garrison duty. Upon occasion, troops were called upon to soothe tensions between whites and plains Indians, but armed confrontations were the exception rather than the rule. In later years, with settlers racing across the continent after the completion of the Transcontinental Railroad, bloodshed would become more commonplace, but in the 1850s Lewis Merrill and his comrades were more likely to fall victim to disease or boredom than to the bows and arrows of red warriors.[1]

He was stationed initially at Jefferson Barracks, Missouri. In the 1850s, Missouri was a frontier where the South and West came together. Populated with restless settlers who migrated from the East ever westward in hopes of building a better life free from the encumbrances of European-style "civilization," the state was a dividing line between the staid world of the eighteenth century and the tumultuous promise of a New World of the nineteenth century. St. Louis, a curious mix of old and new, was the leading city, and Lewis Merrill came to know it well during his service in the 1850s and 1860s.[2]

In the six years between his graduation from West Point and the outbreak of civil war, the young lieutenant moved from one frontier post to another, with a brief stint at Carlisle Barracks, Pennsylvania, sandwiched between his Western duties. Far from exciting or glamorous, his assignments in Missouri and the Nebraska territory were filled with the tedium of army life during peacetime. The more contemplative fellows in his situation reflected on their poor future prospects and reconsidered plans for a civilian career while others took to the bottle, but Merrill left no record of either activity.

Two episodes stand out from Merrill's antebellum career as instructive for his subsequent service fighting guerillas and nightriders. While serving at Fort Leavenworth and Fort Riley, Kansas, he participated in the army's efforts to quell disturbances in "Bleeding Kansas," a crossroads where pro-slavery and anti-slavery forces violently clashed over their respective ideologies and ways of life. The army had first been dispatched as "peacekeepers" by the Pierce administration in 1854. At various times throughout the 1850s, soldiers confronted American Indians, armed guerillas, and assorted

Figure 4.1. Lewis Merrill, a career army officer with long experience fighting guerillas on the frontier, was well suited to lead federal troops against the Ku Klux Klan in South Carolina.

The Roger D. Hunt Collection, U.S. Army Military History Institute

factions of uncertain loyalties. Their tasks were politically delicate and often frustratingly vague; directing military forces to keep the peace through a threat of force left officers with wide latitude for making on-the-spot decisions but little, if any, guidance in resolving specific disputes.[3]

In 1858, he participated in a second guerilla encounter, the so-called Utah expedition. Utah was still a territory in the 1850s, and it was an area plagued by an escalating conflict between the United States government and a militia group, the Nauvoo Legion, operated by the Mormon Church. The confrontation began as a result of the 1856 presidential election when Democrat James Buchanan defeated John C. Fremont of the newly formed Republican Party. During the campaign, the Republicans attacked Buchanan on several issues, including the Democratic Party's lackadaisical attitude toward the "twin relics of barbarism": slavery and polygamy. Had he been inclined to do so, Buchanan was not in a position to ameliorate the effects of slavery, but he thought he could handle polygamy by dismissing Brigham Young, the Mormon governor of the Utah Territory since 1850. The new president appointed a successor to Governor Young, Alfred Cumming, and ordered the U.S. Army to escort the new administrator to his post.

Buchanan had not counted on Governor Young's obstreperous nature or the Mormons' willingness to bear arms against federal troops. The army moved into Utah Territory under the leadership of several officers, most notably Colonel Albert Sidney Johnston, a highly regarded leader who would later join the Confederate States Army and perish in fierce fighting at the Battle of Shiloh in 1862. On September 11, 1857, a week before Colonel Johnston and his men set out for the territory, a group of Mormons slaughtered 120 civilians in southern Utah in what came to be called the Mountain Meadows Massacre. Four days after the massacre, Brigham Young defiantly ordered the Nauvoo Legion to resist federal troops if they entered Utah Territory. In the ensuing month, the Nauvoo Legion harassed the soldiers, and even burned fifty-two U.S. wagons on October 5. Anticipating a long and possibly bloody campaign, Colonel Johnston set up winter quarters at Fort Bridger with the expectation of moving on to Salt Lake City, the Mormon stronghold, in the spring. When spring rolled around, reinforcements arrived and the troops prepared to march. The resulting campaign might have decimated the Mormons had Governor Young not stepped aside and allowed his replacement to take office. The expedition ended with no additional loss of life.[4]

These expeditions taught Lieutenant Merrill valuable lessons about fighting a shadowy enemy that struck without warning before disappearing into the night. When war commenced between North and South in 1861, he was a seasoned professional soldier with experience combating guerillas. He would need all of his experience and professional acumen fighting in Missouri under the command of Major General John Charles Fremont.

Fremont was among the most famous men of his era when the Civil War erupted. He had explored large portions of the territorial United States, and his exploits made him famous as the "Pathfinder of the West." According to one commentator, the "freedom of nature in the Rocky Mountains and the Sierra Nevada nerved every fiber of his being." Fremont was politically well connected, having married Jessie Benton, daughter of prominent Missouri senator Thomas Hart Benton. In 1856, he was the nominee for president of the United States under the banner of a new political party, the Republicans. Although he lost the election to James Buchanan, the future seemed to promise great things for this bona fide American hero.

Fremont returned from Europe in the late spring of 1861 to find St. Louis descending into chaos. President Lincoln ordered him to clear Missouri of rebels, but exactly how this gargantuan task was to be accomplished was unclear. "I have given you *carte blanche*," the president was supposed to have told the famous general. "You must use your judgment and do the best you can." Unfortunately for both Lincoln and Fremont, the latter's best judgment left much to be desired.

Less than a month into his tenure, Fremont became a scapegoat for the Union loss at the Battle of Wilson's Creek southwest of Springfield, Missouri. His subordinate, General Nathaniel Lyon, found himself in dire straits as many of his seven thousand men left military service when their ninety-day enlistments expired, despite the presence of a large Confederate force in the area. The desperate general sent word to Fremont that he required immediate assistance. Believing that he did not command sufficient troops to intercede absent reinforcements, Fremont ordered Lyon to fall back 120 miles to a railhead at Rolla. Before Lyon could execute the order, he engaged the enemy at Wilson's Creek, where he fell to a martyr's death and left his shattered forces in full retreat. Humiliated by a loss in his inaugural effort, the Pathfinder of the West faced the wrath of a dispirited Northern public. Accustomed to adoring crowds and prodigious accolades, Fremont's pride was wounded by his new persona as either an indecisive buffoon or an insidious villain, depending on one's point of view.[5]

Under other circumstances, he might have rallied, for many commanders who later enjoyed sterling reputations blundered at the outset. This was not to be. Fremont's problems also stemmed in part from his flamboyance. One Union soldier, unimpressed with the great man, described Fremont as a

Figure 4.2. Early in his career, Merrill served as chief of cavalry staff for Major General John C. Fremont, pictured here.
The National Archives

"spread-eagle, show-off, horn-tooting general." War or no war, the frontiers-man-cum-gentleman enjoyed his creature comforts; he set up headquarters in a mansion and surrounded himself with layers of aides who marched and preened in full dress regalia, a sight sickening to many soldiers who had tasted battle and knew the alternating drudgery and horrors of war. According to commentator Champ Clark, in addition to his love of pageantry and pomp, Fremont also "displayed a notable disinclination for hard fighting."[6]

From the perspective of the Lincoln administration, all might have been forgiven had Fremont not taken the additional step of placing his commander-in-chief in an untenable position. Without forewarning the president, on August 30, 1861, the major general announced that he was placing the state of Missouri under martial law, a measure that allowed him to execute guerillas without a trial. Any person found to have taken up arms against the government of the United States would have his property confiscated and his slaves freed. This field-level emancipation proclamation transformed Fremont into a hero among abolitionists, but it risked alienating Union loyalists in a key border state.

Exhibiting his well-known concern for the sensibilities of others, Lincoln contacted Fremont "in a spirit of caution, and not of censure" asking that the general withdraw the proclamation. Refusing to recognize a hint, the politically myopic Fremont declined to "change or shade it." "If I were to retract it of my own accord," he wrote in a typically blustery, self-righteous response, "it would imply that I had acted without the reflection which the gravity of the point demanded. But I did not. I acted with deliberation, and upon the certain conviction that it was a measure right and necessary, and I think so still." The day for an emancipation proclamation would come as the nature of the war changed, but that day had not yet arrived in 1861 when John Charles Fremont issued his high-handed reply to Abraham Lincoln. He left his commander-in-chief little choice but to countermand the proclamation. Consequently, the general fell out of favor with the administration and never reclaimed his prewar stature.[7]

As chief of cavalry staff for Fremont, Lewis Merrill bore witness to the great man's painful self-destruction, although Merrill left no written record of his reaction. On April 24, 1861, not long after Fort Sumter capitulated to the Rebels, the young cavalryman was promoted to a first lieutenant in the United States Dragoons. He spent May through August 1861 mustering volunteer regiments into service before orders directed him to join General Fremont's staff in the Department of Missouri. Shortly thereafter, he asked for, and received, permission to organize a cavalry unit, the Second Missouri Volunteer Cavalry Regiment, which became known colloquially as the

Merrill Horse. On August 23, 1861, Merrill assumed the rank of colonel and spent a month at Benton Barracks, Missouri, recruiting more than eight hundred soldiers for the new regiment.[8]

The Merrill Horse served under Fremont's command during the fall of 1861, moving with the general in the campaign against Springfield, Missouri, in September and October. The relationship would not last beyond the autumn. As a result of his ongoing conflicts with President Lincoln and his failure to fight the enemy with vigor, Fremont's days were numbered, and that number was one hundred. Slightly more than three months after he assumed command, the Pathfinder of the West was relieved of duty. He was too important a public figure to be entirely displaced, but the prominent general was shuffled off to another theater where he might do less damage. Observing the situation in Missouri up close, one young lady summarized the general feeling about Fremont's fall from grace: "He had been a girlish idol of mine from reading of his achievements as a Pathfinder, but my illusions vanished, for he was weighed in the balance and found wanting."[9]

After Fremont's departure, Brigadier General (later Major General) Samuel Ryan Curtis assumed part of the Pathfinder's old command. An 1831 graduate of West Point, the somber fifty-six-year-old lawyer and former Iowa congressman had orders to attack southwestern Missouri as part of a three-pronged strategy designed to secure the Mississippi River. Part of Curtis's duty was to drive Confederate General Sterling (Pap) Price, an antebellum governor of Missouri, from his path. General Price had enjoyed early successes at Wilson's Creek and at Lexington on the Missouri River. With a small band of soldiers and guerillas, Price eventually retreated into southwestern Missouri where he engaged in a verbal feud with Confederate General Ben McCullough. Jefferson Davis would later appoint Major General Earl Van Dorn to command both Price and McCullough, but in the meantime Price's Confederate forces remained a thorn in the Union side, if little more.

He may not have represented a major threat to Union forces in Missouri, but Price could not be allowed to launch guerilla operations indefinitely. General Curtis's troops established winter quarters at Sedalia, Missouri, waiting for the spring to come and with it a new offensive to clear out guerillas and halt Price's progress. During the three months they were stationed at Sedalia, the Merrill Horse repeatedly ventured out from the little town to reconnoiter the countryside. The regiment was dispatched to Saline County from December 3 to December 12 and on to Milford from December 15 to December 19.

Figure 4.3.   Merrill served under Major General Samuel R. Curtis during the general's pursuit of Confederate General Sterling Price's forces into Arkansas in 1862–1863.
Picture History

Serving under Merrill in the Second Missouri, Private Sam Baird vividly remembered the regiment's search for guerillas in 1861–1862. Even when the unit was ensconced in winter quarters, "we were almost continuously in the saddle, day and night, scouting after bushwhackers, for the country was full of them. We were going from place to place; Columbus, Warenton, Warington, Boonville, Warsaw, Knobnoster and lots of other places too numerous to mention. At Memphis, Missouri, Moore's Mills and Rose Hill we had hard fighting."[10]

In January 1862, the Merrill Horse was attached to the District of Northeast Missouri, Department of Missouri, an assignment that would last until June 1863. As part of his duty, Merrill commanded the St. Louis Division with his headquarters established in the city. During the seventeen months before the regiment left for Arkansas, Lewis Merrill would hone his skills in combating guerillas. In February 1862, he served as president of a trial and arraignment of several men hauled before a military commission. Seven months later, after his men had scoured the countryside and apprehended three guerillas, he ordered the captives to be executed at Mexico, Missouri, although in two cases he commuted the sentences. In these and other cases that came before him, the young Union officer struggled to be firm but fair. In egregious instances, justice called for the ultimate penalty, but mercy could be extended to men who demonstrated genuine remorse and swore an oath to renounce guerilla warfare.[11]

In the summer of 1863, the Merrill Horse was detached to the Department of Missouri, District of Southeast Missouri, to join an expedition rooting out Confederate forces from Arkansas. The 1860 census showed Little Rock, in the central part of the state, with 3,727 inhabitants—2,874 whites and 853 blacks. Despite its small size, the town was an important crossroads in an important state of the Trans-Mississippi Theater. In July 1863, Major General Frederick Steele came to Helena in eastern Arkansas near the Mississippi border to assume command of Union forces and plan an assault on Little Rock. Steele was a West Point graduate in the same class with Ulysses S. Grant (1843) and well known for his aggressive fighting tactics. If he could not quite muster the organizational skill to excel as a departmental leader, Steele was, in Grant's view, "a first-class commander of troops in battle."

Facing Steele was the same cunning Confederate general that had plagued Federals in Missouri, Pap Price. Price has ascended into command at Helena after General Theophilus Holmes had fallen ill. With only eight thousand men at his command, Price doubted whether he could hold Little Rock if Steele's men launched an all-out offensive, but he presented a brave public face, pronouncing his troops "in excellent condition, full of enthusiasm and eager to meet the enemy." Enthusiasm and eagerness were certainly commendable traits in soldiers, but they were not enough to hold off Steele's forces.

On September 10, after a campaign that lasted forty days, Steele sent Brigadier General John W. Davidson's cavalry across the Arkansas River to advance on the city while other Union forces attacked entrenched Confederates on the north shore. The Merrill Horse was part of the cavalry attack. Sam Baird remembered the preparations: "Our cavalry began to get ready to cross the river at that place [the levy near Price's forts] by fording the stream. We put down a pontoon bridge for the artillery, while Steele's Division kept up the road toward the fort."

At first light, Union batteries opened fire; the Confederates "were so surprised that they fell back and our artillery and cavalry moved quickly across the river. They soon made it pretty hot for us, but we kept driving them and the battle was on 'til about three in the afternoon; then they ran." With surprising ease, the cavalry forced the Confederates to flee, and Little Rock fell into Union hands. By Civil War standards, casualties were small— numbering only 137—with 18 killed, 118 wounded, and 1 missing, although the exact figures were a point of contention in the days that followed.[12]

During the fighting, Lewis Merrill received the only injury of his long military career when he was struck by a ricocheting bullet. The wound seemed slight at the time, but he would struggle with pain and complications from the shooting for the rest of his life. In the meantime, much to Merrill's pleasure, he was awarded the rank of brevet major for the "gallant and meritorious services" he rendered that day. The battle for Little Rock was not a major encounter, but it was the highlight of Lewis Merrill's Civil War career. He never again fought in a head-to-head battle with Confederate forces. For the duration of the conflict, the Merrill Horse was assigned to garrison and escort duty. The regiment fought in minor skirmishes upon occasion, but no further grand cavalry charges were in the offing.

Despite the wound, Merrill rode with his men as the Federals pursued General Price through Arkansas in mid-September. Afterward, he was stationed at Little Rock until March 1864. Although the city was in Union hands, guerilla activities never ceased, and the Merrill Horse engaged in skirmishes throughout the fall and winter. By May 1864, Merrill and his men moved back to St. Louis for a six-month tour of duty. When the Army of Tennessee moved through eastern Tennessee and into Georgia, Merrill was reassigned to fight guerillas in the army's rear. He participated in the

Figure 4.4. Major General Frederick Steele commanded Union forces during the Battle of Little Rock in September 1863, when Merrill was wounded by a stray bullet.
Picture History

expedition against the Mobile and Ohio Railroad before moving to Chattanooga and into Georgia.

From January through September 1865, the regiment escorted trains from Chattanooga to Atlanta. Merrill occasionally assumed command of his volunteer regiment in the field, but he was frequently absent from the ranks and assigned to court martial duty. A month before the war ended, on March 13, 1865, he was promoted to (brevet) brigadier general of U.S. Volunteers. Whatever his talents in the saddle, Merrill was recognized for a superior understanding of military rules and regulations and his ability to adjudicate disputes. He had at last combined his family's two professions—military service and the law—in his chosen career. These skills would serve him well in his battles against the Ku Klux Klan during the postbellum years.[13]

Lewis Merrill had much of which to be proud. Throughout the war, he had shown himself to be a competent cavalry commander imbued with an almost inexhaustible reservoir of patience as well as a precise, gifted legal mind. His men regarded him with respect and a measure of affection. He received several battlefield promotions after engaging in heavy fighting across much of the Trans-Mississippi Theater. At the same time, his service record, while unblemished, did not stand out in the annals of the Civil War. It rankled this ambitious West Pointer that he had not attained the high status afforded many of his peers in uniform. According to one commentator, decidedly underwhelmed by Merrill's performance, his "services seem to have been valuable, but although he was several times recommended for promotion to brigadier general of volunteers, he was still a colonel at his muster-out. It was to be his life-long complaint that his services were never properly recognized or rewarded, and that he had constantly to watch is juniors gain preferment over his head."[14]

Merrill was mustered out of volunteer service on December 14, 1865, but he was a career soldier and chose to remain in uniform as part of the regular army. In 1866, he was stationed again on the frontier, first at Fort Leavenworth, Kansas, and later at Fort Hayes, Kansas. In the latter half of the 1860s, he served as Acting Assistant Inspector-General of the Department of the Platte and as an acting judge advocate. Serving in uniform may have been glorious during the war, but peacetime military service again lost its luster. As was true in the 1850s, army officers found little to recommend a career roaming the plains, guarding railroad tracks, and fighting Indians beneath a fierce sun across an endless, parched landscape.

On November 27, 1868, Merrill was transferred to the Seventh Cavalry with the permanent rank of major. There, while serving under the famed Lieutenant Colonel George Armstrong Custer, Merrill became embroiled in

a controversy that would forever stain his record. It started, as many important cases do, from seemingly innocuous circumstances. The matter involved
charges of fraud filed against a below-average officer in the Quartermaster
Department, and eventually led to charges of corruption leveled against
Lewis Merrill.[15]

The incident began in 1869 when Captain Samuel B. Lauffer was
charged with disobeying orders, engaging in conduct unbecoming an officer, and knowingly making a false return of public property. An assistant
army quartermaster, Lauffer's career was "bleak and colourless." Were it not
for the controversy involving Major Merrill, his name probably would be
lost to history. Like Merrill, Lauffer was a native of the Keystone State. He
was born on February 28, 1826, and spent his early life employed as a clerk.
In August 1863, he was appointed assistant quartermaster of volunteers, a
position he held until he was mustered out of the service in April 1866. After he left the volunteer army, he applied for a civilian position as a store-
keeper for the military. Failing to win that post, Lauffer found a preferable
appointment as a captain and assistant quartermaster in the regular army. He
entered this new phase of his career at Fort Harker, Kansas, in April 1867.[16]

Back in uniform, Captain Lauffer distinguished himself as "a nervous,
timid man too afraid of taking upon himself the smallest responsibility." He
was viewed as honest, albeit an "obstinate, inefficient quartermaster." Post
commanders were at a loss on how to handle this little man. He could not
be brought up on charges if he had committed no offense, but he was so
poorly suited to his duties that he could not be allowed to remain at his
post. As a result, the assistant quartermaster was shuffled from one fort to
another. As soon as he settled into a new assignment and his superiors became aware of his lackadaisical attitude, they longed to be rid of him. Thus,
like a bad penny, he turned up at Fort Wingate, New Mexico, in 1869,
where he again distinguished himself for his lackluster performance and inability to get along with his fellow officers. During his four-month tenure
in New Mexico, Lauffer most notably butted heads with Major Andrew W.
Evans of the Third Cavalry, and their petty dispute erupted into a major
controversy.

The conflict began with the loss of a "public mule." As a member of
the Quartermaster Department, Lauffer was responsible for the care of the
mule, but the animal could not be accounted for after a soldier had borrowed but failed to return it. In the meantime, Major Evans heard tales that
Lauffer intended to submit a falsified affidavit absolving himself of blame
for the missing animal. When the captain persisted in offering the affidavit,
Evans tried in vain to dissuade him from submitting what the latter believed

to be a perjured document. Lauffer countered that the affidavit was true. Rather than allow a false declaration to be entered into the record unchallenged, Evans filed fraud charges against Lauffer. The case was brought before a District of New Mexico court martial in Santa Fe on November 8, 1869.[17]

Acting as judge advocate, Major Merrill prosecuted the case. From the outset, it was evident that the charges against the defendant did not rise to the level of fraud. Lauffer undeniably was a cantankerous fellow, a lazy and unpleasant personality to endure, but not demonstrably fraudulent in his business dealings. The key issue was whether Lauffer should have been allowed to offer an affidavit that he knew to be false. Because no direct evidence showed that Lauffer had misappropriated the mule and, moreover, Major Evans could not say with certainty that Lauffer knew the affidavit to be false, the case collapsed. After five days of *pro forma* testimony, the military tribunal acquitted the defendant. A matter of little consequence appeared to have ended.[18]

Merrill's judgment in prosecuting a questionable case can be excused as his duty; charges had been preferred against Captain Lauffer, and the judge advocate was required to prosecute the matter. Other dealings with Captain Lauffer raise serious questions about Merrill's judgment, however, for Merrill and Captain Henry C. Bankhead of the Fifth Infantry associated with the defendant outside the courtroom. In modern judicial settings, the rule against a prosecutor associating with a defendant with opposing counsel absent is nearly inviolate, and for good reason. Any association, especially of a social nature, raises grave doubts about the impartiality and fairness of the judicial proceeding. In this instance, Merrill, Bankhead, and Lauffer spent their idle hours between court sessions gambling. At the conclusion of their games, Major Bankhead—in essence, a juror in the case—owed money to Captain Lauffer, a subordinate officer and the defendant, who in turn owed money to Major Merrill, the prosecutor. As if this awkward arrangement were not bad enough, Lauffer still owed money to Merrill when the judge advocate left Fort Wingate bound for a new assignment.

A little over a year after the acquittal, in December 1870, Merrill unwisely wrote to Lauffer asking for payment of the outstanding balance of the gambling debt. Suffering from a real or feigned illness, the temperamentally unstable Lauffer replied in a letter dated January 3, 1871. After setting forth a meandering tale of hardship and woe, he finally got to the point. "The money I paid you at Santa Fe New Mexico as Judge Advocate amounting to $200, when on trial before a General Court Martial, I have learned was illegal and improper," the suddenly righteous gambler observed.

Not only did Lauffer believe that he owed no debt, but he demanded "that you will remit by return mail a draft on New York equal to the amount I paid you as above stated."[19]

Merrill viewed Lauffer's reply as a not-so-subtle attempt to welsh on a bet. The audacity was breathtaking; not only did the captain refuse to remit the balance due and owing, but he demanded a return of the monies already paid. Even more worrisome was the reference to the "illegal and improper" character of the debt because it represented a genuine threat to the major's reputation. Lest the message be too subtle, Lauffer left nothing to chance. "If I do not receive said draft within 12 days I will forward copy of this letter through the Adjutant General with full explanation and statement of the whole affair," he concluded.

Ever mindful of the adage that the best defense is a good offense, Lauffer characterized his debt to Merrill and his subsequent acquittal as a quid pro quo transaction. While stationed at Fort Leavenworth in 1870, he told an officer that the judge advocate had deliberately botched the prosecution in exchange for a bribe. The officer wrote to Merrill informing him of the allegations. On January 17, 1871, Merrill explained, "I received a letter from Leavenworth which informs me in substance that an officer there had been informed that an officer named Lauffer had stated that he was willing to make affidavit that he had bartered with me while he was on trial before a Court of which I was Judge Advocate for his acquittal, promising me some five or six hundred dollars, a part of which he had paid me." Alarmed at this turn of events, Merrill reread Lauffer's response to his December 1870 letter "in an entirely new light."[20]

So this was how it was to be: Lauffer would avoid paying his gambling debt by charging the major with corruption. It was an ingenious, if ignoble, strategy. Afraid to allow such a "foul and injurious" charge to stand, Merrill sent a letter to department headquarters asking that a court of inquiry be convened to clear his name. "I will be able to show to the Court that no money transaction ever took place between Captain Lauffer and myself except at cards in company with various other officers, and then under circumstances which left no doubt of their character," he promised.

The adjutant general of the War Department refused to convene a court of inquiry because "no charges of any description against you have been received at these headquarters, and when they are received it will be time enough to convene the Board asked for." Merrill was not satisfied with this response; he took it upon himself to press the matter. In so doing, he further embroiled himself in controversy, this time involving his commanding officer, Lieutenant Colonel Custer.[21]

Merrill believed that Custer had "made himself the medium of accusations made by Mr. Lauffer" and was repeating scurrilous tales impugning Merrill's reputation. The major believed that Custer was upset because Merrill had successfully prosecuted a case against a renowned army officer and Custer associate, George Augustus Armes, who was dishonorably dismissed from the service. In addition, Merrill had been compelled to testify before the "Benzine Board," a formal inquiry into the fitness of certain officers to perform their duties. During his testimony, Merrill denigrated Custer's "method of discipline and ideas of duty." By his own admission, Merrill had been a reluctant participant at the hearings. "The evidence was not volunteered by me, was given in good faith, and pains were taken to avoid unnecessary statements of either facts or names, which might be injurious to persons not directly involved in the inquiries of the board," he later recalled.

One final incident explained Custer's animus toward his subordinate. As Merrill explained, "It is also unfortunately proper for me to refer in terms of criticism in conversation and in an official letter to Department Headquarters to his conduct while my Commanding Officer in putting me in a false position by suppressing the fact that he had granted me leave of absence on an occasion which brought him reproof of the Department Commander, because of my absence."[22]

Whatever the cause, Custer seemed predisposed to regard Merrill with hostility. After the lieutenant colonel learned of the bribery allegations, he corresponded with Captain Lauffer, asking that "you furnish me, if consistent, all the facts and circumstances" regarding the corruption charge, "giving me dates and conversations as nearly accurate as you can." Custer also requested copies of correspondence exchanged between Merrill and Lauffer. "I would of course greatly prefer the original of said letters if you would consent."[23]

When Custer was satisfied that he had examined sufficient evidence of Merrill's corruption, he wrote to the major and asked him to respond to the charges. By the time Merrill received the correspondence, he had moved on to Yorkville to begin his campaign against the Ku Klux Klan. Nonetheless, he found time to write to his commanding officer in a hostile tone dripping with vituperation. Accusing his commander of slandering his character and circulating vicious, unsupported gossip and innuendo, Merrill remarked, "a very small amount of common courtesy, or of that sense of justice, upon which you remark in your present letter, might have suggested to you that upon hearing so vile a slander against an officer of the same regiment as yourself, you should make it your business to see that he

Figure 4.5.   In the late 1860s and early 1870s, Merrill served under a legendary commander, Lieutenant Colonel George A. Custer, in the Seventh U.S. Cavalry. When Merrill departed for South Carolina in 1871, he and Custer were estranged over the 1869–1870 Lauffer case.
The Library of Congress

was informed of it, and had the opportunity to meet it." Because Custer had not filed formal charges and headquarters would not convene a court of inquiry, Merrill felt powerless to address the charges adequately. He reiterated his request for a formal inquiry and invited Custer to file formal charges.[24]

Custer did not reply to Merrill's philippic. Instead, he forwarded the matter to General Terry, commander of the Department of the South. Terry eventually sent the file to the War Department. Several officers, including General William T. Sherman, expressed their support for Merrill. Noting Merrill's "Special Service in South Carolina," Sherman wrote, "I am personally acquainted with Major Merrill and believe he possesses the confidence of the army generally, and can hardly suppose there can be any truth in this story, yet it is of such a nature, that it cannot be denied or overlooked."

The next step was to launch a preliminary investigation that might result in convening a court of inquiry, as Merrill had requested. When the adjutant general asked Lauffer for evidence to substantiate the allegations, however, the former captain, now discharged from military service, confessed that he was "unable to procure sufficient data" because he could not locate "a certain memorandum book, where I entered all monies paid out by myself." The adjutant general then asked Lauffer to swear an affidavit against Merrill even if he could not find his records. Lauffer declined. "I cannot see how I can conscientiously make an affidavit without having the data and facts at hand," he explained.[25]

With Lauffer's failure to produce evidence or swear an affidavit against Merrill, the matter died. The repercussions were far-reaching, however; Custer and Merrill were estranged and their relationship was never repaired. In addition, the taint of corruption followed the major throughout his career. Congress later investigated Merrill when Southern legislators alleged corruption during his time fighting the Ku Klux Klan in South Carolina and the White League in Louisiana. Like the earlier charges in the Lauffer case, no direct evidence of wrongdoing could be proved. Merrill advanced through his career damaged by the whiff of scandal, but he remained unyielding in discharging his duty as he saw fit. Whether he was a scoundrel who was clever enough to escape the righteous hand of justice or an exemplary officer falsely maligned by opportunistic opponents remains an unsettled question. Whatever else could be said of Lewis Merrill, he was a pragmatic, skillful, experienced soldier who knew something of fighting a shadowy faction that would stop at nothing to get what it wanted.[26]

Merrill would need all of his skills to complete his assignment in a region torn asunder by the ravages of guerilla warfare. As the cradle of the Southern Confederacy and a state filled with unreconstructed Rebels, South Carolina proved to be a crucial battleground in the fight to reconstruct the Union. The Ku Klux Klan was but one of many groups resisting the federal government's efforts to restore law and order, but it was among the most powerful and unscrupulous of the armed factions that sprang up across the South. When Merrill and his men arrived in March 1871, they learned the whole story behind the strife and bloodshed in the Palmetto State.[27]

NOTES

1. Samuel Baird, *With Merrill's Cavalry: The Civil War Experiences of Samuel Baird, 2nd Missouri Cavalry, U.S.A.*, with Notes and an Introduction by Charles Annegan (San Marcos, CA: The Book Habit, 1981), 5; George W. Cullum, *Biographical Register of the Officers and Graduates of the U.S. Military Academy at West Point, N.Y. From its Establishment, in 1802, to 1890 with the Early History of the United States Military Academy* (Boston and New York: Houghton, Mifflin and Company, and Cambridge, MA: The Riverside Press, 1891), 624–25; Barry C. Johnson, *Custer, Reno, Merrill and the Lauffer Case: Some Warfare in "The Fighting Seventh"* (London: The Pilot Printing & Publicity Service on Behalf of the English Westerners' Society, 1971), 1–2; Clyde A. Milner II, "National Initiatives," in *The Oxford History of the American West*, Clyde A. Milner II, Carol A. O'Connor, and Martha A. Sandweiss, eds. (New York and Oxford: Oxford University Press, 1994), 171–79; United States Military Academy, *Twenty-Seventh Annual Reunion of the Association of Graduates of the United States Military Academy, at West Point, New York, June 11, 1896* (Saginaw, MI: Seemann & Peters, 1896), 136–37; Wyn Craig Wade, *The Fiery Cross: The Ku Klux Klan in America* (New York and Oxford: Oxford University Press, 1987), 94–95.

2. Cullum, *Biographical Register of the Officers and Graduates of the U.S. Military Academy at West Point, N.Y.*, 624; Johnson, *Custer, Reno, Merrill and the Lauffer Case*, 1; Perry G. McCandless, *A History of Missouri, Vol. III: 1820 to 1860* (Columbia: University of Missouri Press, 1972), 5–6; Christopher Phillips, "'The Crime Against Missouri': Slavery, Kansas, and the Cant of Southernness in the Border West," *Civil War History* 48 (March 2002): 61–64; Robert J. Rombauer, *The Union Cause in St. Louis in 1861: An Historical Sketch* (St. Louis: Nixon-Jones Printing Company, 1909), 297–300; Wade, *The Fiery Cross*, 94.

3. Cullum, *Biographical Register of the Officers and Graduates of the U.S. Military Academy at West Point, N.Y.*, 624; Michael Fellman, "Rehearsal for the Civil War: Antislavery and Proslavery at the Fighting Point in Kansas, 1854–1856," in *Anti-*

slavery Reconsidered: New Perspectives on the Abolitionists, Lewis Perry and Michael Fellman, eds. (Baton Rouge: Louisiana State University Press, 1979), 287–307; Charles Hart, "The Natural Limits of Slavery Expansion: Kansas-Nebraska Act, 1854," *Kansas Historical Quarterly* 8 (Summer 1985): 74–94; Tony R. Mullis, *Peacekeeping on the Plains: Army Operations in Bleeding Kansas* (Columbia: University of Missouri Press, 2004), 1–27, 246; James B. Potts, "North of 'Bleeding Kansas': The 1850s Political Crisis in Nebraska Territory," *Nebraska History* 73 (Fall 1992): 110–18; United States Military Academy, *Twenty-Seventh Annual Reunion of the Association of Graduates of the United States Military Academy*, 136–37; Dale Watts, "How Bloody was Bleeding Kansas? Political Killings in Kansas Territory, 1854–1861," *Kansas History* 18 (Summer 1995): 116–29; Paul E. Wilson, "How the Law Came to Kansas," *Kansas History* 15 (Spring 1992): 18–35.

4. Gerald Patterson, "'To Meet a Rebellion'—The Mormon Confrontation," *American History Illustrated* 7 (December 1972): 10–23; Richard D. Poll and Ralph W. Hansen, "'Buchanan's Blunder,' The Utah War, 1857–1858," *Military Affairs* 25 (Fall 1961): 121–31; Charles P. Roland, *Albert Sidney Johnston of Three Republics* (Austin: University of Texas Press, 1964), chapter 12; "The Utah Expedition: Its Causes and Consequences," *Atlantic Monthly* 3 (March 1859): 361–75, continued in April 1859: 474–91, and May 1859: 570–84; "Winfield Scott and the Utah Expedition," *Military Affairs* (Fall 1941): 208–11. For more on the Utah expedition in general, see also, Durwood Ball, *Army Regulars on the Western Frontier, 1848–1861* (Norman: University of Oklahoma Press, 2001); Hubert H. Bancroft, *History of Utah, 1540–1887* (San Francisco: History Company, 1890), chapters 18 and 19; Robert W. Coakley, *The Role of Federal Military Forces in Domestic Disorders, 1789–1878* (Washington, D.C.: CMH, 1988), chapter 10; Leroy R. Hafen and Ann W. Hafen, eds., *The Utah Expedition, 1857–58: A Documentary Account* (Glendale, CA: Clark, 1958; reprinted 1982); Harold D. Langley, *To Utah with the Dragoons and Glimpses of Life in Arizona and California, 1858–1859* (Salt Lake City: University of Utah, 1974); E. Cecil McGavin, *U.S. Soldiers Invade Utah* (Boston: Meador, 1937).

5. Quoted in Rombauer, *The Union Cause in St. Louis in 1861*, 297. See also, Champ Clark, *Decoying the Yanks: Jackson's Valley Campaign* (Alexandria, VA: Time-Life Books, 1984), 147–48; Doris Kearns Goodwin, *Team of Rivals: The Political Genius of Abraham Lincoln* (New York: Simon & Schuster, 2005), 388–96; James M. McPherson, *Battle Cry of Freedom* (New York: Oxford University Press, 1988), 155–60, 350–51; *Mrs. Hill's Journal: Civil War Reminiscences* (Chicago: R. R. Donnelly & Sons Co., 1980), 47; David Nevin, *The Road to Shiloh: Early Battles in the West* (Alexandria, VA: Time-Life Books, 1983), 29–33; William E. Parrish, "Fremont in Missouri," *Civil War Times Illustrated* 17 (April 1978), 4–8; Russell F. Weigley, *A Great Civil War* (Bloomington and Indianapolis: Indiana University Press, 2000), 87–88.

6. Quoted in Clark, *Decoying the Yanks*, 148. See also, Goodwin, *Team of Rivals*, 389–91; McPherson, *Battle Cry of Freedom*, 155–60; Nevin, *The Road to Shiloh*, 30, 32; Parrish, "Fremont in Missouri," 8–9.

7. Clark, *Decoying the Yanks*, 147–48; Goodwin, *Team of Rivals*, 392–96; McPherson, *Battle Cry of Freedom*, 155–60; Nevin, *The Road to Shiloh*, 32; Parrish, "Fremont in Missouri," 8–10.

8. Baird, *With Merrill's Cavalry*, 5; Cullum, *Biographical Register of the Officers and Graduates of the U.S. Military Academy at West Point, N.Y.*, 624; Johnson, *Custer, Reno, Merrill and the Lauffer Case*, 1; "A Merrill Memorial @ Merrill.family," www .merrill.org.org/genealogy/mm/mm_01_03.html, accessed December 21, 2005; United States Military Academy, *Twenty-Seventh Annual Reunion of the Association of Graduates of the United States Military Academy, at West Point*, 136.

9. Quoted in *Mrs. Hill's Journal*, 44. See also, Baird, *With Merrill's Cavalry*, 5; Cullum, *Biographical Register of the Officers and Graduates of the U.S. Military Academy at West Point, N.Y.*, 624; Johnson, *Custer, Reno, Merrill and the Lauffer Case*, 1; Nevin, *The Road to Shiloh*, 32–33; Parrish, "Fremont in Missouri," 43–45; Rombauer, *The Union Cause in St. Louis in 1861*, 298; United States Military Academy, *Twenty-Seventh Annual Reunion of the Association of Graduates of the United States Military Academy, at West Point*, 136.

10. United States War Department, *War of the Rebellion: A Compilation of the Official Records of the Union and Confederate Armies*, 128 volumes (Washington, D.C.: U.S. Government Printing Office, 1880–1901) [hereinafter abbreviated "OR"], I, Ser. 8, 437–39, 471, 537, 637–38, 639–40. See also, Baird, *With Merrill's Cavalry*, 7–8; Tom Cagley and Parke Pierson, "The Civil War in Arkansas," *America's Civil War* 18 (July 2005): 41; Cullum, *Biographical Register of the Officers and Graduates of the U.S. Military Academy at West Point, N.Y.*, 624; Johnson, *Custer, Reno, Merrill and the Lauffer Case*, 1; Alvin M. Josephy Jr., *War on the Frontier: The Trans-Mississippi West* (Alexandria, VA: Time-Life Books, 1986), 138–41.

11. OR Ser. I, 13, 611, 660, 681; OR Ser. II, 1, 479; OR, Ser. II, V, 99; *Biographical Register of the Officers and Graduates of the U.S. Military Academy at West Point, N.Y.*, 624.

12. Quoted in Baird, *With Merrill's Cavalry*, 20, 22. See also, Cagley and Pierson, "The Civil War in Arkansas," 44; Josephy, *War on the Frontier*, 152–53; Weigley, *A Great Civil War*, 301.

13. Baird, *With Merrill's Cavalry*, 26–46; Cagley and Pierson, "The Civil War in Arkansas," 44; Cullum, *Biographical Register of the Officers and Graduates of the U.S. Military Academy at West Point, N.Y.*, 624; Johnson, *Custer, Reno, Merrill and the Lauffer Case*, 1; Josephy, *War on the Frontier*, 152–53.

14. Quoted in Johnson, *Custer, Reno, Merrill and the Lauffer Case*, 1. See also, Cullum, *Biographical Register of the Officers and Graduates of the U.S. Military Academy at West Point, N.Y.*, 624; United States Military Academy, *Twenty-Seventh Annual Reunion of the Association of Graduates of the United States Military Academy, at West Point*, 136–37.

15. Cullum, *Biographical Register of the Officers and Graduates of the U.S. Military Academy at West Point, N.Y.*, 624; Merrill Military Files, M.103.C.B.1863 (Record Group 94, National Archives & Records Administration, hereinafter RG 94);

United States Military Academy, *Twenty-Seventh Annual Reunion of the Association of Graduates of the United States Military Academy, at West Point*, 136–37.

16. Johnson, *Custer, Reno, Merrill and the Lauffer Case*, 2–3; Merrill Military Files, RG 94.

17. Cullum, *Biographical Register of the Officers and Graduates of the U.S. Military Academy at West Point, N.Y.*, 624–25; Johnson, *Custer, Reno, Merrill and the Lauffer Case*, 3; Merrill Military Files, RG 94; United States Military Academy, *Twenty-Seventh Annual Reunion of the Association of Graduates of the United States Military Academy*, 136–37.

18. Johnson, *Custer, Reno, Merrill and the Lauffer Case*, 3–5; Merrill Military Files, RG 94.

19. Cullum, *Biographical Register of the Officers and Graduates of the U.S. Military Academy at West Point, N.Y.*, 624–25; Johnson, *Custer, Reno, Merrill and the Lauffer Case*, 7; Merrill Military Files, RG 94; United States Military Academy, *Twenty-Seventh Annual Reunion of the Association of Graduates of the United States Military Academy*, 136–37.

20. Johnson, *Custer, Reno, Merrill and the Lauffer Case*, 7–8; Merrill Military Files, RG 94.

21. Ibid.

22. Ibid.

23. Ibid.

24. Stephen E. Ambrose, *Crazy Horse and Custer: The Parallel Lives of Two American Warriors* (New York: Anchor Books, 1996), 338; Johnson, *Custer, Reno, Merrill and the Lauffer Case*, 9–10; Merrill Military Files, RG 94.

25. Johnson, *Custer, Reno, Merrill and the Lauffer Case*, 11; Merrill Military Files, RG 94.

26. Johnson, *Custer, Reno, Merrill and the Lauffer Case*, 11–13; "Major Merrill's Southern Foes," *The New York Times*, New York, NY (February 18, 1886); Merrill Military Files, RG 94; "Sick Man in the Army," *The New York Times*, New York, NY (May 12, 1886).

27. Cullum, *Biographical Register of the Officers and Graduates of the U.S. Military Academy at West Point, N.Y.*, 624–25; "Lewis Merrill Dead," *Yorkville Enquirer*, Yorkville, SC (March 4, 1896); "Major Merrill's Southern Foes"; Merrill Military Files, RG 94; "Sick Man in the Army"; United States Circuit Court [4th Circuit], *Proceedings in the Ku Klux Klan Trials at Columbia, S.C., in the United States Circuit Court, November Term, 1871* (Columbia, SC: Republican Printing Company, State Printers, 1872), 1464–87; Wade, *The Fiery Cross*, 94–95; Jerry L. West, *The Reconstruction Ku Klux Klan in York County, South Carolina, 1865–1877* (Jefferson, NC: McFarland & Company, Inc., 2002), 80–82; Lou Falkner Williams, *The Great South Carolina Ku Klux Klan Trials, 1871–1872* (Athens, GA: University of Georgia Press, 1996), 49; Richard Zuczek, *State of Rebellion: Reconstruction in South Carolina* (Columbia, SC: University of South Carolina Press, 1996), 94–95.

5

"THE DAGGER THAT WAS MADE ILLUSTRIOUS IN THE HANDS OF BRUTUS"

In late April 1865, South Carolina, like other conquered states of the defunct Southern Confederacy, found itself defeated on the battlefield, occupied by Union soldiers, at the mercy of a federal government still reeling from the murder of its chief executive. Prominent South Carolinian Benjamin Franklin Perry was among a handful of locals who took it upon themselves to restore a semblance of order to the state. It was no easy task, for Perry and his colleagues were forced to negotiate from a position of weakness. Fortunately, he rose to the occasion. As President Johnson's choice for provisional governor, this regal planter enjoyed a measure of legitimacy denied his brethren. He had been loyal to the Union before Fort Sumter. Although no friend of the black man, he had opposed secession because he thought—correctly, as it turned out—that war would hasten the demise of slavery. After guns were fired and blood was spilled, he supported his new nation with as much devotion and verve as he could muster.

After four long years of sacrifice and hardship, precisely as he had feared, the South lay prostrate, reeling from wartime losses and economic hardships unimagined in the antebellum era. Nothing if not a pragmatist, Perry recognized that to the victor belong the spoils; however, that brutal realization did not mean that his beloved state must remain subjugated indefinitely. Slaves had long known the virtues of feigned ignorance and a lack of diligence in fulfilling mandates issued from on high, and the provisional governor was determined to rely on similar strategies to resist federal occupation.

Perry and other white Southern opinion leaders unexpectedly found a kindred spirit in the new president, who made it clear that he did not intend to rule with an iron hand. Indeed, Johnson acquiesced when Perry issued a proclamation on July 20, 1865, declaring that all laws in effect at the time of secession were still in effect in South Carolina save measures, such as the prohibition against slavery, that were expressly overturned by Congress. Even in a majority of instances when Southern civilian authority conflicted with military edicts, the president refused to countermand the provisional governors.

Each former state of the Confederacy was required to hold a state constitutional convention to ratify a new series of laws and policies repudiating the Confederate States of America as a precondition for readmission into the Union, but the new policy of home rule allowed defiant Southerners wide latitude for complying with federal requirements. Observing the turmoil at the beginning of the South Carolina convention, (Brevet) Major General John Hatch mused that prewar political leaders "hope to obtain control of the state, and then pass laws with reference to the colored people which shall virtually reestablish slavery." With the president's acquiescence, the old guard stood an excellent chance of achieving its goals.[1]

Delegates to the South Carolina convention repealed the ordinance of secession, but they did not repudiate their actions. Their heads were bloody but defiantly unbowed. In refusing to proclaim secession "null and void," as originally required by the president, South Carolinians tacitly recognized the legitimacy of secession as a political act. To add insult to injury, the delegates nominated former Confederate General Wade Hampton to replace Perry as governor. A wealthy planter and proudly unreconstructed Rebel, Hampton refused the post, but his nomination sent a message to the federal government that South Carolina was unrepentant.

If President Johnson had insisted on obedience with the spirit of the laws as well as the letter, the subsequent history of the state—perhaps of the entire postwar South—might have been different. Alas, all of history is populated with might-have-beens. As it was, the president allowed the Southern states to undermine federal requirements and adopt black codes that would end slavery in name only. If planters were required to free their slaves, so be it; little could be done to reverse the tide of history. The South was required to obey edicts issued from Northern leaders, but that did not stop the white ruling class from imposing harsh conditions on freedmen to such an extent that conditions of near servitude existed.

The state constitutional convention commenced five months after Appomattox, on September 4, 1865, in the same Baptist church where secession had been proclaimed almost five years earlier. Many of the same men were on hand for both events. After repealing the secession ordinance and abolishing slavery, the delegates refused to repudiate the debt incurred in supporting the Confederate States of America. Instead, they focused attention on how political representation would work in a reconstructed state. Should freedmen be granted the franchise and, if so, should their votes count as much as the votes of white men? It was to be one of the contentious issues of Reconstruction, and one of the underlying reasons that the Ku Klux Klan spread to South Carolina in 1868.[2]

Early in the Reconstruction Era, the War Department's Bureau of Refugees, Freedmen and Abandoned Lands attempted to protect newly emancipated slaves, but it faced a daunting task in thoroughly racist South Carolina. Perpetually underfunded and thinly staffed, the bureau could not bring enough resources to bear for a long enough time to change the fundamental socioeconomic status of the black man in the Southern hierarchy. Wade Hampton, one of the more moderate voices among the South Carolina planter elite, labeled the Freedmen's Bureau "that incubus, that hydra-headed monster." In a letter he wrote to President Johnson, Hampton called the bureau "that most vicious institution" because it had been used "by the basest men, for the purpose of swindling the Negro, plundering the white man and defrauding the government."

Whites need not have worried about the long-term effectiveness of the bureau. Federal authorities provided so little support that it was bound to fail. Coupled with President Johnson's indifference toward emancipated slaves, the failure of the Freedmen's Bureau ensured that Southern blacks would be forced to look to their former masters for assistance if they hoped to survive.[3]

A new model of labor relations emerged in the South during 1865. In time, it would solidify and define race relations for a century. Armed with little education, possessing no skills or experience working outside of back-breaking agricultural work, and facing widespread racial discrimination, North and South, blacks had few available choices but to "negotiate" labor contracts with former slave owners. In many cases, these contracts specified that blacks agreed "to work in the same manner as always." Wages were minuscule, barely enough to buy food, clothing, and day-to-day necessities. Facing bleak prospects, freedmen put their wives and children to work in the fields to earn enough money to survive. Reflecting on the dire situation of working for the same planter who had kept him in bondage, a former slave mused, "Freedom wasn't no difference I knows of. I works for Marse John just the same."

After poor crops in 1866 and 1867 reduced the available cash on hand, even planters were forced to seek creative means of compensating former slaves for their work. The sharecropping system was thus born of necessity, but it persisted because it was an effective means of keeping blacks heavily mired in debt and tied to the land. A planter borrowed money from a bank using the land and crops as collateral. Blacks owned no land, so they had no collateral; all they owned was their labor. Therefore, the planter agreed to furnish a small shack, food and clothing, farm animals, and feed and seed to blacks in exchange for their labor. Some planters even established a company store so blacks could buy much-needed provisions on credit until the crop was harvested. This extension of credit acted as a lien on a tenant farmer's meager physical possessions, ensuring that he and his family would remain stationary until harvesting time. When the crop came in and the money was repaid to remove the lien, the tenant had nothing left. He would have to ask for more credit just to survive, thereby ensuring that he would remain on the land through another season.

If this system was exploitative to the laborer, it was little better for the planter. To maximize the return on investment so he could pay the bank note, purchase supplies for his laborers, and realize a profit, a planter was forced to grow high-yield crops, mostly cotton. As the years stretched on and a landowner grew more and more cotton, overproduction forced the price of cotton lower and, even worse, the soil was not replenished of precious nutrients. To make up the difference in each year's declining income, a planter had to grow ever more cotton so he could compensate in volume for what he lost in revenue. This, in turn, continued the same destructive cycle, leading to a depression of the Southern economy that extended well into the twentieth century. It also linked white planters to black laborers in a mutually enervating, embittering relationship of near-poverty and mutual desperation. The poor tenant farmer resented the landowner's miserly paternalism, and the landowner denigrated the black laborer as lazy and stupid, incapable of performing tasks beyond backbreaking manual labor.

Despite the near ubiquity of this stalemate, most white South Carolinians were not planters; they hailed from farming families accustomed to a hardscrabble life. Seething with resentment at battlefield losses, continued federal military occupation, and an inability to improve their station in life, they looked to a social structure that offered them a convenient scapegoat for their plight. Although few had owned slaves or counted themselves among the planter elite, poor whites had vested great faith in the culture of the Old South. They had come of age with a deeply held belief in the supremacy of the white man over the Negro. Even if a fellow fell victim to grinding poverty, at least he could boast that he was not at the bottom of the social stratum. Far below the poorest of the poor whites lay the man who could not escape the squalid conditions of his life, for the color of his skin betrayed him at every turn.[4]

To preserve the traditional social hierarchy, white South Carolinians resisted Reconstruction throughout the 1860s and 1870s. President Johnson may have been a friend to his fellow Southerners, but by 1866 and 1867, he was locked in a bitter duel with Radical Republicans in Congress over the course of federal policy and the continuation of his presidency. As the Radicals wrested control of Reconstruction policy from the president, Southern whites grew increasingly bitter. It was in this atmosphere that the Ku Klux Klan was born.[5]

The first documented appearance of the group in South Carolina occurred in 1868. By that time, the KKK had evolved from its sophomoric origins as a silly social club into something far more sinister and threatening. As with many milestones in the group's history, the circumstances attending the South Carolina Klan's birth are shrouded in mystery. Dr. Charles Clawson is said to have traveled to Tennessee, learned of the Klan's activities there, and introduced a chapter into York County. No evidence suggests a formal tie to the Pulaski Six, Nathan Bedford Forrest's group, or any other Tennessee organization; Clawson seems to have acted on his own impulse and searched for like-minded individuals seeking camaraderie and anxious to express discontent with federal Reconstruction policies.

Another version attributes the origins of the South Carolina group to R. J. Brunson, a Pulaski resident sent in July 1868 by General Gordon, principal author of the Klan Prescript, to organize new dens. Brunson later explained that he spent three months in Rock Hill and surrounding communities before returning home. Assuming that Brunson's tale is accurate, at least one grassroots effort preceded his work. Several groups using the name "Ku Klux Klan" began forming small enclaves in March 1868. In June, a month before Brunson claimed to have arrived in the state, ten residents of York County, probably acting under the auspices of an organization calling itself the Chester Conservative Clan, formed a KKK den. One of the ten organizers, Confederate veteran Iredell Jones, later served as Grand Scribe of his county KKK.[6]

However it came to the state, the Klan was hardly unique. Militant whites mulling over methods for resisting Reconstruction established numerous social clubs and paramilitary organizations to vent their frustration. Former provisional governor Perry was among the more prominent South Carolinians calling for fellow citizens to form Democratic clubs as an alternative to the Republican control of state government, but he was not alone. In early 1868, white militia groups could be seen marching and drilling in preparation for armed confrontation, although the groups stopped short of developing definite plans for violently overthrowing the Republican-controlled state government.

In addition to the timing, the character of the South Carolina Klan is difficult to pinpoint. It did not promote a fixed agenda or a stable, ongoing, clearly identifiable organizational structure. Some groups were social outlets, much as the original Pulaski Klan existed as a fraternal club for overgrown adolescents. Other dens took it upon themselves to patrol the streets and terrorize blacks. In Abbeville County near the Georgia border, stories of night riding and beatings administered against offending freedmen proliferated during the summer of 1868. Local law enforcement officers were reluctant to intervene until rumors of armed blacks assembling in the county pushed them to import guns for whites to carry as a show of force.

Resembling terrorist organizations of a later age, the militant Klan's decentralized nature was both a blessing and a curse for the group. Without a clear structure and organization, its effectiveness was limited; members could engage only in uncoordinated, sporadic, piecemeal campaigns against the enemy. At the same time, however, the shadowy, ill-defined, elusive nature of the secretive guerilla band protected members from reprisals. The authorities could not punish offenders if individuals could not be identified.

Some commentators have described the Klan as the "terrorist arm of the Democratic Party," far more structured and organized than it might have appeared initially. A Klan missive that fell into the hands of David T. Corbin, a Northern-bred United States attorney for South Carolina, outlined the group's mission in florid prose that masked the violent nature of the group. "We are on the side of justice, and constitutional liberty, as bequeathed to us in its purity by our forefathers," the statement read, "and we oppose and reject the principles of the Radical party."

Although it is true that Klansmen shared the general goals of the Democratic Party—primarily ensuring the continuation of white supremacy and undermining Republican-directed Reconstruction policy—it would be a mistake to assume that all Klansmen were politically active. Most rank-and-file Kluxers were not politically sophisticated. They were upset by the continued presence of carpetbaggers and federal troops on South Carolina soil, incensed by the rise of black politicians and political organizations during Reconstruction, and desirous of reasserting social and labor relations as they were before the war, but their understanding and awareness of specific federal policies were tenuous at best. Most whites who joined the Klan had never owned slaves, so the destruction of that institution was not as damaging to their economic status as it had been to the planter elite.

Without assurances that whites would once again control the mechanisms of government and enjoy a superior social status, however, freed blacks represented a threat to the Southern way of life. Opposition to the "Radical Party"—that is, the Republicans—was not so much a declaration of affiliation with the Democratic platform or political principles as it was a rejection of anyone or any entity that supported the freedmen.[7]

The South Carolina KKK received its first public notice around the time of the April 1868 elections. An anonymous advertisement published in the *Yorkville Enquirer* on April 2 employed the typically convoluted, euphemistic language of the Klan. At the top of the advertisement, the acronym "K.K.K." was followed by a warning that the "dismal hour draws nigh for the meeting of our mystic Circle." In that hour, the "Shrouded-Knight will come with pick and spade" to engage in "the ritual of the dead." Although some men might be frightened at such an hour when "the lightnings flash althwart the heavens" and "the thunders roll," the "Past Grand Knight of the Sepulcher will recoil not."

Enquirer publisher Lewis Grist felt compelled to explain to readers that "K.K.K." was an abbreviation for a "singularly secret and doubly mysterious and hideous organization known as the 'Ku-Klux-Klan,' which is rapidly spreading over the country." Despite the subsequent portrayal of Yorkville as a nest of Kluxers with nary a dissenting voice to be heard, Grist was the exception that proved the rule. He expressed regret that the secret society had spread to his community. "It has inspired no small degree of terror among certain classes in the West, and has become of sufficient importance to induce General Thomas, commanding the Tennessee Department, to send to Washington for more troops to suppress it." With the Klan's penchant for violence, Grist mused, "We believe no good can result from such organizations, and regret to hear of the K.K.K. in our midst."[8]

Notwithstanding the *Yorkville Enquirer's* reservations, governor-elect Robert K. Scott, a carpetbagger who would grapple with the Klan throughout his tenure in office, warily observed that several state newspapers wrote "approvingly" of the group. Within months of assuming office, the new governor received dozens of petitions and calls for assistance from terrified citizens, white and black, who had encountered the Klan. In some areas of the state, blacks were not satisfied to stand by idly and wait for government to come to their aid. They organized their own militia groups, some under the auspices of local organizations called Union Leagues, to train freedmen in military tactics should they need to defend themselves from assaults by armed nightriders. When whites learned that black militia groups were being formed, they responded in kind, leading to an escalating arms race that worried the governor. He would spend much of the next three years raising the alarm and seeking federal assistance as the Klan and black militia groups grew in strength and power across the Palmetto State.

A race war on the back roads of South Carolina seemed a genuine possibility in the late 1860s and early 1870s. From the perspective of whites, the 1868 elections had been calamitous. Governor Scott was a carpetbagger from Ohio. Most state legislators were Republicans as well as carpetbaggers, and some were even more odious, for they were black. Whites controlled the state senate, but blacks dominated the House of Representatives and therefore enjoyed a numerical superiority in the General Assembly. A new state constitution authorized some federal government interference into state affairs and required adherence to U.S. constitutional amendments outlawing slavery and extending due process and equal protection guarantees to all citizens. It was almost too much for a proud, defiant, angry white man to endure.

After a new state constitution was adopted in April 1868, South Carolina formally reentered the Union. In June, Congress abolished the Second and Third Military Districts and created the Department of the South to oversee Reconstruction policy in the states. In the meantime, the War Department handed over administrative and judicial functions to state governments. Normally, this transfer of power would have been welcomed, but with carpetbaggers and blacks ensconced in state offices, it served only to increase the anger felt by disaffected whites. In a letter to Governor Scott, former governor Milledge L. Bonham expressed the fear felt by many whites anxious to avoid bloodshed. "When a war of races shall be inaugurated," Bonham warned, "it requires no prophet to predict the result." Bonham and others urged Scott to declare martial law to ensure the existence of law and order, especially in the mountainous areas of northwestern South Carolina.[9]

Not anxious to call for federal troops, the governor contacted Colonel L. D. Childs, a friend and confidant of influential planter and former Confederate general Wade Hampton. Despite Hampton's denunciation of the Freedmen's Bureau and his decidedly anti-Northern views, the general could be counted on to champion law and order as well as social stability. Rumors later circulated that Hampton himself was a Klansman. Whether the stories were true or not, Governor Scott was shrewd in eliciting a well-respected South Carolinian to assist in keeping the peace. He knew as he spoke to Childs that the colonel would carry the gist of the conversation back to Hampton. Therefore, the governor provided great detail about threats of violence and the imminent intervention of armed federal soldiers unless something or someone soothed tensions, especially in the white community. Demonstrating a penchant for histrionics he would use repeatedly in later discussions with federal officials, Scott promised that if violence erupted between blacks and whites in South Carolina, the resulting melee "could be compared to nothing but the bloody revolution of Robespierre in France." In a subsequent face-to-face meeting with Hampton, the governor outlined the risks and reiterated the possibility of federal intervention. Given the rising hysteria and violence in the countryside, it was hardly an idle threat.

Hampton got the message. Although he was officially retired from politics—and would remain in the political wilderness until his successful gubernatorial campaign in 1876—he recognized that damage in a race war would harm the interests of all South Carolinians, not simply the freedmen. On October 23, newspapers across the state printed remarks Hampton had delivered to state Democrats asking that they make "earnest efforts in the cause of peace and the preservation of order." The general's simple plea for law and order saved the day, and Scott's savvy appeal to a leading citizen of the state paid handsome dividends. Although the Ku Klux Klan did not disappear from the landscape, it lapsed into ineffectual silence for almost eighteen months.[10]

By the time the 1870 elections rolled around, Northern carpetbaggers had controlled the machinery of state government for more than five years. Governor Scott had been charged with bribery, and the South Carolina General Assembly was widely regarded as riddled with corruption. In the words of one commentator, A. A. Taylor, the legislature "had become dominated by a group of tricksters who could do almost any questionable thing ostensibly in the interest of the public welfare." Although the number of federal troops on South Carolina soil was minimal, resentment over the continued Northern military presence festered nonetheless. Many white Southerners felt they had been ground under the boot heels of federal oppression long enough. Realizing that Ulysses S. Grant would win the presidency and the Republicans were temporarily on the ascendancy in 1868, disgruntled whites and the state Democratic Party had reluctantly acquiesced when they heard General Hampton's entreaties. In allowing violence to subside, however, whites did not forgive or forget the countless indignities, large and small, real and imagined, that they suffered. Their bitterness grew. Violence could not be averted indefinitely; if something did not change in 1870, whites were prepared to take matters into their own hands, even if that meant reviving the dormant KKK.[11]

Figure 5.1. Fearing that Governor Scott would request assistance from armed federal troops, former Confederate general (and future redeemer governor) Wade Hampton, shown here late in his life, urged an end to Klan violence in South Carolina during Reconstruction.
Picture History

A few episodes between the 1868 and 1870 elections hinted at the potential for violence. In 1869, the state legislature passed a new militia law and authorized the governor to purchase two thousand arms. While the militia was in training, the governor could raise a company of one hundred or more men and dispatch them to any area where violence threatened to shatter the calm. In the summer of 1869, Governor Scott exercised his new authority when he sent three hundred Winchester rifles to Edgefield in Abbeville County to put down an outbreak of violence. The largest number of incidents continued to occur in the northwestern part of the state, especially in York County.[12]

In October 1869, William Wright, a black York County resident, complained that he had been whipped by Klansmen and, to make matters worse, they burned down the house he was renting. The white man who owned the house also complained. Consequently, local constables organized a largely black militia company comprising seventy men armed with the state's Winchester rifles. They elected a white man, John R. Faris, to lead the company. The new militia company patrolled the streets searching for suspects to apprehend and bring to trial. Only one masked marauder, Abraham Sapoch (sometimes spelled "Sepaugh" or "Sapaugh"), could be identified, and even he could not be held in custody after he produced an acceptable alibi. Sapoch was not satisfied with his narrow escape from prosecution. He preferred charges against Wright for perjury and false arrest. In an ironic twist of logic, South Carolina style, Wright was eventually convicted and sent to prison. Finding no evidence of masked vigilantes roaming the countryside, the jury expressed outrage at the unwarranted presence of a Negro militia company, which amounted to little more than a "public nuisance." In fact, the jury went so far as to suggest that tales of the Ku Klux Klan were merely a convenient pretext for Republicans to suppress Democratic voting strength in South Carolina.[13]

The Wright case held an ominous lesson for Governor Scott and other carpetbaggers occupying positions in state government. Republicans might be nominally in power, but white citizens would not settle for the status quo. Turning their attention to the 1870 elections, conservative whites vowed to wrest control from carpetbaggers, scalawags, and freedmen, all of whom were seen as sources of widespread corruption. A "Citizen's Party"—later renamed the "Union Reform Party"—emerged as a mechanism for maverick Republicans to unite with disgruntled Democrats and build a winning coalition. Judge Richard Carpenter, a Republican, accepted the new party's nomination for governor, and he was joined by former Confederate General Matthew Calbraith Butler, a Democrat, as the candidate for lieutenant governor. The party pledged to replace "the present corrupt government with competent men of known integrity and honor" and to rise above "the absolute and sharp antagonism between the races."

As promising as such a new party and platform appeared to be, the Union Reform Party was a sham. Conservative whites had long opposed Republican control of state government; promises of rooting out corruption and reconciling whites and blacks was a trick designed to capitalize on general discontent with the party in power. Some freedmen were not fooled by the chicanery; others, perhaps more gullible or opportunistic for their own ends, supported the campaign. Jonas Byrd, described as "a respectable Negro from Charleston," took to the stump for the Union Reform Party on numerous occasions and "rendered much service" for the party in the black community. Other "substantial citizens of Charleston" from the black community assisted the party, including the well-known opinion leaders Aaron Harper, Stephney Riley, W. E. Marshall, Joseph Edmonton, and W. Sneed. Even Adam Jackson, labeled "one of the most influential colored preachers of St. James Santee Parish," labored to reform politics-as-usual in South Carolina.[14]

Worried that the Union Reform Party would dilute its voting strength, Republicans fought to retain black support in the coming elections. Robert Brown Elliott, a black Republican reputed to be unwaveringly honest after he had resigned from state government because he was incensed over rampant corruption, warned that reformers were not to be trusted. Observing that the coalition of white Southerners and blacks anxious for reform would not last, he argued, "Today we are welcomed by those who have always declared that we are not fit to occupy a position entrusted to us." This curious pact could only lead to trouble for freedmen. "It behooves us to be careful of these men," Brown advised.

James L. Orr, a former governor, cautioned that reform, if it were to come at all, must emanate from the Republican ranks. Whites would be well advised to join with the dominant party rather than to continually oppose change. "Suppose one hundred of the most intelligent white citizens of each county had gone, in good faith, and with frank sincerity, into the Republican organization," he reflected. "Can it be doubted that their intelligence and moral strength would have secured honest nominees?"[15]

Despite opposition from the Democrats as well as the Union Reform Party, Republicans retained control of state government in 1870. Charges of fraud and intimidation were rife, but all sides seemed culpable. Tales circulated that on election day militias marched in the streets, polling places were moved to new locations at the last minute, and ballot boxes were tampered with to add or subtract votes, as needed. In the end, Governor Scott was reelected with 85,071 votes in his favor and 51,537 cast for his opponent.

Despite the solid majority supporting him, the governor recognized that a large group of white South Carolinians was disturbed by the results. Many white "reformers" had been so convinced of success that the election loss struck them as incontrovertible evidence of corruption and shady dealings. The Charleston *Daily News* declared that "the solid black vote cast against the nominees of the Reform Party" was viewed by would-be reformers as "a declaration of war by the negro race against the white race, by ignorance against intelligence, by poverty against actual or potential wealth." Coupled with stories about black militias forming in enclaves throughout the state and repeated tales of Republican corruption, discontented whites simply had reached the limits of their tolerance. In this contentious political arena filled with emotionally charged rhetoric, the revival of groups such as the Ku Klux Klan became almost inevitable. A Klan circular distributed late in 1870 summarized whites' bitterness: "Defeated on the battle-field, defrauded at the ballot box, we have but one remedy—The dagger that was made illustrious in the hands of Brutus."[16]

The aftermath of the 1868 elections had been an uncertain time in South Carolina, but the inevitability of the Republican presidential victory and the calming words of Wade Hampton and other white conservative leaders had eased tensions. The situation two years later was far more volatile. Many whites had exhausted their patience. No longer could they turn a blind eye to the abuses perpetrated by Republicans in power. No longer could they tolerate blacks banding together in militia units and issuing veiled and sometimes no-so-veiled threats against the white community. No longer could they tolerate the presence of federal troops in their beloved state. Something had to be done. If the formal mechanisms of government were unavailable, a large minority of white citizens did not object to relying on informal means of redress.

Despite his victory in the election, Governor Scott was vilified at every quarter. One black representative expressed the frustration that many freedmen felt when he declared that Scott was "criminally guilty, and should be dealt with accordingly." Whites saw him as a carpetbagger in league with Republicans and federal forces anxious to subjugate the state. Despite repeated pleas to President Grant, Attorney General Akerman, and other federal officials to intervene, the beleaguered Scott found little to encourage him that help was on the way.

Figure 5.2. Alarmed by escalating violence in the upcountry, South Carolina's Reconstruction governor, Robert K. Scott, asked for federal assistance in controlling Klan activities.
The Ohio Historical Society

The first wave of violence erupted shortly after the results of the 1870 elections were announced. In Laurensville, a white man and the local constable engaged in fisticuffs. A group of black militiamen that had assembled to aid the constable grew frightened when shots were fired. They ran into the local armory, which was then surrounded by a mob of white men firing into the building. As the shooting intensified, several men broke through the back window and fled. By the time the melee ended, two black men had been killed inside the armory and another man was shot dead as he ran out the back. Altogether, at least nine Republicans were killed in rioting.

When they learned of the episode, two Negro militia companies assembled, armed and ready for battle, awaiting orders from the governor to spring into action. Recognizing that the presence of black militiamen only heightened tensions, Governor Scott wisely gave no such order. In fact, he did exactly the opposite. He ordered all militia units to travel to Columbia and surrender their arms. He also declared martial law in Laurens, Newberry, Spartanburg, and Union Counties.[17]

Frightened whites were convinced that black militia companies planned future military action against their homes and communities. As if to prove that such fears were well founded, blacks in and around York County responded to perceived threats in a confrontational manner that only exacerbated the hostility. Recognizing that white law enforcement officers would not protect them—indeed, those same officers probably were responsible for the outrages—Negro militia companies assumed a high-profile presence in black communities. It was every former slave owner's worst nightmare come to life: armed black men marching lockstep through the countryside with loaded rifles resting on their shoulders. Exhibiting their firepower and occasionally discharging rifles into the air, the militiamen reassured the black community that the freedmen would not succumb to violence without putting up a fight.

Other blacks responded with less fanfare, but in an equally unsettling manner. Shortly after the Laurensville riot, an unknown person or persons set fire to white property owners' homes and businesses. Mysterious fires became commonplace in nine upstate counties during that fall and winter. Lawson Brown's meat house burned to the ground. Dennis Crosby's gin house was destroyed along with 600 pounds of cotton and 1,400 bushels of cotton seed. Hugh Warren, S. N. Miller, and Mrs. Jane Thomasson, among others, were targets of arsonists. Two could play at the terrorism game; the Klan was not the only group to avail itself of darkness.[18]

Whites responded in a predictable fashion; they, too, sought comfort and safety through organized resistance. In November 1870, a group of men met in Columbia and formed the Council of Safety. The group's self-professed goal was to defend the property and lives of white people from any blacks who might seek to inflict harm. Membership was extended to "approved white men" eighteen years old and above who swore an oath of loyalty and secrecy. To ensure secrecy would exist, members were designated by letters of the alphabet instead of using names.

Within a few months, Councils of Safety had grown up in several areas of the state. A pamphlet circulated explaining that the "objects of this organization are, first, to promote the peace, enforce the laws and protect and defend the persons and property of the good people of the state; and, second, to labor for the restoration of constitutional liberty, as taught by our forefathers, and to reform abuses in the government, state and national." In another section, the pamphlet promised that its "operations shall be two-fold: 1. Political, social and moral, under the forms of established law. 2. Physical, according to the recognized principles of the law of self-defense."[19]

For all of its audacious threats and muscular, intimidating prose, the Council of Safety failed to capture a large membership. Many whites shared its goals of self-defense and propagation of white values, but the organization existed for only a few months. The historical record is murky on this point, but it is possible that local Councils of Safety reinvigorated the Klan. Dormant after the 1868 elections and General Wade Hampton's appeals to preserve the peace, the KKK had been absent from the South Carolina political scene for almost two years. Its leaders patiently bided their time, searching for an opportunity for the Klan to reemerge from the shadows, hailed as a savior of the white race.

At last, the time was ripe. When the Council of Safety did not galvanize white opposition against black militias and the ignominy of Republican rule, old ideas, rejected two years earlier as dangerous to the peace, suddenly seemed palatable. The disappointing results of the 1870 elections reinforced the discontent felt by many whites. The Southern economy remained dismal, with few prospects for improvement. Fears about armed confrontations with black militia companies shot through almost every white community in the state. These deteriorating conditions emboldened Klan leaders, who once again unfurled their banners and hatched their schemes. All they needed to don their robes was a precipitating event, a spark to set the kindling of resentment ablaze. A series of mysterious fires sweeping through the South Carolina Upcountry provided exactly the kind of incendiary spark needed to ignite a conflagration.

Learning that a group of freedmen had threatened to burn the town of Yorkville, on January 22 the Klan circulated a notice promising to kill ten black men and two whites if more fires were set. And so a new round of depredations began. Someone shot up county treasurer Edward Rose's house, but he was not home at the time. Tim Black, a Rock Hill resident, was not as lucky. He was shot eighteen times and his throat was slit with a knife. On February 25, the Klan attacked Anderson Brown, a freedman suspected of arson. Dragged from his house, Brown was shot repeatedly, including once in the head. The murder of Jim Williams in March may have been revenge for the spate of fires as well. KKK killings occurred in other parts of the state, too. In February, a black county commissioner, Henry Nash, was murdered. Two freedmen were lynched in Williamsburg, and a house full of blacks was attacked in Chester around the same time. The victims shared a common bond: They harbored Republican sentiments.

Despite stories circulated by Democrats contending that stories of such nighttime atrocities were the creation of fanciful imaginations, Captain Felix Torbell of the Eighteenth U.S. Infantry confirmed that at least two murders occurred during this period. In Torbell's opinion, the Ku Klux Klan was responsible. The group's goal was to "break the spirit of local loyalty, so that control of the state may be first secured."[20]

The South Carolina Klan at this time truly was the "invisible empire." Dens sprang up in South Carolina and North Carolina, but their origins and operations were unclear. Some evidence suggests that Spartanburg resident J. Banks Lyle, a Confederate veteran and state legislator, may have been the leader of the upcountry KKK, but even this conclusion is not certain. Many accounts suggest that Major James W. Avery served as head of the York County Klan. Familiar with military hierarchy and command structures from their service in the Confederate States Army, Lyle and Avery occasionally participated in nighttime raids, but generally they issued orders and served as strategists in lieu of assuming field command. Whenever possible, they preferred to work with other former Confederate officers who knew how to obey orders and guard secrets.

The socioeconomic makeup of Klan members seems to have varied throughout the state. According to the Reverend R. A. Holland of Warm Springs, North Carolina, despite later depictions of Klansmen as uncouth country bumpkins, "members of the K.K.K. were gentlemen of fine education, struggling manfully to retain and sustain their manhood, and to give their children as a heritage of the war a higher civilization than perhaps they themselves had enjoyed." Other sources suggest that the group was "composed of low-type men, and did not enjoy among respectable contemporaries the esteem with which later generations have invested it." Commentators Francis Simkins and R. H. Woody dismiss rank-and-file Kluxers with a simple observation: "The fact that [the Klan] flourished most extensively in the hill counties of the state, where the uncultured whites were predominant, is an indication of the type of membership."[21]

Many—perhaps most—adult white males in the South Carolina Up-country participated in Klan activities or at least sympathized with the group. The numbers remain difficult to pinpoint with precision. Researcher Allen Trelease concludes that between 1,800 and 2,300 men eventually took part in York County Klan activities, but another researcher, Jerry L. West, argues that these figures are inflated. Whatever the actual numbers, by March 1871, it was clear that the problem was growing and something had to be done. Governor Scott had complained to the Grant administration many times; his repeated requests were easy to dismiss as histrionics. One contemporaneous observer noted, "I think that the general disposition at that time in the North was to assign the K.K.K. to the category of horse play."[22]

Uncertain that federal authorities would lend a hand, on March 13, 1871, the governor met with seventeen of South Carolina's "best citizens" to develop a plan for curbing violence and bloodshed. For his part, Scott pledged to refrain from imposing martial law, promised to disband militia companies in the upstate area, and agreed to replace several local officials deemed anathema to white community leaders. In exchange for these actions, the citizens said they would use their "utmost influence" to ensure that peace prevailed. Because some of the citizens with whom he crafted the agreement probably were in league with the Klan, the governor's deal seemed to be little more than a craven attempt to bargain with terrorists by giving in to their demands. With few resources at hand and no guarantees that assistance would be forthcoming, however, Scott faced bleak prospects in mid-March 1871. He had few realistic options but to capitulate.[23]

The same day that Scott met with the leading citizens of the state, former provisional governor Benjamin Franklin Perry sent his successor a public letter outlining "two things which you can do, and should do, the sooner the better." Perry suggested that Scott completely disarm the black militia, thereby completing the steps he had taken after the Laurensville riot, and "appoint good and intelligent men to office." The phrase "intelligent men," he did not have to say, referred to white men. In Perry's view, the "colored people of South Carolina behaved well during the war and would have continued to do so but for the unprincipled carpet-bagger, who came among them and stirred up hatred to the whole white race by the most artful and devilish appeals to their fears and bad passions."

The comment about unprincipled carpetbaggers must have been especially galling to Governor Scott, who was often criticized by whites because he was a former official of the Freedmen's Bureau as well as an Ohio native. Nonetheless, coupled with the advice he received during his meeting with the leading citizens, Scott felt he had no choice. He ordered the

Figure 5.3.　The KKK moved into South Carolina in 1868—the same year the group rose to prominence throughout the South—but the Klan reached its greatest prominence in the state in 1870–1871. This drawing from the December 19, 1868, edition of *Harper's Weekly* shows soldiers posing in Klan garb seized in Huntsville, Alabama.
Picture History

black militias to disarm. Unfortunately, this action engendered the opposite reaction from what Scott intended. Instead of appeasing whites, disbanding the black militias and caving in to white demands were seen as a sign of weakness. Far from assuaging white concerns, the disarmament order encouraged Klansmen and others to terrorize blacks and Republicans with newfound vigor. If state leaders could be brought to heel with threats of violence, imagine what power could be exercised through actual violence.[24]

As the governor tried to eke out a truce with the hostile white population, he received assistance at last, belated though it was. Finally recognizing the volatile atmosphere in South Carolina above all other states suffering from Klan abuses, the Grant administration intervened. Late in March, General William T. Sherman reorganized several army regiments serving on the Great Plains. Having corresponded with Governor Scott on numerous occasions, Sherman's subordinate, General Alfred Terry, was convinced that the KKK represented a genuine threat to the Carolina countryside. Once he had sufficient troops at his disposal, General Terry dispatched Companies B, E, and K of the Seventh U.S. Cavalry to the South Carolina upcountry to provide relief.

In the beginning, their mission was limited. The plan was for the troops to assist local law enforcement officials in keeping the peace. Despite congressional inquiries, reports from other federal troops, and increasing evidence that the Klan was as dangerous as the stories suggested, federal officials were not yet convinced that the problem was as pervasive as Scott suggested. General Terry suspected that the Seventh Cavalry would encounter a depth of lawlessness previously unknown, but he needed proof. If the Grant administration was expected to take drastic steps such as increasing the presence of the U.S. Army, invoking authority under various federal statutes, and perhaps even curtailing the writ of habeas corpus, federal leaders needed cold, hard facts at hand. Prosecuting the Klan would not be possible until someone exposed the Invisible Empire to the light of day. Major Lewis Merrill was to be the point man in the investigation.[25]

As three companies of the Seventh U.S. Cavalry made their way to South Carolina, President Grant elevated the importance of federal efforts to curb Klan violence in a statement he issued on March 23, 1871. Denouncing "combinations of armed men, unauthorized by law," the president urged Congress to enact legislation allowing the federal government to punish Klansmen who engaged in violence. He issued a second statement on May 3, promising to use all the powers provided by the recent Ku Klux Klan Force Bill to ensure compliance with the law; however, he stopped short of ordering martial law or suspending habeas corpus. Those drastic

steps might become necessary in the future, he intimated, but until he had
more facts at his command, he would not act further. Soldiers of the Seventh Cavalry would have to penetrate the secret world of the Klan and document their nefarious activities before the Grant administration would
bring the full might of the federal government to bear against the Invisible
Empire.[26]

NOTES

1. Eric Foner, *Reconstruction: America's Unfinished Revolution, 1863–1877* (New
York: Francis Parkman Prize Edition, History Book Club, 2005; originally published by HarperCollins, 1988), 187–88, 192, 293–94; Robert Selph Henry, *The
Story of Reconstruction* (New York: Konecky & Konecky, 1999), 53–54; Francis B.
Simkins, "The Ku Klux Klan in South Carolina," *Journal of Negro History* 12 (Oc-
tober 1927): 608–11; Alrutheus Ambush Taylor, *The Negro in South Carolina Dur-
ing Reconstruction* (Washington, D.C.: The Association for the Study of Negro Life
and History, Inc., 1924), 186–87; Allen W. Trelease, *White Terror: The Ku Klux Klan
Conspiracy and Southern Reconstruction* (Baton Rouge: Louisiana State University
Press, 1971), 70; Wyn Craig Wade, *The Fiery Cross: The Ku Klux Klan in America*
(New York and Oxford: Oxford University Press, 1987), 21, 26; Jay Winik, *April
1865: The Month That Saved America* (New York: HarperCollins, 2001), 380–83;
Richard Zuczek, *State of Rebellion: Reconstruction in South Carolina* (Columbia, SC:
University of South Carolina Press, 1996), 12–14.

2. Foner, *Reconstruction: America's Unfinished Revolution*, 199–201; Henry, *The
Story of Reconstruction*, 87–89; Richard W. Murphy, *The Nation Reunited: War's Aftermath* (Alexandria, VA: Time-Life Books, 1987), 33–34; Zuczek, *State of Rebellion*,
10–16.

3. Michael Les Benedict, "Preserving the Constitution: The Conservative Basis
of Radical Reconstruction," *The Journal of American History* 61 (June 1974): 78;
Foner, *Reconstruction: America's Unfinished Revolution*, 168–69; Henry, *The Story of
Reconstruction*, 118–19, 470; John Porter Hollis, *The Early Period of Reconstruction in
South Carolina* (Baltimore, MD: The Johns Hopkins Press, 1905), 107–29; Thomas
Holt, *Black Over White: Negro Political Leadership in South Carolina During Reconstruc-
tion* (Urbana: University of Illinois Press, 1977), 28–29; Edward G. Longacre, *Gen-
tleman and Soldier: The Extraordinary Life of General Wade Hampton* (Nashville, TN:
Rutledge Hill Press, 2003), 255; Murphy, *The Nation Reunited*, 36–39; Zuczek,
State of Rebellion, 17.

4. Foner, *Reconstruction: America's Unfinished Revolution*, 106–08, 404–11; Lacy
K. Ford, "Rednecks and Merchants: Economic Development and Social Tensions
in the South Carolina Upcountry, 1865–1900," *Journal of American History* 71 (September 1984): 294–318; George M. Frederickson, "Masters and Mudsills: The
Role of Race in the Planter Ideology of South Carolina," *South Atlantic Urban*

Studies 2 (1978): 34–48; Asa H. Gordon, *Sketches of Negro Life and History in South Carolina*, 2d. ed. (Columbia: University of South Carolina Press, 1929), 158–61; Henry, *The Story of Reconstruction*, 363–65; Murphy, *The Nation Reunited*, 42–44, 123–24; Julie Saville, *The Work of Reconstruction: From Slave to Wage Laborer in South Carolina, 1860–1870* (Cambridge, UK: Cambridge University Press, 1994), 138–39. An alternate view—that "the central problem of Reconstruction in the South was not race or labor, but a lack of capital"—can be found in Heather Cox Richardson, "A Marshall Plan for the South? The Failure of Republican and Democratic Ideology during Reconstruction," *Civil War History* 51 (December 2005): 378–87.

5. David Herbert Donald, *The Politics of Reconstruction, 1863–1867* (Baton Rouge: Louisiana State University Press, 1965), 3–17; Holt, *Black Over White*, 28–35; Herbert Shapiro, "The Ku Klux Klan During Reconstruction: The South Carolina Episode," *Journal of Negro History* 49 (January 1964): 34–55; Simkins, "The Ku Klux Klan in South Carolina," 608–11; J. C. A. Stagg, "The Problem of Klan Violence: The South Carolina Up-Country, 1868–1871," *Journal of American Studies* 8 (December 1974): 303–18; Trelease, *White Terror*, 72; Zuczek, *State of Rebellion*, 55–61.

6. Douglas Summers Brown, *A City Without Cobwebs: A History of Rock Hill, South Carolina* (Columbia: University of South Carolina Press), 142; Kermit L. Hall, "Political Power and Constitutional Legitimacy: The South Carolina Ku Klux Klan Trials, 1871–1872," *Emory Law Journal* 33 (Fall 1984): 925–26; Stanley F. Horn, *Invisible Empire: The Story of the Ku Klux Klan, 1866–1871* (Montclair, NJ: Patterson Smith, 1969), 216–17; Francis B. Simkins and R. H. Woody, *South Carolina During Reconstruction* (Chapel Hill: The University of North Carolina Press, 1932), 457–59; Taylor, *The Negro in South Carolina During Reconstruction*, 188–89; Trelease, *White Terror*, 72; Wade, *The Fiery Cross*, 62–63; Jerry L. West, *The Reconstruction Ku Klux Klan in York County, South Carolina, 1865–1877* (Jefferson, NC: McFarland & Company, Inc., 2002), 38–40; Zuczek, *State of Rebellion*, 55–63.

7. Brown, *A City Without Cobwebs*, 143; David Everitt, "1871 War on Terror," *American History* 38 (June 2003): 27; Foner, *Reconstruction: America's Unfinished Revolution*, 342–43; John Hope Franklin, *Reconstruction After the Civil War*, 2d. ed. (Chicago: The University of Chicago Press, 1961), 153–62; Frederickson, "Masters and Mudsills," 43–44; Robert J. Kaczorowski, "Federal Enforcement of Civil Rights During the First Reconstruction," *Fordham Urban Law Journal* 23 (Fall 1995): 156–57; "Notes," *Harper's Weekly* (March 25, 1871): 259; Elaine Frantz Parsons, "Midnight Ramblers: Costume and Performance in the Reconstruction-Era Ku Klux Klan," *The Journal of American History* 92 (December 2005): 815–16, 830–36; Louis F. Post, "A Carpetbagger in South Carolina," *Journal of Negro History* 10 (January 1925): 40; Simkins, "The Ku Klux Klan in South Carolina," 608; Trelease, *White Terror*, 72–73; West, *The Reconstruction Ku Klux Klan in York County, South Carolina*, 34–44; R. H. Woody, "The South Carolina Election of 1870," *The North Carolina Historical Review* 8 (April 1931): 178; Zuczek, *State of Rebellion*, 55–63.

8. Foner, *Reconstruction: America's Unfinished Revolution,* 342–43; "K.K.K.," *Yorkville Enquirer,* Yorkville, SC (April 2, 1868); Trelease, *White Terror,* 72–73; Wade, *The Fiery Cross,* 94–104; West, *The Reconstruction Ku Klux Klan in York County, South Carolina,* 34–37; Joel Williamson, *After Slavery: The Negro in South Carolina During Reconstruction, 1861–1877* (Chapel Hill: The University of North Carolina Press, 1965), 260–61; Zuczek, *State of Rebellion,* 61, 90, 94.

9. James S. Allen, *Reconstruction: The Battle for Democracy, 1865–1876* (New York: International Publishers, 1937), 98–102; Henry, *The Story of Reconstruction,* 313–15; Holt, *Black Over White,* 29–35, 102–03; Shapiro, "The Ku Klux Klan During Reconstruction: The South Carolina Episode," 44; Otis A. Singletary, "The Negro Militia During Radical Reconstruction," *Military Affairs* 19 (Winter 1955): 177–86; Stagg, "The Problem of Klan Violence: The South Carolina Up-Country, 1868–1871," 316–17; Trelease, *White Terror,* 116, 350, 361, 368; Williamson, *After Slavery,* 260–61; Woody, "The South Carolina Election of 1870," 177; Zuczek, *State of Rebellion,* 50, 54, 57, 59.

10. Richard Nelson Current, *Those Terrible Carpetbaggers* (New York: Oxford University Press, 1988), 148; "Governor Scott's Proclamation," *Yorkville Enquirer,* Yorkville, SC (October 29, 1868); Longacre, *Gentleman and Soldier,* 254–57; Trelease, *White Terror,* 349–50; West, *The Reconstruction Ku Klux Klan in York County, South Carolina,* 47; Zuczek, *State of Rebellion,* 59–61.

11. Current, *Those Terrible Carpetbaggers,* 222–27; David Everitt, "1871 War on Terror," 27–28, 31; Shapiro, "The Ku Klux Klan During Reconstruction: The South Carolina Episode," 55; Simkins, "The Ku Klux Klan in South Carolina," 610–11; Simkins and Woody, *South Carolina During Reconstruction,* 457–64; Taylor, *The Negro in South Carolina During Reconstruction,* 191–98; Trelease, *White Terror,* 350–61; West, *The Reconstruction Ku Klux Klan in York County, South Carolina,* 47, 62–63, 64–76; Woody, "The South Carolina Election of 1870," 179–82; Zuczek, *State of Rebellion,* 61–63.

12. Holt, *Black Over White,* 29–31; Singletary, "The Negro Militia During Radical Reconstruction," 177–82; Taylor, *The Negro in South Carolina During Reconstruction,* 190–93; Trelease, *White Terror,* 349; Lou Falkner Williams, *The Great South Carolina Ku Klux Klan Trials, 1871–1872* (Athens: University of Georgia Press, 1996), 22–23; Zuczek, *State of Rebellion,* 71–75.

13. "King's Mountain Township," *Yorkville Enquirer,* Yorkville, SC (February 3, 1870); "Ku Klux Klan Trial," *Yorkville Enquirer,* Yorkville, SC (May 5, 1870); Trelease, *White Terror,* 349–50; West, *The Reconstruction Ku Klux Klan in York County, South Carolina,* 134–36; Williams, *The Great South Carolina Ku Klux Klan Trials,* 107–9.

14. Current, *Those Terrible Carpetbaggers,* 222–27; Foner, *Reconstruction: America's Unfinished Revolution,* 414–15; Henry, *The Story of Reconstruction,* 415–16; Simkins and Woody, *South Carolina During Reconstruction,* 448–53; Taylor, *The Negro in South Carolina During Reconstruction,* 195–97; Trelease, *White Terror,* 350–51; Woody, "The South Carolina Election of 1870," 174–79; Zuczek, *State of Rebellion,* 76–83.

15. Quoted in Taylor, *The Negro in South Carolina During Reconstruction*, 196–97. See also, Current, *Those Terrible Carpetbaggers*, 225–27; Simkins, "The Ku Klux Klan in South Carolina," 610–11; Simkins and Woody, *South Carolina During Reconstruction*, 457–64; Trelease, *White Terror*, 351; Woody, "The South Carolina Election of 1870," 174–79; Zuczek, *State of Rebellion*, 76–83.

16. Allen, *Reconstruction: The Battle for Democracy, 1865–1876*, 101–02; Henry, *The Story of Reconstruction*, 415–17; Taylor, *The Negro in South Carolina During Reconstruction*, 197–200; Trelease, *White Terror*, 351–52; Williams, *The Great South Carolina Ku Klux Klan Trials*, 25–29; Woody, "The South Carolina Election of 1870," 174–79; Zuczek, *State of Rebellion*, 80–83.

17. Allen, *Reconstruction: The Battle for Democracy, 1865–1876*, 99; Brown, *A City Without Cobwebs*, 143; Everitt, "1871 War on Terror," 27–28; Foner, *Reconstruction: America's Unfinished Revolution*, 427–28; Hall, "Political Power and Constitutional Legitimacy," 927–28; Henry, *The Story of Reconstruction*, 416; Horn, *Invisible Empire*, 228–30; James E. Sefton, *The United States Army and Reconstruction, 1865–1877* (Westport, CT: Greenwood Press, 1967), 222–26; Shapiro, "The Ku Klux Klan During Reconstruction: The South Carolina Episode," 44–46; Simkins and Woody, *South Carolina During Reconstruction*, 457–63; Singletary, "The Negro Militia During Radical Reconstruction," 186; Trelease, *White Terror*, 349–53; Williamson, *After Slavery*, 261–65; Woody, "The South Carolina Election of 1870," 179–80; Zuczek, *State of Rebellion*, 88–93.

18. Foner, *Reconstruction: America's Unfinished Revolution*, 427–28; Hall, "Political Power and Constitutional Legitimacy," 925–26; Henry, *The Story of Reconstruction*, 416; Simkins and Woody, *South Carolina During Reconstruction*, 457–61; Singletary, "The Negro Militia During Radical Reconstruction," 177–80; Zuczek, *State of Rebellion*, 88–93.

19. Hall, "Political Power and Constitutional Legitimacy," 926–28; Horn, *Invisible Empire*, 230–31; Simkins and Woody, *South Carolina During Reconstruction*, 458; Singletary, "The Negro Militia During Radical Reconstruction," 182; Trelease, *White Terror*, 352; Williams, *The Great South Carolina Ku Klux Klan Trials*, 23–25; Zuczek, *State of Rebellion*, 89.

20. Brown, *A City Without Cobwebs*, 143–46; Current, *Those Terrible Carpetbaggers*, 227–28; Foner, *Reconstruction: America's Unfinished Revolution*, 430–32; Gordon, *Sketches of Negro Life and History in South Carolina*, 78–79; Henry, *The Story of Reconstruction*, 415–16; Simkins and Woody, *South Carolina During Reconstruction*, 458–59; Williamson, *After Slavery*, 264–66.

21. Holland quoted in West, *The Reconstruction Ku Klux Klan in York County, South Carolina*, 40–41. See also, Franklin, *Reconstruction After the Civil War*, 153–55; Parsons, "Midnight Ramblers," 815–16; Simkins and Woody, *South Carolina During Reconstruction*, 460; Trelease, *White Terror*, 352–53; Williamson, *After Slavery*, 263–65.

22. Quoted in Post, "A Carpetbagger in South Carolina," 40. See also, Current, *Those Terrible Carpetbaggers*, 227–30; Shapiro, "The Ku Klux Klan During Recon-

struction: The South Carolina Episode," 44–46; Stagg, "The Problem of Klan Violence: The South Carolina Up-Country, 1868–1871," 317; Taylor, *The Negro in South Carolina During Reconstruction*, 193–201; Trelease, *White Terror*, 352–53, 369–70; West, *The Reconstruction Ku Klux Klan in York County, South Carolina*, 80–81.

23. Everitt, "1871 War on Terror," 28; Horn, *Invisible Empire*, 231–32; Shapiro, "The Ku Klux Klan During Reconstruction: The South Carolina Episode," 44–45; Williamson, *After Slavery*, 265; Richard Zuczek, "The Federal Government's Attack on the Ku Klux Klan: A Reassessment," *South Carolina Historical Magazine* 97 (January 1, 1996): 50, 52.

24. Quoted in Current, *Those Terrible Carpetbaggers*, 229. See also, Everitt, "1871 War on Terror," 28; Horn, *Invisible Empire*, 231–32; Shapiro, "The Ku Klux Klan During Reconstruction: The South Carolina Episode," 44–45; Simkins, "The Ku Klux Klan in South Carolina," 608–23; Stagg, "The Problem of Klan Violence: The South Carolina Up-Country, 1868–1871," 316–17; Zuczek, *State of Rebellion*, 93, 106, 148.

25. Brown, *A City Without Cobwebs*, 146–52; Everitt, "1871 War on Terror," 27–28; Hall, "Political Power and Constitutional Legitimacy," 925–26; Post, "A Carpetbagger in South Carolina," 41–43; Sefton, *The United States Army and Reconstruction, 1865–1877*, 222–25; Shapiro, "The Ku Klux Klan During Reconstruction: The South Carolina Episode," 46; Simkins, "The Ku Klux Klan in South Carolina," 640–41; Taylor, *The Negro in South Carolina During Reconstruction*, 197–202; Trelease, *White Terror*, 369–70; Wade, *The Fiery Cross*, 93–94; West, *The Reconstruction Ku Klux Klan in York County, South Carolina*, 80–81; Williams, *The Great South Carolina Ku Klux Klan Trials*, 38–39; Lou Falkner Williams, "The South Carolina Ku Klux Klan Trials and Enforcement of Federal Civil Rights, 1871–1872," *Civil War History* 39 (March 1993): 49–50; Zuczek, "The Federal Government's Attack on the Ku Klux Klan: A Reassessment," 52–54; Zuczek, *State of Rebellion*, 93–95.

26. Brown, *A City Without Cobwebs*, 146–48; Everitt, "1871 War on Terror," 31; Hall, "Political Power and Constitutional Legitimacy," 925–26; Henry, *The Story of Reconstruction*, 449; Horn, *Invisible Empire*, 232; V. C. Jones, "The Rise and Fall of the Ku Klux Klan," *Civil War Times Illustrated* 2 (February 1964): 16–17; Kaczorowski, "Federal Enforcement of Civil Rights During the First Reconstruction," 158–160; Jean Edward Smith, *Grant* (New York: Simon & Schuster, 2001), 544–46; Trelease, *White Terror*, 387–91, 402–05; Wade, *The Fiery Cross*, 89; Williams, *The Great South Carolina Ku Klux Klan Trials*, 42.

6

"A PERVERSION OF MORAL SENTIMENT AMONG THE SOUTHERN WHITES"

The South Carolina Upcountry is nestled between two great river systems—the Savannah to the west and the Pee Dee to the east. Between the two rivers lies a hundred-mile swath of land sometimes referred to as the Piedmont region. A study in contrasts, the Piedmont region includes the Sand Hill area in the northeast and the Blue Ridge Mountains tucked in the northwestern corner of the state. Traveling from north to south, steep hills gradually slope down to rolling hills peppered with a multitude of loblolly pines and plentiful scrub brush. Two smaller rivers—the Broad and the Catawba—flow through the region, feeding numerous tributaries that provide much-needed water to people and animals. Throughout most of its history, the Piedmont has been a rural region populated by small farms where residents barely eke out a living growing cotton, tobacco, and vegetables. Cities and wealth are conspicuously absent.

York County lies in the heart of the Piedmont region. In 1871, it was bordered by North Carolina to the north, Chester County to the south, Union and Spartanburg Counties to the west, and Lancaster County to the east. Local historians brag that Hernando De Soto passed through what would become York County during his search for gold in North America during the 1540s. If so—and the evidence is inconclusive—he undoubtedly encountered the Catawba Indians, a Native American tribe that numbered around six thousand during much of the sixteenth century.[1]

South Carolina became a colony of the English Crown in 1670, but the Piedmont region was largely ignored by whites until the dawn of another era. European settlers arrived in the area in large numbers between 1750 and the outbreak of the American Revolution in 1775. Although not yet identified as a distinct region, the Piedmont supplied men and materiel to the American cause when the British launched their South Carolina offensive in 1780. Five years later, the South Carolina legislature officially carved out a county bearing the name "York" from surrounding counties. Some residents referred to the entire northwestern corner of the state as the "Piedmont region" or, more colloquially, the Upstate or Upcountry, a designation differentiating it from the South Carolina Low Country.

The first U.S. census, conducted in 1790, listed 6,604 residents of York County. Historians of the Old South sometimes write of the planter elite as if the class was ubiquitous in the South Carolina landscape, but few wealthy farmers were present in the Upcountry. They tended to congregate in the Low Country, however, especially near the more prosperous tidal areas close to Charleston. Of the York County residents listed in the first census, most were subsistence farmers. The census identified 923 residents as slaves. Nine men who might be called moderately successful planters owned approximately a quarter of the slaves; the remainder was dispersed among smaller families and business owners. About 15 percent of York County's population lived in bondage in 1790 compared with a 30 percent statewide average.

By 1786, at the center of the county, Fergus's Cross Roads marked the spot where six roads converged, and the village of York eventually arose from the crossroads. In May 1809, a future member of the South Carolina House of Representatives, William D. Martin, visited the village and recorded his impressions. "Its local situation is pleasant and interesting," he observed. "The [site] is on a plane of some length, near the centre of which is a small eminence, on which is built a Court House, a neat brick building. The private houses, also, are principally of brick, and very far excel those usually built in similar places."[2]

This county populated with charming little hamlets remained virtually unchanged until at least the 1840s. By 1841, the village of York, commonly referred to as the "York Court House," was incorporated as a town, Yorkville. Around this time, the cotton gin, a decades-old invention recently introduced into the Piedmont, revolutionized the economy and ensured that slavery would remain an integral part of Upcountry life despite the relative poverty of the region. Anxious to fill their coffers after suffering through many years of modest planting, farmers leapt at the opportunity to harvest a cash crop. Before this new invention came along, it had been too risky and cumbersome to devote vast acreage to a crop that would require enormous labor resources to realize a profit, no matter how lucrative it might be in the long run. By the mid-nineteenth century, however, cotton was king in York County, as it was across the Deep South. Farmers enjoyed another benefit when the railroad expanded into the area in 1851. Numerous crossroads and small towns grew up alongside the tracks. Rock Hill, situated immediately south of Charlotte, North Carolina, became an important Upcountry town that owed its existence to the steam locomotive.

As a result of its rural character, agriculture was an indispensable part of life in the Piedmont region. During the antebellum years, almost 93 percent of the residents raised crops or worked on the land while the average across the United States stood at 78 percent. Only 13 percent of the York County population was employed, even part time, in industry.[3]

The Civil War disrupted life in the Upcountry, although no major engagements were fought in northwestern South Carolina. Fiercely loyal to the South, a large percentage of the 5,500 white male population of York County enlisted in the Confederate States Army in 1861. Fourteen infantry companies joined the ranks, to say nothing of the men who served in various cavalry and artillery regiments organized elsewhere in South Carolina. By war's end, the York District had suffered the highest casualty rate of any South Carolina county. To make matters worse, the more prosperous farmers returned to find their fields fallow, their debts mounting, and their sons and male relatives missing, dead, wounded, or incapacitated. It was not uncommon to see larger landowners selling their acreage to satisfy their creditors. Even when a farmer could hold onto his land, he knew little of farming techniques or strategies for replenishing nutrients in the soil. As a result, the average farmer worked fewer acres than he had during the antebellum years, and each acre produced smaller and smaller yields as the years passed. Gradually, the local economy drifted deeper into recession, leaving many residents embittered by federal Reconstruction policies, Yankee indignities, and changing social mores that allowed free blacks to roam the countryside while whites who previously had been their social superiors—perhaps their masters—struggled to survive.[4]

The 1870 census listed 24,286 people living in York County. Of that total, approximately 1,500 residents called Yorkville home. Taken together, the county and town populations were almost equally divided between blacks and whites, although blacks held a slight advantage in the county. Yorkville residents were proud of their quaint village, but they probably were envious of the adjacent town of Rock Hill, which served as the railroad junction between Charlotte and Columbia. In time, Rock Hill would eclipse its older neighbor in population numbers and importance to the Upcountry.[5]

Figure 6.1. Organized groups of freedmen gathering under the auspices of the Union League alarmed white citizens in South Carolina during Reconstruction.
The York County Historical Commission

When the Seventh United States Cavalry arrived in Columbia in mid-March 1871, the Ku Klux Klan's reign of terror in York County had subsided, although the respite was brief. Passions and tempers could not be held in check for long. Whites were especially alarmed when they saw blacks parading through the Upcountry as part of well-drilled Union Leagues. Whether these paramilitary groups organized to protect blacks from armed white vigilantes were the cause or the result of Klan abuses remains an open question—perhaps it was a little of both—but their presence heightened tensions in an already tense time and place. The appearance of three new federal cavalry companies only added to the mounting fears of the white community.

Major Lewis Merrill first came to the Upcountry by rail with ninety men under his command. Setting up camp near Yorkville, he was cautiously optimistic that peace could be restored with minimal disruptions to civilian life. He was a professional soldier who had seen much during his time serving in the army, and he was initially skeptical of the tales he heard about KKK outrages. During his months of service in the Piedmont, however, he was disappointed to learn that the ostensibly reasonable demeanor of the town's leading citizens and the relative tranquility of events were merely a façade. Yorkville was a powder keg waiting to blow.

Throughout his career in uniform, Merrill had demonstrated his willingness and ability to engage guerilla forces with firmness and tenacity. In his earlier engagements out West and in the Union army, he was accustomed to exercising considerable discretion in choosing how he would fight the enemy. Whether battling Plains Indians, the Nauvoo Legion, or bands of rebel guerillas, he understood the fundamental principles of a successful military campaign: remain vigilant; be willing to adapt to changing, uncertain developments; and do not hesitate to bring all available resources to bear on a problem.

During his early months stationed in South Carolina, the major found the situation markedly different than anything he had experienced previously. The Grant administration was reluctant to antagonize Southerners any more than was necessary. Already viewed as obdurate and tyrannical, federal officials were loath to send reinforcements only to find that a premature reaction triggered yet more bloodshed and opposition. As a consequence of this timid policy, Merrill and his troops found themselves in the unenviable position of supporting local law enforcement officials but devoid of authority to take active measures to curb Klan violence. The Enforcement Acts of 1870 and 1871 allowed the U.S. military to assist civil authorities in restoring law and order when confronted with a riotous mob, but it stopped short of providing the broad authority Merrill thought he needed to eradicate the Klan. Even if he had tried to be proactive, the major knew that his force of ninety men could not hope to defeat the KKK, which enjoyed far larger numbers.[6]

Frustrated by the passive indifference and sometimes active collusion of locals with the Klan, Merrill chose to make the best of a bad situation. If orders from Washington required him to stand by passively awaiting refinement of federal policy, at least he could use his time to gather facts about which Klan stories were true and which were fabricated. "It was necessary that the commanding general of the department should be kept advised of the true state of facts here," he later testified. "In order that my reports might be accurate, I took pains to keep myself well informed of what was transpiring, and to investigate with care such cases as offered any opportunity to get at facts." This clear sense of purpose would prove to be Merrill's greatest asset.[7]

In the aftermath of the Elias Hill beating at the hands of Klansmen and Merrill's meetings with prominent York County citizens in an effort to curb further violence, the major began interviewing witnesses, many of whom

spoke to him on the condition of anonymity. Blacks who had been terrorized by nightriders were understandably fearful of retaliation if their coop-
eration with federal troops became widely known, but a substantial number
of freedmen nonetheless ignored the obvious risks and supplied Merrill
with crucial information. Several former KKK members also provided invaluable insight into the thinking, scheming, and customs of the group, although, according to some witnesses, their recollections sometimes had to
be "refreshed" with monetary inducements. The credibility of two former
Klansmen turned informants, Kirkland L. Gunn and Charles W. Foster, was
later challenged when cases were brought to trial in federal court because
the men had been granted immunity from prosecution and supposedly were
compensated for their testimony, although they vehemently denied the latter allegation. Another informant, Samuel G. Brown, proved to be so unreliable that he contradicted himself and recanted portions of his testimony
on the witness stand.

Despite occasional misinformation, inaccurate details, and contradictory testimony, Merrill's informants, black and white, revealed a widespread
pattern of Klan activity that shocked the young officer. He realized that
Klan members' shadowy maneuvers and hidden identities shielded them
from scrutiny, which made an accurate summary of the facts difficult, if not
impossible. Even if an investigator somehow managed to gather information and bring a criminal case against Klansmen, the fear that gripped the
local community, especially blacks, and the generally sympathetic attitude
exhibited by whites in the county all but guaranteed that the Klan would
not be broken. As the interviews progressed, Merrill became convinced that
the only effective strategy would be for federal authorities to handle the investigation and prosecution of the group.[8]

On May 25, he inadvertently engendered controversy when he
telegraphed his superiors requesting authority to arrest suspects and hold
prisoners under lock and key until a trial could be arranged. After congressional enactment of the Ku Klux Klan Force Bill in April, the relatively limited scope of the Enforcement Acts—which had hampered Merrill's efforts
during his first few months in Yorkville—could be circumvented. The new
federal statute could serve as the basis for more stringent, effective federal
law enforcement than previously had been possible.

Unbeknownst to Merrill, the telegraph operator was a Klan member.
When the young fellow read the contents of the telegram to his brethren,
they were incensed. Before Merrill could even receive a response from
Washington, local Klansmen had assembled to discuss their options. They
contemplated attacking Merrill's troops, but the more sober-minded mem-

bers realized that an armed assault ultimately would lead to defeat. The Klan had escaped vigorous federal prosecution by hiding in shadows and darkness. It was simple to deny the existence of the group or, if its existence was verified, to explain that it was merely a social club organized with benign motives. If the KKK fought soldiers and spilled their blood, it would awaken the might of the federal government. More regiments would pour into the county within days or weeks, and their arrival would signal the beginning of the end. The Klan might succeed in driving Merrill and part of the Seventh Cavalry from the area, but reinforcements would overwhelm them. The Klan might triumph in a short guerilla campaign against three cavalry companies, but it could never hope to wage a long, drawn-out, bloody war against the U.S. Army.[9]

Although ill-advised, an attack almost occurred, in any case. A splinter group of Klansmen, still upset at Merrill's interference and anxious to frighten him and his men, plotted to sneak up and fire indiscriminately into the camp. As long as they did not show themselves, how could the episode be attributed definitively to the KKK? Unfortunately for the mob, Merrill's informants—derisively labeled "Pukers" or "Pukes"—told him of the plot beforehand. Recognizing that he could use the information to his advantage, Merrill circulated a rumor that he knew of the plan as well as the identity of the participants. Several prominent citizens, including Dr. J. Rufus Bratton, suddenly approached the major and offered to help prevent further violence if he would reveal his sources. Delighted that his scheme had worked, Merrill declined to name names. Exactly as he had anticipated, the startling depth and unknown origin of his information were worrisome to community leaders. An attack never came.[10]

Ironically, if the Klan had attacked, the major's task would have been easier; he would have possessed unequivocal evidence that the group was dangerous to public safety. In the absence of an armed assault, Merrill's insights and sensibilities were shared only by a handful of his superiors, notably General Alfred Terry and Attorney General Amos T. Akerman. To convince a larger group of federal authorities, especially skeptical members of Congress, of the dangers of the Klan, he needed to prepare a case against the offenders as though he were again serving as a judge advocate in a court martial.

Merrill's legal acumen and military experience served him well in York County. He collected and sifted through a large body of facts and testimony from informants, and this information served as the basis for a detailed summary of his findings. Dated June 9, 1871, Merrill's careful, methodical report to General Terry was the first and probably the most detailed accounting of the Klan's activities during Reconstruction. The major outlined the hierarchical structure of South Carolina Klan dens and described the various officers and their duties. The Pukers had taught him well. Merrill explained how Klan members communicated through a series of secret signs and code words as well as bars of musical notations. "Beyond doubt the object of the organization in this vicinity is to terrify the negroes into obeying the whites in voting or to compel them to stay away from the polls," he wrote. Federal troops were virtually powerless to prevent outrages owing to their role supporting white law enforcement officials who were either Klansmen or Klan sympathizers.[11]

General Terry was stunned at the details in the report. Never had so much information and data been assembled about this shadowy group. Clearly, Major Merrill had been the right man for the assignment, despite his earlier controversy in the Lauffer case. Confident that he possessed the facts necessary for federal prosecutors to act against the KKK, the general forwarded Merrill's report to the War Department with a cover letter lauding his subordinate as "an officer of great intelligence, and I think that the utmost confidence may be placed in his representations."[12]

Merrill's report was unquestionably an important initial step in prosecuting the Klan, but it also underscored a fundamental problem in initiating a criminal case. Almost all criminal laws were created and enforced at the state level. If state officials were active Klan participants, prosecuting cases would be difficult. Moreover, in light of the large number of Klansmen roaming through the Southern states, even if evidence could be collected and presented in court, the number of cases probably would overwhelm federal resources. With no hope of pursuing Klansmen in every area, General Terry recommended that Merrill's report become the basis for striking at the KKK in the South Carolina Upcountry. If a small number of selective prosecutions could move forward against known Klan leaders, the *in terrorem* effect might force rank-and-file Klansmen to reconsider their affiliation with the gang.[13]

With Merrill's report in hand, a three-man subcommittee of the Joint Select Committee to Inquire into the Condition of Affairs in the Late Insurrectionary States visited South Carolina in June and July. Merrill met with subcommittee members and presented transcripts of informant testimony regarding whippings, arson, and murders perpetrated by the KKK in the Upcountry. As he led them through the labyrinthine workings of the Klan, his command of detail and the thoroughness of his records impressed the two Republican subcommittee members, although Democrat Philadelph Van Trump was not convinced. He held firm to the long-standing Democratic

Figure 6.2.   The freight depot was the first sight that greeted visitors arriving by rail in Yorkville, South Carolina.
The York County Historical Commission

party line that stories of the Ku Klux Klan were wild exaggerations or out-right fabrications. Sensing a political motivation, Congressman Van Trump pressed the major to admit that he was a Republican intent on smearing Democrats by compiling a dossier filled with lies and innuendo.

Coming so soon after the Lauffer imbroglio, Van Trump's insinuations seemed especially offensive. "I am an officer in the Army," Merrill assured the congressman, "bred up in a school which taught me that officers of the Army were not proper persons to mix in politics."

"Are you known here as a pronounced Republican?"

"If I am, I do not know it."

Van Trump would not abandon his thesis. "Are you not a Republican?"

Merrill was adamant that partisanship did not unduly influence his conclusions. "Perhaps in the main my political opinions coincide more nearly with the Republican than with any other party on questions relating to public affairs." Nonetheless, the major's party affiliation was beside the point. He insisted that he did not actively take part in political affairs and "am not decided in expressing political opinions, except it be in social or domestic conversation."[14]

Van Trump remained skeptical of the major's report, but the Republican subcommittee members were convinced, especially after they witnessed an unsettling series of events. A local U.S. congressman, Alexander S. Wallace, was well known as an anti-Klan crusader who repeatedly had pressed the Grant administration for assistance in battling the KKK. His efforts made him enormously unpopular throughout the district, particularly in Yorkville, where the Klan was strong. One evening while the congressman was dining at Rawlinson's Hotel with Major Merrill and the Republican members of the subcommittee, a disgruntled local man, J. H. Berry, spied the gentlemen. In a fit of pique, Berry grabbed a pitcher of cream and approached their table, apparently intent on dousing the congressman as a demonstration of righteous indignation. Mr. Rawlinson, owner of the hotel, happened to be in the dining room at that instant and, recognizing trouble at hand, attempted to intervene. He caught Berry's arm at the instant the assailant was swinging the pitcher. Consequently, the cream missed Congressman Wallace, although it drenched subcommittee member Job Stevenson of Ohio.

Wallace and Stevenson instantly shot to their feet and reached into their coat pockets. It seemed likely the men would produce pistols, and guns would blaze throughout the dining room. Thankfully, they withdrew only handkerchiefs. Rawlinson hustled Berry from the room and had the man arrested for assault and battery. Such was the local temperament that Berry was hailed as a hero while Congressman Wallace was ridiculed with a silly nickname, "Buttermilk" Wallace, which stayed with him for the rest of his life. As York County incidents went, the affair was little more than an amusing interlude, but it reflected the sensibilities of Yorkville residents.[15]

A far more serious event followed the dinner. Aware that the subcommittee was in town to investigate stories of Klan abuses, local blacks assembled outside the hotel to serenade the members in an impromptu concert. A crowd of angry whites, already infuriated that agents of the federal government dared to meddle in their affairs, heckled the serenaders. Despite provocation on both sides of the racial divide, the assemblage might have dissolved peacefully if the local constable, William H. Snyder, a Klansman, had not exacerbated tensions by threatening to arrest a black musician, Tom Johnson. Johnson recognized a trumped-up charge—obstructing a sidewalk—when he heard it. He resisted. During the ensuing scuffle, Snyder whipped out a pistol and shot Johnson five times, striking the young man in the face, back, arms, and shoulder.

Figure 6.3.   This photograph shows Main Street in Yorkville, South Carolina, during the nineteenth century. This sleepy little town was a scene of enormous unrest and violence in 1870–1871.
The York County Historical Commission

The brawl, already serious, would have degenerated into an even bloodier melee but for Major Merrill. Wading into the crowd, he spoke to the blacks and asked them to disperse. He also asked the mayor, a KKK member, to send the whites away. Chaos was averted, but barely. Blacks recognized that the incident was a pretext for jailing or shooting them in large numbers. If that were the case, Merrill's intercession had indeed saved the day. The mayor emerged from the ruckus a hero in the eyes of the white community, but any attempt to portray Yorkville to the subcommittee as a peaceful, idyllic little town plagued only by exaggerated stories of civil unrest was shattered.[16]

Realizing that the Ku Klux Klan had infiltrated the highest ranks of local government and acting on that realization were two entirely different matters, for the wheels of Congress turned slowly. As the subcommittee visited other states and collected evidence and testimony, Major Merrill and his men were forced to stand by in a supporting role. Federal troops could intercede if they witnessed depredations; otherwise, they were relegated to patrolling the forests of York County and searching the ranks of local citizens for Pukers to buttress their case. In a report he later submitted to Congress, Merrill expressed his frustration as spring gave way to summer and summer dissolved into autumn:

> In my previous reports I have repeatedly expressed the opinion that the local civil authorities were powerless to cope with the strength of the Ku Klux conspiracy, even if willing to make the attempt, and I have been compelled to believe that the desire to make the attempt was entirely wanting. It is impossible to believe that such numerous crimes should be repeated almost daily for month after month, with no instance of punishment and hardly the commonest formality of investigation, and at the same time to credit the assertions of the civil functionaries that they were sincerely zealous in their duties, and desirous of bringing the offenders to justice. The pretense that it was impossible to detect the criminals was transparent, and I have been able, with the very limited means at my command, to trace numbers of the crimes far enough to make it certain that an honest, fearless, and vigorous discharge of duty by the civil officers would have brought to light all the facts needed to bring the offenders to trial.[17]

Despite his assumption that the South Carolina courts would not prosecute Klansmen with alacrity, the major believed he had an obligation to present evidence before the civil courts of York County. The fall session commenced on Monday, September 18, 1871. When he learned in a letter from Senator Scott that the judge presiding over the cases, William M. Thomas, had asked the senator for witnesses' affidavits and information on Klan crimes in the county, Merrill was momentarily encouraged.

His hopes were dashed when he listened to the judge's charge to the county grand jury. Although he was not overtly hostile to the federal government, Judge Thomas intimated that all the fuss over the Ku Klux Klan in York County was exaggerated. After sharing his opinion that martial law was undesirable, the judge questioned the federal government's commitment to investigating the charges. He also implied that the court had asked for copies of the affidavits that Senator Scott and the congressional subcommittee had collected when they visited the county, but he had yet to receive a reply. The judge's remark could be interpreted any number of ways, some benign, some suspicious. Perhaps the mails were slow and the response was delayed. Perhaps Senator Scott and the subcommittee simply did not care what happened in York County. Perhaps no affidavits existed.

It was a crafty performance. Without openly defying federal authorities, Judge Thomas presented such a vague, general picture of the "dark cloud of trouble hanging over York County" that the grand jury would have little grounds for indicting anyone for anything. As if that were not enough, he peppered his speech with allusions to the importance of home rule—"It is high time that we understood that if we wish to govern ourselves we must show that we can do so"—always careful to admonish jurors to do their duty. Nowhere did he mention the evidence of the Klan murders and beatings investigated by Major Merrill. Was Judge Thomas unaware of nighttime activities in York County or had he been deliberately obtuse in his grand jury charge?

Observing Thomas's oration from the back of the courtroom but unable to interrupt the tirade, Merrill was incredulous. The Seventh Cavalry was acting under orders to assist civil authorities, not displace them; thus, he could do little apart from witness the session and scribble copious notes for his report to General Terry. Powerless to countermand the jury charge, Merrill nonetheless penned a letter to the judge outlining the facts he had assembled concerning Klan activities in the county and offering to share his information before the next day's session. "In justice to yourself I can only infer that you had no knowledge of the numerous crimes that have occurred during the vacation of the court," he explained in his letter. Merrill undoubtedly believed the judge knew exactly what he was doing, but Thomas was not the only official who felt compelled to keep up appearances.

In a perfunctory reply, Judge Thomas agreed to meet with Merrill the following day in judge's chambers. At the appointed time, the major appeared along with his assistant, Captain Owen Hale, whom he brought to take notes. After exchanging customary pleasantries, the men got down to business. As Merrill and Hale later reconstructed the dialogue, Judge Thomas asked, "Do you not think that in the present 'nascent and infantile' state of public sentiment in opposition to the Ku-Klux outrages it would be inexpedient to stir up these things by an investigation; that this sentiment which has just begun to show itself would become more powerful if these things were not stirred up?"

Merrill replied that he was not familiar with the South Carolina courts and could not tell Judge Thomas how to run his courtroom; however, he believed that expediency was not the paramount issue. Instead, the grand jury should be presented with all the credible information collected so the jurors could choose to indict or not, as they saw fit. From the charge presented the previous day, the grand jury did not have sufficient information upon which to act. Thomas alternated between proclaiming the grand jury ready to perform its duty and lodging a litany of protests. "Do you think it expedient to stir up this thing?" he asked repeatedly. When he realized that

Judge Thomas did not intend to "stir up this thing" no matter what he said, the major fell silent.

If he entertained doubts about Thomas's good faith during their meeting in chambers, the judge's performance in open court resolved the ambiguity. The sessions were a farce. In Merrill's opinion, expressed later in his official report, Thomas "did not honor the obligations of his office." The judge was so sympathetic to the KKK that, in the major's words, the proceedings "convinced me that public sentiment was so far under Ku-Klux control that no hope would be reasonably entertained that the court would vigorously attempt its duty, even under the strongest pressure of such facts as I could lay before it."

On rare occasions when the judge allowed evidence and testimony to be presented, the grand jury was no more willing to listen than he was. The session lasted for ten days, but no action was taken apart from ridiculing Merrill's reports and questioning the reliability of his evidence. In each case brought before the court—including the notorious murders of Jim Williams and Tom Roundtree—the jurors reported a similar finding: "We do not regard it as sufficiently definite to authorize any special presentation from us." At the conclusion of the September term, foreman A. L. Hutchinson closed the grand jury report with a comment that could have applied to every Ku Klux Klan case presented that month. "Information was furnished the grand jury by Major Merrill to the effect that six persons had recently been whipped in the southeastern part of this county. After careful examination of the facts we ascertain that no such outrage occurred in this county. The officer alluded to as making the report expressed himself as satisfied as to his mistake, and proffered to correct any erroneous report of the affair that may have emanated from him."

Merrill was anything but satisfied with the grand jury's findings. "I offered them a mass of information in regard to hundreds of crimes," he reported, "none of which they examined with more than the most transparent pretense of getting at the facts." The conclusion was inescapable: York County's leading white citizens were sympathetic to, and probably complicit with, the Ku Klux Klan, as evinced by the grand jury report. He would later discover that many grand jurors were in fact active Klansmen— perhaps as many as one-third—and two jurors probably participated in the murders he had investigated.[18]

The major was apoplectic. The Klan would never be brought to justice if federal troops could only assist civil authorities, many of whom were in league with the Klansmen. Rushing from Yorkville to Columbia, he found U.S. attorney David T. Corbin and expressed his frustration with the proceedings, "so broad a farce" and a "ghastly mockery of justice." Fortunately, Attorney General Akerman was in transit from Raleigh, North Carolina, where he had been collecting evidence about the illicit activities of the North Carolina Ku Klux Klan. Anxious to confer with the attorney general, Merrill met Akerman at the Columbia train depot. Together they traveled, along with Corbin, to Yorkville.

The local grand jury had disregarded the evidence, but Merrill's dossier impressed Akerman and Corbin. The depth and breadth of the information was difficult to ignore or deny. Moreover, the transcripts and affidavits confirmed Akerman's findings from his investigations in North Carolina. The major was so passionate in arguing his case and so meticulous in documenting abuses, the attorney general later told General Terry that Merrill was "resolute, collected, bold and prudent, with a good legal head, very discriminating between truth and falsehood, very indignant at wrong, and yet master of his indignation." In Akerman's view, Merrill "performed a difficult service with admirable success." No one but the most myopically partisan Democratic hack could doubt the veracity of the evidence. Merrill had finally done what no one before him had been willing or able to do: He had exposed the Invisible Empire to sunlight, undoubtedly the best disinfectant for exposing masked vigilantes operating in darkness. This vindication from his superiors must have come as welcome attention for a man still reeling from the negative scrutiny he had received in the Lauffer case.[19]

As he sifted through the interview transcripts, Akerman realized that the federal government faced a daunting task, yet he had no option but to proceed with federal prosecutions. He agreed with Merrill that soldiers serving in a supporting role would never curb Klan violence as long as local law enforcement officials were in league with nightriders. His only recourse was to invoke the authority of the Ku Klux Klan Act signed by the president in April.

Before contacting Grant, Akerman met privately with Corbin and Governor Scott to explain his decision. Although he had vacillated about whether the federal government should increase its presence in the state, Scott recognized the wisdom of moving forward—as long as the Grant administration was fully committed to prosecuting the cases. The governor could not support federal KKK prosecutions if the president and the Justice Department were unwilling or unable to see this thing through to the conclusion. Akerman assured him of continued federal support. The governor's repeated pleas to Grant for assistance had borne fruit, although whether for good or ill remained to be seen.

Akerman journeyed to Louisville, Kentucky, to confer with General Terry. From there, he traveled to Dayton, Ohio, to present his evidence to President Grant, who was visiting the area. On October 10, the attorney general returned to South Carolina and assured the president by telegram that the troops were prepared to arrest suspected Klansmen as soon as the president authorized such action. Two days later, Grant issued a preliminary proclamation before suspending the writ of habeas corpus. Identifying "unlawful combinations and conspiracies" in nine Upstate counties—Chester, Chesterfield, Fairfield, Lancaster, Laurens, Marion, Newberry, Spartanburg, and York—he ordered all persons involved in the illegal activities to cease and desist and surrender their arms and costumes within five days. The preliminary proclamation was a last chance for KKK members to lay down their arms, hang up their robes, and resume lawful activities in their communities. Failure to comply would force the president to issue a final proclamation suspending habeas corpus. Once the writ was unavailable to criminal defendants, federal soldiers would comb the countryside arresting Klansmen for trial in federal court.

The nine counties identified in the list were curious choices. The Klan was not especially active in Fairfield, Lancaster, and Chesterfield counties, and Marion County was not even in the Upcountry but across the state toward the coast, suggesting that this reference was a mistake. In the haste to have the president issue a preliminary proclamation, someone had mistaken Akerman's designation of "Union" County as "Marion" County. After the error was discovered, it was corrected in a subsequent proclamation. The lack of attention to detail was not troubling to federal authorities; a message had been sent.

And a powerful message it was. KKK leaders were well aware of Akerman's activities and they could guess the gist of his recommendations to the president. Anticipating the eventual suspension of habeas corpus and invocation of the Ku Klux Klan Act, the leaders were worried. Their lives as vigilantes meting out punishments without accountability were at an end. Well-to-do leaders with money at their disposal and destinations in mind abandoned their families and fled to other states. In some instances, they took refuge in foreign countries. After observing this flurry of activity in mid-October, Merrill remarked that "many of the Ku-Klux leaders, suspecting that measures were being devised to bring them to justice, and with the cowardice which has characterized all their infamous crimes, fled, leaving their poorer followers and ignorant dupes to stand sponsors for the crimes of which they had been the chief authors and instigators."[20]

Not surprisingly, even those Kluxers who stayed in the Piedmont were reluctant to step forward and surrender their arms or retire their Klan robes.

To do so publicly was to violate the KKK oath of secrecy, and no small measure of embarrassment would result. For a fellow to admit to neighbors, family, and friends that he had engaged in illegal conduct was a potential source of shame. Although many Upcountry whites sympathized with the Klan in general, no individual wanted to announce unequivocally his complicity in rapes, beatings, and murders, to say nothing of fears of federal prosecution and possible retribution from the black community.

When it was clear to Akerman that the preliminary proclamation would have little practical effect, he sent word to the president that a final proclamation was required. In a missive he transmitted on October 16, the attorney general reiterated the need for strong action. Because the Klan controlled civil government, juries, and social institutions in northwest South Carolina, only the U.S. Army, acting under color of federal law in a time of rebellion, could prevent KKK outrages. "I am justified in affirming that the instances of criminal violence perpetrated by these combinations within the last twelve months in the above named counties would be reckoned by the thousands," he explained.

The president agreed. He knew Democrats and pro-Southern whites would regard his action as a first step toward a military dictatorship, but he believed he had little choice if he hoped to stop the Klan. According to Article I, § 9, Clause 2 of the U.S. Constitution, "The privilege of the Writ of Habeas Corpus shall not be suspended, unless when in Cases of Rebellion or Invasion the public Safety may require it." Recognizing that a state of rebellion existed in South Carolina, on October 17 the president, acting as commander-in-chief of the armed forces pursuant to Article II of the Constitution, suspended habeas corpus in the nine Upstate counties "during the continuance of such rebellion," the first time in American history a president had felt compelled to undertake such drastic measures during peacetime. Linking his action to the language of Article I, § 9, Grant explained, "In my judgment the public safety requires that the privileges of the writ of habeas corpus be suspended." This bold directive was necessary if federal troops were to round up suspects and stop the KKK "rebellion."

Typically, a lawful arrest requires a warrant to be served on a suspect by civil authorities empowered to enforce criminal law in the jurisdiction where the arrest occurs. After the defendant is taken into custody in accordance with the terms of the warrant, he must be arraigned before a judge. During the arraignment, the defendant enters a plea and the question of bail may be heard and decided. If authorities fail to follow the appropriate procedure, a defendant possesses a constitutional right to apply for a court order—the writ of habeas corpus—requiring an arraignment, the filing of formal criminal charges and, if appropriate, a time set for trial. In the absence of an arraignment, a defendant must be released from custody.

If the writ is unavailable, however, the defendant's status is unclear. He might be detained, presumably for an indefinite time, until law enforcement officers proceed with the case. In light of Major Merrill's reports that Upcountry civil authorities were sympathetic to the Ku Klux Klan, allowing the state's criminal justice system to follow normal procedures would be ineffective. Moreover, considering the time and logistics required for the army to scour the area and arrest numerous suspects, the suspension of habeas corpus was the only practical tactic for bringing South Carolina Klansmen to justice.[21]

White citizens of the Piedmont region viewed the proclamation as evidence of the encroachment of federal power on the states, another offense in a long line of indignities stretching back to the early years of the century. York County resident Mary Davis Brown echoed the fears of Southern whites when she noted in her diary that "it is reported that martial law is declared and that the yankeys will commence arresting the men at eney time." Her sons fled the county bound for "parts unknown," leaving behind a "broken harted Father & Mother." Almost every Upcountry family was affected directly or indirectly. The streets of Yorkville took on a haunted look; where once they bustled with horses and men conducting business, now they were empty save for soldiers on patrol. Despairing for their solvency, merchants closed up shop early or sent merchandise back to distributors, citing a lack of customers as the reason.[22]

Observing the frantic reaction of citizens on the eve of the arrests, a New York *Tribune* correspondent wrote, "the place had the look of a town in war time recently captured by an invading army," and citizens "had the look of excitement and despondency always observable in the inhabitants of a conquered town." A week later, in an attempt to quell panic, the *Yorkville Enquirer* reported that the "authorities are reticent in regard to their movements and intentions, and we can only publish facts as they transpire, deeming conjectures and sensational paragraphs—such as will flood many of the papers at a distance—as quite superfluous, and in tendency injurious."[23]

Regardless of whether the newspaper eschewed "conjectures and sensational paragraphs," excitement and anxiety spread throughout the Upcountry that month, and with little wonder. After bivouacking in York County impotently for almost seven months, federal soldiers were prepared for action. They did not have long to wait. Beginning on October 19, soldiers efficiently combed the countryside for suspects, arresting dozens of men who had not fled to more hospitable environs. According to the *Yorkville Enquirer*,

Figure 6.4.   This photograph shows a broad view of Congress Street, Yorkville, South Carolina. In October 1871, a witness described the scene as having "the look of a town in war time."
The York County Historical Commission

"[o]n Thursday last, the military authorities at this place commenced making arrests. Several citizens of the town were arrested while in the pursuit of their avocations, and many persons from the county, while in town on business, were also detained and lodged in prison." Lest word spread about the arrests and alert Klansmen living outside the city limits, concerted action was required. "About the same hour that the arrests commenced in town, the military began to move, squadrons of cavalry marching out in various directions, for the purpose of arresting those in the country against whom accusations had been made for violations of the 'Ku-Klux' and 'Enforcement' Acts of Congress." By the end of the month, seventy-nine alleged offenders languished in the York county jail. Dozens more were rounded up in surrounding counties. By January 8, 1872, 472 men had been arrested in the Upcountry. The figure rose to 533 by April, when the attorney general prepared his annual report.[24]

The *Yorkville Enquirer* reported in a straightforward, matter-of-fact manner that the arrests were orderly and generally without incident. "It may be proper here to state that very few arrests have been made after night, the larger number having been made during the day time," an October 26 story explained, "and, so far as we have been able to learn, no show of resistance to authority has been made." This calm, almost detached perspective was distinctly a minority view in South Carolina that autumn. Most state newspapers were controlled by Democrats, and they wailed against the blatant disregard for constitutional protections by overzealous soldiers under the command of anti-Southern Radical Republicans.[25]

A typical Democratic recounting of federal soldiers attempting to arrest a suspected Klansman placed the episode at night and featured a predicable cast of characters, complete with heroes and villains. The tale usually conjured up a worried but defiant mother—the heroine—shielding a small, frightened child from well-armed, capricious federal soldiers—the villains—hell bent on tearing the homestead apart. The soldiers looted and plundered as they searched for the man of the house, an innocent victim facing trumped-up charges unfairly lodged against him by carpetbaggers, scalawags, and vindictive freedmen.

A story printed in the Rock Hill newspaper, the *Lantern*, on June 22, 1872, beautifully illustrates the major themes and serves as a classic in the genre. Recalling a nocturnal visit—"between twelve o'clock and daybreak"—to the home of a suspected Klan leader, the reporter regales readers with the exploits of "Mrs. Avery, the brave-hearted wife of Dr. Edward T. Avery, who it will be remembered escaped by flight last winter from the clutches of Jeffrey Bond's Court of Injustice." The tale continues in the histrionic style of the day:

Mrs. Avery was summoned to the front door by a loud and continuous rapping. Demanding of the party who was at the door and what they wanted, they replied that they wished to be admitted to the house. Mrs. Avery then requested that she be allowed to dress, she being in her night attire. This request was civilly granted. . . . Performing a hasty toilet she returned and opened the door being accompanied by her little son Edward. At the door stood several soldiers in Federal uniforms.

"Have you orders to do this thing?" demanded the brave hearted lady.

"Yes," was the prompt reply by a sergeant who stepped forward.

Just at that moment a voice called out from the road, thirty or forty steps away, "Sergeant, do your duty!"

Mrs. Avery, being a little inquisitive in such matters, proceeded with her questioning.

"Who are your orders from—Merrill?"

"No, from the Deputy County Marshall," replied the sergeant. As he said this he drew a pistol, perceiving which Mrs. Avery remarked, pointing to the weapon, "That is the authority you generally act under. I am a defenseless woman. You can come in!"

After Dr. Avery could not be found, the soldiers departed, leaving the reporter to reflect on "a most orderly retreat from the bloodless field." The moral of the tale does not mention the Ku Klux Klan; it ridicules the soldiers and their cause. "Thus ended this grand military expedition, the purpose of which was to effect the capture of one poor *one-handed* man."[26]

White Southerners were so embittered and the prose published in the Democratic newspapers was so vitriolic that, decades later, a commentator, recalling the scene, summarized the feelings of Upcountry whites long after the events had transpired. The "arrests were generally made after midnight with the head of the household routed from his bed and taken away without any explanation to the terrified family. Later it was written that 'even Merrill's subordinate officers were ashamed of his ruffianism in 1871.'"[27]

Merrill was not oblivious to the Southern reaction. "At first much indignation was expressed at what Ku-Klux sympathizers chose to designate the 'arbitrary arrests,' the 'tearing away of innocent men from their families,' and similar expanded distortions of facts," he noted in a report to his superiors. "Later developments have shown that, if all their clamor was the expression of honest feeling, rather than the chattering of such as sought to conceal crime by exciting public sympathy, they had been either criminally indifferent or amazingly ignorant of what had been enacted under their eyes." In the major's opinion, genuine Klan members and participants "were greatly in the minority." As for the rest of the population, he divided them into three classes: residents who approved of the Klan's methods and purposes but took no active part in their depredations; residents who sympathized with the group "more because of their inexpediency than of their wickedness"; and "by far the smallest class, those who had no sympathy with its objects, or anything but condemnation for its acts, but who had come to learn that security from personal indignity required silence." Only active Klan participants needed to fear federal prosecution, but ferreting out active and inactive Klansmen was not always a simple task.

It was also no simple task to arrest the right people. In an era before consistent street addresses, Social Security and tax identification numbers, and driver's licenses offered a standard means of identification, the soldiers were forced to rely on incomplete or inaccurate information. Thus, they arrested two men with the same name and held both suspects until they could determine which fellow was the proper defendant. A thirteen-year-old boy, the son of a Klan leader, was arrested for having participated in a KKK raid until the troops released him on the grounds that he was too young to be responsible for his actions. Several suspected offenders were released after they produced alibis that were later corroborated by reliable witnesses. Despite these understandable errors, the number of men mistakenly arrested was surprisingly small, thanks in no small measure to Major Merrill's thorough investigation and his penchant for insisting on multiple sources of information and identification whenever possible.[28]

Aside from offenders apprehended by soldiers, the number of men who voluntarily surrendered was staggering. During October and November, federal authorities were unprepared for the deluge of bodies in the county jail. "Conspirators against the well-being of society, of every grade of criminality, have come in and surrendered by the score," Merrill remarked. "Day after day, for weeks, men came in in such numbers that time to hear them confess and means to dispose of or take care of them both failed, and I was powerless to do anything more than secure the persons of those most deeply criminal and send the rest to their homes on their personal parole to be forthcoming when called for."[29]

Federal officials had good reason to be magnanimous; they did not have a sufficient number of troops to quell a riot should detainees grow disaffected and rowdy. With few exceptions, U.S. troops treated prisoners leniently, allowing the men to exercise outdoors and receive visitors. Occasionally, the soldiers marched their wards through Yorkville as if on parade. Merrill later boasted that his men had behaved in exemplary fashion: "No complaint has been made of even the smallest impropriety of conduct or want of courtesy toward the prisoner, or toward citizens with whom their duty brought them in contact." For their part, ladies from the surrounding community paid their respects to the men by bringing picnic baskets filled with food and drink.

Merrill's ability to temper justice with mercy during this difficult time was illustrated by an event that occurred not long after the arrests commenced. The major and his assistant, a self-proclaimed carpetbagger named Louis Post, were attending to business one evening when a messenger appeared with an appeal from a prisoner anxious to speak with Merrill.

"Bring him here at once," the major ordered. Turning to Post, he said, "at last, one of the big ones wants to puke." He had many informants, of course, but finding new sources of information was always greeted with excitement.

Much to Merrill's surprise, the prisoner brought before him was not a Klan leader eager to cut a deal, nor did he seek to "puke" new information. Instead, he was a worried father who explained that his son was sick, and he needed to tend to the boy.

"How old is your boy?" Merrill asked.

"Fourteen."

"How ill is he?"

"My wife don't think he'll live 'til morning."

Merrill had nothing to gain by allowing the prisoner to return home. In fact, if he granted permission and the fellow failed to return, which seemed likely, the major could face a court martial. He knew better than most officers the intricacies of a court martial proceeding. After hesitating for a few brief moments, he said, "You may go." Witnessing the surprising scene, Post was even more surprised to learn that the Klansman later returned.[30]

Despite the relatively benign treatment and numerous instances of leniency and mercy, self-styled martyrs raised a hue and cry at the indignity of their circumstances. Confederate veteran Iredell Jones of Rock Hill, a man thought to be the Grand Scribe of his county's KKK den, complained that he was a victim of "persecution" and was "innocent of any crime whatever," yet he was made to "suffer a heavy penalty without even being allowed a hearing." Some men wrote letters to Democratic newspapers alerting them to the travesty of justice but, considering the unusual circumstances, the arrests and detentions were orderly and without serious incident. Merrill noted that unfounded criticism by whites suspected of being Kluxers vexed his men and "were very trying to their patience and forbearance," but they did not retaliate. As a result, "just cause of complaint has been absent."[31]

Exactly as General Terry had foreseen when he first read Merrill's report, the numbers overwhelmed not only federal troops in South Carolina but also prosecutors. Attorney General Akerman and U.S. Attorney Corbin decided they had no choice but to classify offenders according to their degree of criminality. Klan leaders and persons who directly participated in serious crimes such as murder and rape would be bound over for trial while their followers—those persons who aided and abetted but did not directly participate—and perpetrators of misdemeanors would be released on bail or their own recognizance after confessing to their deeds. The attorney general was under no illusion that selective prosecutions would immediately destroy a pervasive force as powerful as the Klan, but if he could undermine its attractiveness, destroy its cachet, and strike terror in the hearts of men who until recently had struck terror in the hearts of others, perhaps the group would slowly dissolve. In a letter he wrote to General Terry, Akerman confided, "I feel greatly saddened by this business. It has revealed a perversion of moral sentiment among the Southern whites, which bodes ill to that part of the country for this generation."[32]

Most defendants were released on bail while still residing in the York County jail. The remaining men were transported to Columbia, the state capital, where they would be bound over for trial in federal court beginning in November. In their absence, white citizens of the Piedmont region settled back into a routine of eking out a living from the land. The bitterness remained but whites did not have to wait many years before they reclaimed positions of power in state and local governments throughout the South.

With the expiration of President Grant's second term early in 1877, Reconstruction effectively ended, and Southern governments were "redeemed." Carpetbaggers, scalawags, and federal soldiers were gone from South Carolina. In their place was a new name and presence, "Jim Crow," the derisive label for laws segregating blacks from white society. The new order rendered groups such as the Ku Klux Klan superfluous; whites did not employ extralegal means of controlling blacks when legal means were at their disposal.

In the meantime, freedmen enjoyed a brief interlude after the 1871 arrests, secure in the knowledge that the power of the Ku Klux Klan was broken, at least for the moment. They never forgot the actions of the Republican Party in restoring law and order to Upstate South Carolina. For many decades, blacks would vote, when they were allowed to vote at all, the Republican ticket. It was during a different era in a different century when blacks deserted the party of Lincoln and Emancipation to join the ranks of the Democratic Party.

Union Leagues still existed in the Southern states after the fall of the Klan, but they declined in importance. Different tools and strategies would be needed to fight Jim Crow. Armed resistance would do nothing but provoke whites in power and inevitably lead to lynchings, beatings, and violent reprisals conducted under the color of law, a far cry from the night riding of hooded desperadoes.[33]

By the end of 1871, Major Merrill had reclaimed much of the good reputation he had enjoyed before the Lauffer case blackened his name. "As all the arrests were made upon information which I furnished the attorney general, it is gratifying to be able to vindicate the carefulness of my investigations," he later wrote. He would spend many months writing reports as well as testifying before congressional committees and in court proceedings before enjoying a brief leave of absence to recuperate from the "exhaustion of brain power" that an army surgeon deemed "consequent upon close and protracted mental application to duties incident to his official position at Yorkville, S.C."

After his respite ended, the major reported for similar duty compiling information on the White League, a white supremacist group in Louisiana.

Later, he was again assigned to posts on the Great Plains. More controversy would accompany his career, including charges of bribery lodged against him for his service in South Carolina and a series of debt collection actions that would hound him well into retirement, but no one could deny that he had been instrumental—arguably the single most important figure—in breaking the power of the South Carolina Ku Klux Klan.[34]

NOTES

1. Douglas Summers Brown, *A City Without Cobwebs: A History of Rock Hill, South Carolina* (Columbia: University of South Carolina Press), 8–9; *History of York County* (Yorkville: York County Historical Commission, 1995), 1–2.

2. Brown, *A City Without Cobwebs*, 139–41; *History of York County*, 2–4; Jerry L. West, *The Reconstruction Ku Klux Klan in York County, South Carolina, 1865–1877* (Jefferson, NC: McFarland & Company, Inc., 2002), 2; Stephen A. West, "Minute Men, Yeomen, and the Mobilization for Secession in the South Carolina Upcountry," *Journal of Southern History* 71 (February 2005): 75–104.

3. Brown, *A City Without Cobwebs*, 139–41; *History of York County*, 2–4; West, *The Reconstruction Ku Klux Klan in York County, South Carolina*, 1–2.

4. Brown, *A City Without Cobwebs*, 135–41; *History of York County*, 6–7.

5. Eric Foner, *Reconstruction: America's Unfinished Revolution, 1863–1877* (New York: Francis Parkman Prize Edition, History Book Club, 2005; originally published by HarperCollins, 1988), 430; *History of York County*, 7; West, *The Reconstruction Ku Klux Klan in York County, South Carolina*, 1–3, 15–16.

6. "Arrival of a Cavalry Company," *Yorkville Enquirer*, Yorkville, SC (March 30, 1871); William Blair, "The Use of Military Force to Protect the Gains of Reconstruction," *Civil War History* 51 (December 2005): 396–97; Kermit L. Hall, "Political Power and Constitutional Legitimacy: The South Carolina Ku Klux Klan Trials, 1871–1872," *Emory Law Journal* 33 (Fall 1984): 925; Thomas Holt, *Black Over White: Negro Political Leadership in South Carolina During Reconstruction* (Urbana: University of Illinois Press, 1977), 30–32; James E. Sefton, *The United States Army and Reconstruction, 1865–1877* (Westport, CT: Greenwood Press, 1967), 224–25; Herbert Shapiro, "The Ku Klux Klan During Reconstruction: The South Carolina Episode," *Journal of Negro History* 49 (January 1964): 46; Otis A. Singletary, "The Negro Militia During Radical Reconstruction," *Military Affairs* 19 (Winter 1955): 177–82; Hans L. Trefousse, *Reconstruction: America's First Effort at Racial Democracy* (New York: Van Nostrand Reinhold Company, 1971), 137–46; Allen W. Trelease, *White Terror: The Ku Klux Klan Conspiracy and Southern Reconstruction* (Baton Rouge: Louisiana State University Press, 1971), 371–72; United States Circuit Court [4th Circuit], *Proceedings in the Ku Klux Klan Trials at Columbia, S.C., in the United States Circuit Court, November Term, 1871* (Columbia, SC: Republican Printing Company,

State Printers, 1872), 743–48; United States Congress, *Report of the Joint Select Committee to Inquire into the Condition of Affairs in the Late Insurrectionary States*, 42 Cong., 2 Sess., No. 22 (1872), Vol. V, 1406–15, 1477; Wyn Craig Wade, *The Fiery Cross: The Ku Klux Klan in America* (New York and Oxford: Oxford University Press, 1987), 93–99; West, *The Reconstruction Ku Klux Klan in York County, South Carolina,* 80–84; Richard Zuczek, "The Federal Government's Attack on the Ku Klux Klan: A Reassessment," *South Carolina Historical Magazine* 97 (January 1, 1996): 52; Richard Zuczek, *State of Rebellion: Reconstruction in South Carolina* (Columbia, SC: University of South Carolina Press, 1996), 93–94.

7. Quoted in: United States Congress, *Report of the Joint Select Committee*, Vol. V, 1464. See also, Barry C. Johnson, *Custer, Reno, Merrill and the Lauffer Case: Some Warfare in "The Fighting Seventh"* (London: The Pilot Printing & Publicity Service on Behalf of the English Westerners' Society, 1971), 1–2; United States Military Academy, *Twenty-Seventh Annual Reunion of the Association of Graduates of the United States Military Academy, at West Point, New York, June 11, 1896* (Saginaw, MI: Seemann & Peters, 1896), 136–37; Wade, *The Fiery Cross,* 94–95; West, *The Reconstruction Ku Klux Klan in York County, South Carolina,* 85; Zuczek, *State of Rebellion,* 94–95.

8. Foner, *Reconstruction: America's Unfinished Revolution,* 431; Stanley F. Horn, *Invisible Empire: The Story of the Ku Klux Klan, 1866–1871* (Montclair, NJ: Patterson Smith, 1969), 240–41; Robert J. Kaczorowski, "Federal Enforcement of Civil Rights During the First Reconstruction," *Fordham Urban Law Journal* 23 (Fall 1995): 157; Francis B. Simkins and R. H. Woody, *South Carolina During Reconstruction* (Chapel Hill: The University of North Carolina Press, 1932), 462–63; Wade, *The Fiery Cross,* 95–97; Zuczek, *State of Rebellion,* 95–97.

9. "Arrival of a Cavalry Company," *Yorkville Enquirer,* Yorkville, SC (March 30, 1871); David Everitt, "1871 War on Terror," *American History* 38 (June 2003): 27–28, 30–31; Foner, *Reconstruction: America's Unfinished Revolution,* 454–59; Kaczorowski, "Federal Enforcement of Civil Rights During the First Reconstruction," 157; Richard W. Murphy, *The Nation Reunited: War's Aftermath* (Alexandria, VA: Time-Life Books, 1987), 98–99; United States Congress, *Report of the Joint Select Committee,* Vol. V, 1464; West, *The Reconstruction Ku Klux Klan in York County, South Carolina,* 80–83.

10. Everitt, "1871 War on Terror," 31; Louis F. Post, "A Carpetbagger in South Carolina," *Journal of Negro History* 10 (January 1925): 43–45; Sefton, *The United States Army and Reconstruction, 1865–1877,* 225; United States Congress, *Report of the Joint Select Committee,* Vol. V, 1481; West, *The Reconstruction Ku Klux Klan in York County, South Carolina,* 84.

11. Quoted in Wade, *The Fiery Cross,* 97. See also, Sefton, *The United States Army and Reconstruction, 1865–1877,* 224–25; Francis B. Simkins, "The Ku Klux Klan in South Carolina," *Journal of Negro History* 12 (October 1927): 611; West, *The Reconstruction Ku Klux Klan in York County, South Carolina,* 84.

12. Trelease, *White Terror,* 402–03; Wade, *The Fiery Cross,* 97–98; Zuczek, *State of Rebellion,* 97–98.

13. Wade, *The Fiery Cross*, 102–03; Lou Falkner Williams, "The South Carolina Ku Klux Klan Trials and Enforcement of Federal Civil Rights, 1871–1872," *Civil War History* 39 (March 1993): 49–50; Zuczek, "The Federal Government's Attack on the Ku Klux Klan: A Reassessment," 54.

14. Quoted in Wade, *The Fiery Cross*, 98–99. See also, Everitt, "1871 War on Terror," 31; Horn, *Invisible Empire*, 232–34; "The Ku-Klux Committee," *Yorkville Enquirer*, Yorkville, SC (July 27, 1871); Simkins, "The Ku Klux Klan in South Carolina," 640–41; Trelease, *White Terror*, 374–75; United States Congress, *Report of the Joint Select Committee*, Vol. V, 1463–87, especially 1470; West, *The Reconstruction Ku Klux Klan in York County, South Carolina*, 84–86; Zuczek, "The Federal Government's Attack on the Ku Klux Klan: A Reassessment," 54; Zuczek, *State of Rebellion*, 97.

15. "The Barry-Wallace Difficulty," *Yorkville Enquirer*, Yorkville, SC (August 3, 1871); Trelease, *White Terror*, 375; United States Congress, *Report of the Joint Select Committee*, Vol. III, 1533–34; West, *The Reconstruction Ku Klux Klan in York County, South Carolina*, 84–86.

16. "Street Affray," *Yorkville Enquirer*, Yorkville, SC (July 27, 1871); Trelease, *White Terror*, 375–76; United States Congress, *Report of the Joint Select Committee*, Vol. III, 1533–34; West, *The Reconstruction Ku Klux Klan in York County, South Carolina*, 86.

17. Quoted in United States Congress, *Report of the Joint Select Committee*, Vol. III, 1600. See also, Trelease, *White Terror*, 369–71; Wade, *The Fiery Cross*, 95; West, *The Reconstruction Ku Klux Klan in York County, South Carolina*, 84–85; Zuczek, *State of Rebellion*, 94–97.

18. Horn, *Invisible Empire*, 234–35; "Report of the Grand Jury," *Yorkville Enquirer*, Yorkville, SC (October 5, 1871); Everette Swinney, *Suppressing the Ku Klux Klan: The Enforcement of the Reconstruction Amendments, 1870–1877* (New York: Garland, 1987), 212–13; Trelease, *White Terror*, 376–77, 401–3; United States Congress, *Report of the Joint Select Committee*, Vol. III, 1600–4; Wade, *The Fiery Cross*, 99–100; West, *The Reconstruction Ku Klux Klan in York County, South Carolina*, 87–88; Lou Falkner Williams, *The Great South Carolina Ku Klux Klan Trials, 1871–1872* (Athens: University of Georgia Press, 1996), 45; Zuczek, *State of Rebellion*, 97–99.

19. Horn, *Invisible Empire*, 234; Simkins, "The Ku Klux Klan in South Carolina," 641; Trelease, *White Terror*, 402–03; Wade, *The Fiery Cross*, 99–100; West, *The Reconstruction Ku Klux Klan in York County, South Carolina*, 86; Williams, "The South Carolina Ku Klux Klan Trials and Enforcement of Federal Civil Rights, 1871–1872," 48–50.

20. Everitt, "1871 War on Terror," 31; Hall, "Political Power and Constitutional Legitimacy," 925–26; Robert Selph Henry, *The Story of Reconstruction* (New York: Konecky & Konecky, 1999), 449; Horn, *Invisible Empire*, 235–36; Kaczorowski, "Federal Enforcement of Civil Rights During the First Reconstruction," 157–58; Murphy, *The Nation Reunited*, 98–99; Simkins and Woody, *South Carolina During Reconstruction*, 462–63; Alrutheus Ambush Taylor, *The Negro in South Carolina During*

Reconstruction (Washington, D.C.: The Association for the Study of Negro Life and History, Inc., 1924), 201; Trelease, *White Terror*, 403; United States Congress, *Report of the Joint Select Committee*, Vol. III, 1602; Wade, *The Fiery Cross*, 99–100; West, *The Reconstruction Ku Klux Klan in York County, South Carolina*, 89; Williams, *The Great South Carolina Ku Klux Klan Trials*, 46–47; Zuczek, *State of Rebellion*, 98.

21. Blair, "The Use of Military Force to Protect the Gains of Reconstruction," 396; Everitt, "1871 War on Terror," 31; Hall, "Political Power and Constitutional Legitimacy," 925–26; John Hope Franklin, *Reconstruction After the Civil War*, 2d. ed. (Chicago: The University of Chicago Press, 1961), 164–65; Henry, *The Story of Reconstruction*, 449; Murphy, *The Nation Reunited*, 99; Trelease, *White Terror*, 403; Wade, *The Fiery Cross*, 100; West, *The Reconstruction Ku Klux Klan in York County, South Carolina*, 88–90; Williams, *The Great South Carolina Ku Klux Klan Trials*, 46–47; Zuczek, *State of Rebellion*, 98.

22. "Arrests of Citizens," *Yorkville Enquirer*, Yorkville, SC (October 26, 1871); Trelease, *White Terror*, 405; West, *The Reconstruction Ku Klux Klan in York County, South Carolina*, 89–90; Williams, *The Great South Carolina Ku Klux Klan Trials*, 47–48.

23. "Arrests of Citizens," *Yorkville Enquirer*, Yorkville, SC (October 26, 1871); Trelease, *White Terror*, 405; West, *The Reconstruction Ku Klux Klan in York County, South Carolina*, 90–96.

24. Quoted in "Arrests of Citizens," *Yorkville Enquirer*, Yorkville, SC (October 26, 1871). See also, Everitt, "1871 War on Terror," 31–32; Simkins, "The Ku Klux Klan in South Carolina," 641–42; Simkins and Woody, *South Carolina During Reconstruction*, 463; "The Situation," *Yorkville Enquirer*, Yorkville, SC (November 2, 1871); Wade, *The Fiery Cross*, 100–1; West, *The Reconstruction Ku Klux Klan in York County, South Carolina*, 90–96; Williams, *The Great South Carolina Ku Klux Klan Trials*, 47–48; Zuczek, *State of Rebellion*, 98–99.

25. Quoted in "Arrests of Citizens," *Yorkville Enquirer*, Yorkville, SC (October 26, 1871). See also, Foner, *Reconstruction: America's Unfinished Revolution*, 434; Trelease, *White Terror*, 404–7; Wade, *The Fiery Cross*, 101.

26. Quoted in Brown, *A City Without Cobwebs*, 149–50. For more on nocturnal arrests or the lack thereof, see also, Horn, *Invisible Empire*, 238–39; Simkins, "The Ku Klux Klan in South Carolina," 641–42; Taylor, *The Negro in South Carolina During Reconstruction*, 202.

27. Quoted in Louise Pettus, "Samuel B. Hall & Maj. Lewis Merrill," *The Quarterly* (Rock Hill, SC: York County Genealogical and Historical Society, 1997), n.p. See also, Horn, *Invisible Empire*, 238–39; Simkins, "The Ku Klux Klan in South Carolina," 641–42.

28. Quoted in United States Congress, *Report of the Joint Select Committee*, Vol. III, 1602–3. See also, Trelease, *White Terror*, 401–3; West, *The Reconstruction Ku Klux Klan in York County, South Carolina*, 89–96; Williams, *The Great South Carolina Ku Klux Klan Trials*, 48–49; Zuczek, *State of Rebellion*, 98–99.

29. Quoted in Trelease, *White Terror*, 403–4. See also, West, *The Reconstruction Ku Klux Klan in York County, South Carolina*, 90–96; Williams, *The Great South Carolina Ku Klux Klan Trials*, 48–49; Zuczek, *State of Rebellion*, 98–99.

30. Everitt, "1871 War on Terror," 32; Post, "A Carpetbagger in South Carolina," 45–46; Wade, *The Fiery Cross*, 101–2; Williams, *The Great South Carolina Ku Klux Klan Trials*, 48–49.

31. Everitt, "1871 War on Terror," 32; Kaczorowski, "Federal Enforcement of Civil Rights During the First Reconstruction," 175–76; Trelease, *White Terror*, 401–3; United States Congress, *Report of the Joint Select Committee*, Vol. III, 1605; Williams, *The Great South Carolina Ku Klux Klan Trials*, 48–49.

32. Wade, *The Fiery Cross*, 102–3; West, *The Reconstruction Ku Klux Klan in York County, South Carolina*, 97; Williams, *The Great South Carolina Ku Klux Klan Trials*, 48–49; Zuczek, "The Federal Government's Attack on the Ku Klux Klan: A Reassessment," 56; Zuczek, *State of Rebellion*, 99–100.

33. Holt, *Black Over White*, 30–35; Kaczorowski, "Federal Enforcement of Civil Rights During the First Reconstruction," 164–65; Singletary, "The Negro Militia During Radical Reconstruction," 181–86; Taylor, *The Negro in South Carolina During Reconstruction*, 202–3.

34. Amos T. Akerman to William W. Belknap, January 8, 1872, in Merrill Military Files, M.103.C.B.1863 (Record Group 94, National Archives & Records Administration); Merrill Military Files, RG 94; Sefton, *The United States Army and Reconstruction, 1865–1877*, 226; Shapiro, "The Ku Klux Klan During Reconstruction: The South Carolina Episode," 46; Williams, *The Great South Carolina Ku Klux Klan Trials*, 49–50.

7

"AS FAR AS I CAN LEARN, THE PROSECUTING LAWYERS HAVE MANAGED THE BUSINESS ABLY"

The federal government's prosecution of the South Carolina Ku Klux Klan commenced in the Fourth Federal Circuit Court, which included South Carolina, in Columbia during the November 1871 term. It was immediately clear to everyone that the Klan trials would judge not only the guilt of the defendants in individual cases but they would serve, in the words of one commentator, as "a forum of constitutional experimentation in the service of political objectives." The political objectives included the Grant administration's attempt to reestablish law and order in a Southern state where extralegal forces—the KKK—had circumvented legal forces commanded by the Republican-controlled state government. The legal issues would be decided by the court's interpretation of the Enforcement Act of 1870, which guaranteed the political rights of freedmen under the new Fourteenth and Fifteenth Amendments, and the Ku Klux Klan Act of 1871, which authorized the president to suspend the writ of habeas corpus.[1]

Attorney General Amos T. Akerman and federal soldiers stood by to assist as necessary, but responsibility for trying the cases fell on the shoulders of two seasoned attorneys, David T. Corbin and Daniel H. Chamberlain. Corbin served as the U.S. attorney for South Carolina, a position he had held since 1867. Born and bred in the North, Corbin was another hated carpetbagger that populated the state's government during Reconstruction, although he was not as objectionable to Southerners as most of his colleagues. At least one source suggested that Corbin enjoyed a "reputation of being one of the most conservative and fair of the Republican Party." He began his career practicing law during the antebellum years. Similar to Akerman, Corbin was a graduate of Dartmouth College but, unlike the attorney general, he sided with the Union during the Civil War. After the war, he came to South Carolina as a Freedmen's Bureau agent. Corbin later served in the state senate, as a delegate to the 1868 constitutional convention, and as a commissioner to revise the state statutes. He was intimately familiar with South Carolina's tortured history of race relations and its strong antipathy toward federal authority.

Chamberlain, too, was well versed in legal and political matters in South Carolina. A native of Massachusetts and an abolitionist early in his life, he graduated from Yale University and attended Harvard Law School until he left to serve as an officer in the Fifth Massachusetts Cavalry, a black regiment, during the war. He headed south to settle the affairs of a friend after Appomattox but he stayed in South Carolina to try his hand at cotton planting. Disappointed when he did not amass a fortune, Chamberlain turned to politics and found his niche. His vigorous, impressive oratory at the state constitutional convention brought him to the attention of influential Republicans. He won election as attorney general in 1868 and later would serve as the last Reconstruction governor before Wade Hampton and the Democrats "redeemed" the state in the 1876 election.[2]

As they prepared their cases, Corbin and Chamberlain faced two distinct challenges. The obvious challenge was the enormous task of combing through the affidavits, transcripts, and piles of notes that Major Merrill had accumulated during his investigation. Locating and preparing witnesses, identifying relevant documents, and presenting the material in an easily understandable format for the grand jury would prove to be formidable chore but not impossible. The far more difficult challenge of developing and implementing a successful strategy for applying federal law to state-level crimes would make or break the prosecution's case.

During the eighty-two-year history of the nation under the U.S. Constitution—from 1789 until 1871—the federal courts had exercised minimal jurisdiction, hearing few cases apart from technical matters involving federal treaties, tariffs, and contract disputes. Prior to passage of the Fourteenth and Fifteenth Amendments, an aggrieved party could not seek redress in a federal court if a state violated his constitutional rights. Principles of federalism articulated in the landmark case of *Barron v. Baltimore* indicated that Bill of Rights protections applied only to the actions of the federal government. The Civil War amendments changed this constitutional scheme, but the idea of federal courts exercising concurrent, overlapping jurisdiction with state courts was such a novel concept that no one knew how federal judges would rule if their jurisdictional authority were questioned by defense attorneys in criminal cases.

Figure 7.1. South Carolina attorney general Daniel H. Chamberlain, pictured here, a carpetbagger who later served as governor, prosecuted the Ku Klux Klan cases in federal court along with U.S. attorney David T. Corbin.
South Caroliniana Library, University of South Carolina, Columbia

Aside from the jurisdictional issues, Corbin and Chamberlain recognized that a winning strategy could not ignore race. Federal courts could draw potential jurors from a larger pool than the state courts, but in light of the widespread power of the Ku Klux Klan in the Southern states, the impartiality of any white juror, no matter where he resided, would be suspect. Merrill's list of prosecution witnesses included a substantial number of blacks who had been victimized by the nightriders. Historically, the testimony of black men against white men in Southern courts had been problematic. In some cases, blacks were not allowed to testify against whites. Even when their testimony was permitted, juries tended to view blacks as inherently inferior to whites. Consequently, white jurors seldom believed testimony offered by blacks, or if they believed it, they afforded it little weight in their deliberations. If the prosecutors hoped to win the case, seating black jurors would be a crucial factor in their strategy.[3]

The cases were scheduled to be heard by two federal judges, Hugh Lennox Bond, a circuit judge of the Fourth Federal Circuit, and George Seabrook Bryan, the federal district judge for South Carolina. Born in Baltimore, Maryland, in late 1828, Bond graduated from New York University. He spent much of his career pursuing the dual goals of advancing in politics and in the legal profession. Along with Henry Winter Davis, he was a founding member of the Maryland Republican Party. Throughout his career, he had demonstrated a strong commitment to civil and political rights for blacks tempered by a pragmatic streak that prevented him from being labeled a "Radical Republican," although he appeared to embrace most of the Radical Republican ideology of the time.

In 1861, he demonstrated genuine moral and physical courage while serving as a judge on the Baltimore County Criminal Court by charging a grand jury to return an indictment against a mob of Confederate sympathizers that attacked soldiers of the Sixth Massachusetts Regiment as they marched through the city. Despite his predilection for Republican politics, it would be a mistake to assume that Bond was a Republican hack. He could be, and often was, fiercely independent. In an age when judges frequently mixed politics with legal analysis and seldom distinguished the two, Bond insisted on adhering to a strict constructionist interpretation of the law whenever possible, even if it went against his political affiliation. As a judge in a conservative border state during the Civil War, the jurist demonstrated his ability to balance the state rights sensibilities of pro-Confederate Marylanders with the need to preserve law and order under the federal Constitution.

In April 1870, President Grant appointed the forty-one-year-old judge to the federal bench despite resistance from the Congress. The U.S.

Senate confirmed the appointment by a slim margin of only seven votes. If any judge would be sensitive to the plight of KKK victims, Judge Bond would be the one. At the same time, his strict constructionist tendencies suggested that broad expansion of federal power under new and mostly untested constitutional amendments and federal statutes would not be a foregone conclusion. Corbin and Chamberlain would have to craft persuasive arguments grounded in recognized, well-worn constitutional jurisprudence to convince Judge Bond of the need for increased federal authority over issues usually confined to the province of the states.[4]

He was joined on the bench by Judge George Seabrook Bryan. In many ways, Judge Bryan was a polar opposite of the younger and more vigorous Judge Bond. A Whig-turned-Democrat and former slaveowner, Bryan was appointed to the federal district court by President Andrew Johnson in February 1866. Born in Charleston on May 22, 1809, he had lived among the South Carolina elite all of his life. His kinship ties were strong, as were his allegiance to the state's first families and his belief in the primacy of local customs and traditions. During his tenure on the federal court, he clashed with the Union military commander in Charleston, General Daniel Sickles, when Bryan demanded that the civil court be reconvened and trials by jury supplant military tribunals operating under martial law. Sickles resisted, so Bryan contacted President Johnson, who already was exhibiting decidedly pro-Southern proclivities, for assistance. Although he did not approve of the KKK's violent methods, Judge Bryan was unquestionably pro-Southern. He could be counted on to require clear evidence of guilt before he would rule in favor of the federal government. Moreover, he shared Judge Bond's reluctance to engage in novel constitutional interpretation.

Despite their shared adherence to strict constructionism, it was apparent that the two judges would not agree on many matters of judicial style, temperament, and courtroom management. Bond was an extrovert who was not above bullying his brethren now and again. Bryan was hardly a fragile figure, but he preferred thoughtful, contemplative repose to the bare-knuckle wheeling and dealing endemic to partisan politics. Recognizing that the Democrats were lobbying Bryan to see things their way with promises of future high office, Bond confronted his fellow judge early in the proceedings. As Bond later described the encounter in a letter to his wife, Anna, he "went to [Bryan] the other day & frightened him to death. I stormed at him & told him, if he wanted his salary increased (you know he is always talking about that) he had just better [not] keep the court sitting doing nothing but posing about the smallest matter in the world day after day." Bond succeeded in venting his frustration, but he did not change the judge's behavior. "I am in a peck of trouble with old Bryan. The democrats have got hold of him—visit him in crowds & persuade him to be a stick between our legs at every step." Elsewhere, he confided in Anna, "I am sick of him & altogether disgusted & he is with me."[5]

The animosity between the two judges boded well for the defense. Conservative South Carolina Democrats recognized an opportunity to undermine Republican political power in the state as well as prevent an expansion of federal jurisdiction that would inevitably result from victories in the Ku Klux Klan cases. Although his affiliation with the Klan has been subject to debate, leading South Carolinian Wade Hampton led his fellow Democrats on a quest to secure the best possible defense counsel. He headed a legal defense fund that eventually collected $10,000, a sizable sum, and employed two able lawyers, both former attorneys general of the United States, to represent the defendants.[6]

Former U.S. senator Reverdy Johnson was one of the most prominent constitutional scholars of his day. Already seventy-five years old at the start of the Klan trials, his long career stretched back to 1815, when he began practicing law with some of the most esteemed lawyers of the Maryland bar, including Luther Martin, William Pinkney, and Roger B. Taney. The latter association would prove to be especially propitious. Four decades after his initial contact with Taney, Johnson represented the slaveowner in *Dred Scott v. Sanford*, the infamous case where the U.S. Supreme Court held that slaves were property and not entitled to protection under the Constitution. Taney, Johnson's former colleague, was serving as Chief Justice of the U.S. Supreme Court when he penned the majority opinion in arguably the worst decision—certainly among the most controversial—in American constitutional history. In a passage referring to slaves, Taney explained that the "question before us is, whether the class of persons described in the plea in abatement compose a portion of this people, and are constituent members of this sovereignty? We think they are not, and that they are not included, and were not intended to be included, under the word 'citizens' in the Constitution, and can therefore claim none of the rights and privileges which that instrument provides for and secures to citizens of the United States." If Taney has been subject to the opprobrium of history, Reverdy Johnson was not far behind. Although an attorney need not share his client's legal, political, or moral views, neither is he required to represent a client that espouses views he finds morally repugnant. Johnson's zealous defense of the Southern cause in numerous cases before and after the war suggests that he subscribed to the widely held opinion that blacks were inferior to whites and therefore deserving of lesser legal protections.[7]

Between his admission to the Maryland bar and his participation in *Dred Scott*, Johnson alternated between practicing law and holding political office. From 1821 until 1825, he served in the Maryland State Senate. He was a U.S. senator representing Maryland as a Whig from 1845 through 1849, when he resigned his seat to serve as President Zachary Taylor's attorney general. After Taylor's death, Johnson resigned his post and returned to his law practice. Personally opposed to secession, he held a variety of positions for the federal government during the Civil War. In 1863, he was returned to the U.S. Senate representing Maryland, a position he held until he resigned in July 1868 to serve as the U.S. minister to England. In that role, he negotiated the Johnson-Clarendon Treaty that settled disputes arising out of the Civil War. When the Senate refused to ratify the treaty and Ulysses S. Grant became president, Johnson returned home and resumed his law practice.

For all intents and purposes, this illustrious septuagenarian had retired from public life when Southern Democrats approached him about representing the defendants in the South Carolina KKK trials. A proponent of limited federal authority under the U.S. Constitution, Johnson believed that the Civil War amendments and the Enforcements Acts passed by Congress represented a genuine threat to the reserved powers of the states under the Tenth Amendment. He was aghast at President Grant's decision to suspend the writ of habeas corpus. In his reading of the Constitution, the writ could be suspended only when a rebellion existed. Like most Democrats, Johnson did not believe that the alleged activities of the Ku Klux Klan, assuming they had occurred in the first place, constituted a "rebellion." He held no special affinity for the individual defendants, but he was anxious to use the federal courts as a mechanism for restoring what he viewed as the proper constitutional balance of power between the federal government and the states.[8]

His co-counsel was Henry Stanbery, an Ohio Democrat known as a vehement critic of federal Reconstruction policy. Although not as well known as Johnson, Stanbery was an accomplished advocate in his own right. According to commentator David Miller DeWitt, "Stanbery was a remarkably handsome man of imposing presence. As a lawyer he stood in the front rank of his profession, and he carried his preeminence with dignity and grace. He possessed a persuasive manner, his voice was musical, and his elocution finished." Similar to Johnson, the sixty-eight-year-old Stanbery had enjoyed a stellar career—in his case stretching back almost half a

Figure 7.2.   Former Maryland Democratic senator Reverdy Johnson, a well-known constitutional lawyer, headed the defense team in the Ku Klux Klan trials.
Picture History

century. Born in New York City in 1803, he graduated from Washington College and gained admission to the bar in 1824. He served as Ohio's first attorney general after the position was created in 1846, and four years later became a delegate to the Ohio constitutional convention. After he left the Ohio attorney general's office in 1851, Stanbery spent the next fifteen years in private legal practice. He rose to national prominence when President

Andrew Johnson nominated him for a seat on the U.S. Supreme Court. The nomination failed to win Senate confirmation, but President Johnson secured the requisite votes to have his friend installed as U.S. attorney general. Two years later, Stanbery resigned to head Johnson's defense team when the president was impeached. He shared Johnson's belief that the U.S. Constitution was a document limiting federal authority in favor of the states, and he saw the Ku Klux Klan trials as a convenient forum from which to propound his constitutional philosophy.[9]

With this accomplished cast of characters, the cases promised high drama. On November 28, 1871, the first day of the trial, attorneys, judges, and newspaper reporters squeezed into the state capitol in hopes of witnessing the proceedings. Blacks and whites milled about in the hallways, awaiting their turn in the witness chair.

Demonstrating its typical biases against freedmen, the Democratic press disparaged "lazy and idle negroes who were paid and clothed at government expense" to testify as witnesses to Klan abuses. As for the larger legal and political issues, the *Charleston Daily Courier* observed that the "Constitution of the United States is on trial. In the history of this country no questions more important have ever arisen or been presented to a judicial tribunal for adjudication than are those which will arise in the trials now about to take place." Although the observation was exaggerated, it reflected the concern shared by Democrats and Republicans alike that the verdicts handed down in the cases would shape federal-state relations for years to come.[10]

Judge Bond later explained his thinking as he surveyed the throngs stuffed into the courtroom gallery and spilling into the corridors. "I fear that we will not be able to control the court, tempers run very high, and the populace is unsettled." He was already perturbed at Judge Bryan's failure to locate a sufficient number of potential jurors—a "venire," in legal parlance—to hear the cases. Internal Revenue agents had been directed to compile a list of one hundred potential jurors from each district, but white citizens had failed to heed the summons. Perhaps they feared perjuring themselves if they were forced to swear they had never participated in Klan activities. Alternatively, they may have feared the scrutiny they would receive from friends and neighbors if they sat in judgment of their peers. Whatever the reason, the absence of a requisite number of men to constitute a venire presented the first major obstacle to trying the Klan.[11]

The attorneys were not naïve; they knew the makeup of the jury would be a crucial factor in determining the outcome of the cases. If they could win this round, the rest of the case would be promising. To no one's surprise, prosecutor David Corbin rose from his seat and challenged the venire as "irregularly" selected, citing the legal requirement that jurors' names must be drawn in the presence of the clerk of court and the marshal. Because the clerk had allowed a child to draw the names in the absence of the marshal, the results were tainted. Defense attorney Reverdy Johnson opposed Corbin's motion, arguing that this anomaly amounted to nothing more than a technical deficiency that ought not to affect the trial. After the lawyers traded barbs, Corbin expressed his concern that an irregularly drawn jury might provide grounds for an appeal if the defendants were convicted. Johnson offered to waive all objections regarding the manner in which the jury was selected. After considering the defense attorney's offer, the next day Corbin agreed to withdraw his challenge.

The compromise did not resolve all contentious issues about the venire. Johnson proposed that the selection process should be limited to residents of the counties in which the Klan was most active—that is, the Piedmont region—because those residents were most affected by the trials and they were the defendants' peers. Although he did not say it, Johnson probably thought that jurors from the Upcountry counties would be more hesitant to convict their friends and neighbors. Recognizing this strategy as a ploy to stack the jury, the prosecution team objected, suggesting instead that jurors hail from all districts throughout the state. With Bryan's acquiescence, Judge Bond agreed with the prosecution; he dispatched marshals to compile additional names from each district of the state.

Drawing names for the venire from across the state provided a distinct advantage to the prosecution. Because many whites again refused to appear in response to the jury summons, two-thirds of the people who appeared for service on the petit, or trial, jury were black. The twenty-one-member grand jury included fifteen blacks. The foreman, Benjamin K. Jackson, was white, but he was a Republican and presumably unsympathetic to the Klan.

Attorneys in Southern courts traditionally resisted racially mixed juries; they considered it beneath their dignity and social position to address blacks in open court. Similarly, white jurors objected to sharing physical proximity and social status with blacks in the jury box. Judge Bond's decision to allow blacks to serve on the venire and his ruling that limited the defense team's peremptory challenges to ten—which ensured that Johnson and Stanbery could not remove all blacks from the jury—served notice that the defendants would be judged by a race of people they had victimized.[12]

After the jury was selected, the prosecution assumed the burden of proof in presenting a case against the Klansmen. Working with Amos T. Akerman, Corbin and Chamberlain had fashioned a novel, multifaceted constitutional argument reflecting the attorney general's penchant for legal experimentation. First, they contended that although the Bill of Rights in the U.S. Constitution historically applied only to the federal government, the Fourteenth Amendment had altered the traditional arrangement of federalism. Because the Fourteenth Amendment specifically referred to states in language similar to the Fifth Amendment's constitutional protections against actions undertaken by the federal government, the intent was to apply, or "incorporate," Bill of Rights protections to state action through the Fourteenth Amendment. In short, if the prosecution could demonstrate that the Klan had, in fact, caused harm to citizens of any color or partisan stripe, the individual defendants were guilty of violating federal law.

Second, Corbin and Chamberlain argued that "state action," a necessary component of the prosecution's case, should be broadly interpreted. Although most Klansmen were not acting officially as members of state government when they perpetrated their crimes, the prosecutors contended that the defendants' actions were tantamount to acting under the color of state law. South Carolina law enforcement officers and local trial judges refused to enforce the law and protect freedmen when the Klan struck, in effect lending the imprimatur of the state to the Klan.

Finally, Corbin and Chamberlain argued that the Fifteenth Amendment guaranteed all male citizens of suitable age, of whatever race, the right to vote. The amendment expressly prohibited the denial or abrogation of voting rights "by the United States or by any State." If the Klan prevented blacks from voting through threats and intimidation, this action clearly violated the Fifteenth Amendment and brought the offenders under the jurisdiction of the federal courts. Unlike their first two arguments, using the Fifteenth Amendment as grounds for trying the Klansmen did not require an expansive interpretation of the Constitution.[13]

To no one's surprise, Johnson and Stanbery opposed a broad interpretation of the Fourteenth and Fifteenth Amendments as well as the Enforcement Acts. The argument that the Fourteenth Amendment nationalized the Bill of Rights was especially novel. If such an expansive interpretation were adopted by the court, it would fundamentally alter well-established principles of federalism that had governed the republic since its inception. As for the definition of "state action," the defense contended that a broad interpretation would make a state liable for innumerable actions by private citizens far beyond what any state could reasonably be expected to control. As for the protection of voting rights in the Fifteenth Amendment, it should be limited to specific instances where the federal or state governments specifically and unequivocally interfered with voting. Applying the amendment to

instances when a group of private defendants allegedly engaged in violent
actions away from the ballot box was an unconscionable expansion of federal power.[14]

The first KKK case testing these theories was *United States v. Allen
Crosby*, which involved several alleged Klansmen that had terrorized a black
family. The facts were all-too-typical of Klan outrages in the South Carolina Upcountry. Amzi Rainey, a black militiaman described as a "most respectable mulatto" with "an excellent character," awoke in the middle of
the night to find six rowdy Klansmen at his door. Unlike some freedmen—
Jim Williams and Elias Hill, for example—Amzi Rainey was not a rabble-
rouser, nor had he threatened violence toward the white community. His
offense was his public support of U.S. Congressman Alexander S. Wallace—
the same "Buttermilk" Wallace involved in the incident at Rawlinson's hotel during the congressional subcommittee's visit to Yorkville during the
summer of 1871. In addition to his affinity for Congressman Wallace,
Rainey was known to be a Republican, as were virtually all politically active Southern blacks.

To punish the freedman's audacity, masked nightriders herded Rainey's
family into the yard. Brandishing guns and shouting epithets, the offenders
savagely beat the man's wife while she cradled a baby in her arms. An unknown number of men raped his daughter in full view of the family. When
another of Rainey's daughters, a small child, begged, "please don't kill my
pappy," a Klansman shot the little girl in the forehead, although luckily for
the family it was only a glancing blow. She survived.

Rainey survived as well, but he paid a high price. The mob dragged
him into the woods where they beat and stabbed him with knives. They
probably would have killed him had he not pleaded for his life, promising
never again to support the Republican Party. In possession of his life, if not
his dignity, Rainey recovered sufficiently to complain about the assaults and
rape to local law enforcement officers, an act of immense bravery in that
time and place. He even identified one assailant as Allen Crosby, a white
man he knew to be a KKK member. Despite the credibility and specificity
of Rainey's complaint, the local sheriff took no action to bring the perpetrators to justice. Under the circumstances where local and state officials allowed lawlessness to reign supreme and refused to intervene, *Crosby* was a
promising case to test whether the court would accept the prosecution's expansive interpretation of the U.S. Constitution.[15]

Corbin and Chamberlain filed an eleven-count indictment arguing
that Crosby and his codefendants had violated the Enforcement Act of 1870
by intimidating Rainey, thereby interfering with his right to vote under the

Fifteenth Amendment. In addition, the prosecutors contended that the new statutes and constitutional amendments enacted after the Civil War imposed an obligation on the federal government to protect its citizens. Instead of viewing the Constitution as a list of actions the federal government could not perform—the notion of "civil liberties" protecting citizens from government oppression—this new perspective reframed the Constitution as a document providing positive civil and political rights—that is, actions the federal government must perform on behalf of its citizens. Among the rights secured by this interpretation included the right to vote, the right to enjoy a variety of privileges and immunities associated with citizenship, and the right to be free from unreasonable searches and seizures in one's home. This last point depended on the incorporation of the Fourth Amendment protection against unreasonable searches and seizures through the Fourteenth Amendment and applied to the states. Almost as an afterthought, the indictment charged the defendants with burglarizing Rainey's house in the process of denying him his constitutional rights.[16]

The defense moved to quash all counts of the indictment, arguing that the prosecutors' novel interpretations of the Constitution defied long-standing conventions of legal construction. They met with a receptive audience. The judges did not agree with each other on many points of law, but both Bond and Bryan were philosophically predisposed to read the Constitution strictly. Acknowledging that Congress possessed authority under the Fourteenth and Fifteenth Amendments to punish defendants who harmed blacks' voting rights in specific instances, the judges refused to rule that this acknowledgment necessarily meant that the U.S. Constitution guaranteed the right to vote in instances where only general acts of violence were alleged. The judges also rejected the idea that the Fourth Amendment was incorporated through the Fourteenth Amendment and applied to the states. The right against unreasonable searches and seizures, Judge Bond explained, "is not derived from the constitution, but it existed long before the adoption of the constitution, at common law."[17]

The loss of their novel constitutional arguments dealt a severe blow to the prosecution, but they were not beaten. Two counts of the indictment—the charge of a general conspiracy and the charge of a conspiracy to harm Rainey because he had voted in a congressional election—survived the motion to quash. Judge Bond explained that congressional authority to protect voters who wished to participate in federal elections existed even before the Reconstruction amendments and statutes were enacted. The burglary charge split the court, with Bryan reluctant to allow ordinary state crimes to fall under the purview of the federal judiciary. Bond disagreed; he entertained the

possibility that a federal burglary crime involved a violation of civil rights—
a position curiously at odds with his strict constructionist views in other areas of constitutional law.

Unfortunately for Amzi Rainey, the case was never tried. The KKK
trials were broader than the interests of individual Klansmen and their victims, which meant that individual litigants might be denied a day in court
in pursuit of a larger purpose. Both the prosecution and defense were
searching for a test case to be certified to the U.S. Supreme Court where
the outcome could establish clear, controlling legal precedent for years, perhaps decades, to come. *Crosby* was a poor vehicle for each side. Because so
many of their expansive constitutional arguments had been quashed,
Corbin and Chamberlain did not believe that *Crosby* was an appropriate
case to send up to the high court. It simply did not provide a forum for testing new legal remedies available under federal law. Confident that the
Supreme Court would stick closely to precedent and reject fanciful new
constitutional theories, the defense also was anxious to have a case certified.
The alternative was to spend months, perhaps years, slogging through
dozens of cases, interviewing hundreds of witnesses, and arguing minor,
technical points of law that would not get at the central federalism issue
lurking at the heart of the Ku Klux Klan prosecutions.

With each side anxious to dispose of *Crosby*, a compromise was soon
worked out. During a lengthy debate about whether each defendant was
entitled to ten peremptory challenges to prospective jurors for each individual defendant or whether the ten challenges applied to the entire group
of defendants, Corbin severed one case—the charges filed against Sherod
Childers—from Allen Crosby's case. Judge Bond once again disagreed with
Judge Bryan, preferring the ten peremptory challenges to apply to the entire group while Bryan supported the alternative. Bond ultimately went
along with Bryan's view so the cases would not be mired in a controversy
over a relatively minor, ancillary issue. In the same spirit of compromise,
Judge Bond also persuaded the defendants Crosby and Childers to plead
guilty to what amounted to lesser charges than those originally filed. The
guilty pleas carried a penalty of eighteen months in federal prison and a
$100 fine, although Childers later received a presidential pardon.[18]

With Amzi Rainey's complaint off the docket, the prosecution could
then turn its attention to *United States v. James W. Avery*, a more promising
case for certification to the U.S. Supreme Court. Because it included conspiracy and murder charges filed against the defendant, Major James W. Avery, for his part in planning and executing the plot against Jim Williams, the
black militia captain hanged on the night of March 6, 1871, the case raised

the important factual and legal issues that both sides wanted the Supreme Court to decide. Avery and his co-conspirator, J. Rufus Bratton, had fled to London, a city in Ontario, Canada, when federal troops rounded up the suspects in October, but the case would proceed without them.

Major Merrill had identified the named defendant, a well-to-do merchant, as the leading Klansman in the Piedmont region. Avery undoubtedly ordered most, if not all, of the nighttime raids against freedmen during the height of the KKK's York County reign of terror in 1870–1871. If Avery directed strategy, acting as a kind of strategic general officer, Bratton was his trusted field commander, directing ground operations. It was little wonder that the two men fled the country when the arrests commenced in October 1871. They were the type of defendants who evinced the "deep criminality" Akerman had targeted for prosecution.[19]

When *Avery* was certified in the U.S. Supreme Court, it raised two issues requiring clarification. First, an issue arose whether the Second Amendment, which guarantees the right to bear arms, was incorporated through the Fourteenth Amendment and applied to the states. Second, the question of whether the federal courts could impose capital punishment in civil rights cases was at issue. In preparing the case, Corbin included an indictment for conspiracy under the first Enforcement Act. He added a murder charge as well, although it would be difficult to prove because Avery was absent from the scene when Jim Williams was lynched.

Unfortunately for the prosecutors, in March 1872, the Supreme Court ruled that it lacked jurisdiction to hear the case on its merits because the lower federal courts possessed discretion in determining whether to quash parts of an indictment. Therefore, the issues certified to the U.S. Supreme Court were more appropriately decided by the circuit court. Given the difference of opinion between Bond and Bryan in *Avery*, Corbin and Chamberlain were not confident that the circuit court could decide the salient issues. Even worse from the prosecutors' perspective, the high court's ruling provided no guidance on resolving the novel constitutional questions raised in the indictment. The practical effect of the Supreme Court's determination that it lacked jurisdiction was to ignore the incorporation issues, a blow to the prosecution's argument for expanding federal constitutional authority.[20]

Corbin and Chamberlain had no choice but to press on, regardless of the setback. With *Crosby* and *Avery* sidetracked by unresolved legal issues, the first KKK case tried in the circuit court during the November 1871 session was styled *United States v. Robert Hayes Mitchell*. The matter grew out of the same fact setting involved in *Avery*, namely the Jim Williams murder. According to the indictment, the defendant was part of the large group of Klansmen that participated in the infamous raid and lynching. Testimony indicated that the defendant was not among the dozen men who accompanied Dr. Bratton in reconnoitering the property and hanging Jim Williams, but Mitchell participated with the mob and therefore was a co-conspirator.

Despite the judges' reluctance to accept new constitutional interpretations, Corbin reiterated his incorporation argument. It was to no avail. Bond and Bryan were as unsympathetic as ever. Without incorporation in their arsenal, the prosecutors were forced to turn their attention to the dual conspiracy charges, a far more promising avenue than relying on constitutional grounds. To prove the first charge, a general conspiracy, the prosecution had to demonstrate that a group of men acting under the banner of the Ku Klux Klan knowingly sought to hinder blacks from voting, and the defendant was part of this group. On the second charge, the prosecution was required to show that Mitchell and the Klan specifically set out to harm Jim Williams because he had exercised his right to vote on a prior occasion.

At this point, Major Merrill's diligence in uncovering the workings of the KKK and documenting its goals and activities proved to be invaluable. Corbin and Chamberlain produced a copy of the Ku Klux Klan constitution and bylaws to show that the organization existed in the South Carolina Upcountry. Although the Klan was protected by its shadowy workings and strict oath of secrecy, after a written version of the constitution and by-laws fell into the prosecutors' hands, the group's existence and purposes were difficult to deny. The documents made it plain that "No person of color shall be admitted into this order." Anyone who failed to carry out his duties as a Klansman or violated the oath of secrecy "shall meet the fearful penalty and traitor's doom, which is Death! Death! Death!" A series of eyewitnesses and affidavits from former Klansmen and victimized freedmen unequivocally demonstrated the existence of a conspiracy.[21]

The prosecution paraded witnesses before the court to show that the defendant was a member of the Klan and had been one of the seventy masked men assembled on horseback at the Briar Patch muster ground on Howell Mill Road west of Yorkville on the night in question. The witnesses agreed, however, that Mitchell hid in the woods while Bratton and a smaller group of Klansmen routed Jim Williams from his house, threw a rope around his neck, lynched him to a nearby tree limb, and left a sign around his neck, "Jim Williams on his big muster."

Rather than deny the existence of the Klan in the face of overwhelming evidence to the contrary, defense countered that the organization was not devoted to denying freedmen their voting rights. The group's sole purpose, Johnson and Stanbery averred, was to protect frightened Upcountry whites from the dangers lurking everywhere in the Piedmont. A purely defensive organization, the Klan patrolled streets and forests, in the words of the constitution and by-laws, to provide "mutual aid to each other in sickness, distress and pecuniary embarrassment." Recognizing the fragility of Southern womanhood, the constitution noted, "Female friends, widows and their households, shall ever be special objects of our regard and protection."[22]

Defense counsel Henry Stanbery admitted that Mitchell had participated in the raiding party on the night of March 6, but not for the purpose of killing Jim Williams. As far as Mitchell knew, the Klan's avowed purpose was to disarm a dangerous Negro and protect vulnerable white families from violent black militiamen. "This young man supposed he was going for what he considered a proper purpose, and what I would consider a proper purpose if I had lived in that neighborhood," Stanbery argued. "When you get Dr. Bratton, deal with him. But for God's sake, don't make this young man his scape-goat."[23]

The predominantly black jury was not hoodwinked by the defense, especially after Reverdy Johnson repeatedly uttered disparaging remarks about blacks. Professing his lack of prejudice, the haughty Johnson revealed his true feelings a few minutes later while arguing that whites were justified in taking up arms against a black militia. "In the name of justice and humanity, in the name of the rights for which our fathers fought, you cannot subject the white man to the absolute and uncontrolled dominion of an armed force of a colored race," he exclaimed. Following a short deliberation, the jury found Mitchell guilty on the second count of the indictment—taking part in the conspiracy against Jim Williams—but not guilty of general conspiracy. Mindful that the defendant had not participated in the actual lynching, Judge Bond announced a relatively light sentence—eighteen months in prison and a $100 fine.[24]

Assessing the federal case against the Ku Klux Klan at the conclusion of the *Mitchell* trial, the prosecution had cause for both optimism and pessimism. On the one hand, prosecutors Corbin and Chamberlain had used Lewis Merrill's meticulously documented investigative dossier to expose the terrible secrets of what amounted to a paramilitary, terrorist organization. Any objective observer attending the trial or reading the transcripts learned of numerous instances of Klan night riding and violence, of a disenfranchised black population quaking in fear, of a white population either sympathetic to the KKK cause or too frightened to speak out, and of a portion of the South Carolina Upcountry where civil government was broken almost beyond repair. The Klan was not a chivalrous "defensive" band of

Figure 7.3.   This drawing, produced in 1870, depicts a Ku Klux Klan mode of torture.
Picture History

brothers fulfilling a noble purpose, it was a mob practicing its own brand of vigilante justice against freedmen, Republicans, and anyone who dared oppose its members. Despite overwhelming state and local sentiment in favor of the Ku Klux Klan, the prosecutors demonstrated that it was possible to pierce the veil of the secret brotherhood and punish wrongdoers even if they hid behind robes and masks and worked under cover of darkness. This was no small achievement in the South Carolina of 1871.

On the other hand, the trial had lasted three long, arduous weeks and only one defendant—a relatively insignificant Klansman, at that—had been convicted. His light sentence was hardly the comeuppance designed to frighten would-be terrorists from fulfilling their duty as they saw it. The leaders behind the South Carolina Klan had fled to other areas, most notably Canada, where they seemed beyond the reach of prosecutors. Even without the leaders at hand, hundreds of additional cases awaited trial, although a majority of defendants had not displayed the "deep criminality" that Attorney General Akerman had established as a primary criterion for punishment. In the meantime, the statutory and constitutional bases that would allow the federal government to prosecute Klan members while forgoing an excruciating case-by-case adjudication were unavailable owing to the judges' unwillingness to accept expansive constitutional theories. In short, the men who deserved the harshest punishment were long gone, and the legal tools necessary to punish the remaining defendants were largely unavailable.[25]

Despite a mixed record of success, the prosecution slogged through the next set of cases. *Mitchell* had provided a winning formula—parading eyewitnesses before the jury to testify about the existence of the KKK in the South Carolina Upcountry followed by testimony linking a particular defendant to a Klan conspiracy—and Corbin and Chamberlain used it to good effect in subsequent proceedings, including the second South Carolina Ku Klux Klan case brought to trial, *United States v. John W. Mitchell and Thomas B. Whitesides.* Unlike Robert Hayes Mitchell, defendants John Whitley Mitchell and Thomas B. Whitesides were prominent members of the Hickory Grove community in York County and therefore far more influential in organizing and operating the South Carolina Klan than the vast majority of defendants awaiting their day in court. The former was a well-known Klan chieftain and Whitesides, like Rufus Bratton, was a prominent physician.

Corbin and Chamberlain filed a four-count indictment. The first count, as usual, alleged the existence of a general Klan conspiracy. The second count charged that the defendants engaged in a special conspiracy to injure a black Union League Republican, Charles Leech (sometimes spelled "Leach"), during a raid in which the defendants had participated. Count three charged that the raid was launched because Leech had voted in 1870, which tied the criminal action to remedies provided by the Enforcement Act. The final count charged that Leech was prevented from voting in the future by the defendants' actions.

Prosecutors introduced far more evidence than they needed against Mitchell and Whitesides. With a large number of newspaper reporters on hand, Corbin and Chamberlain were anxious to publicize a litany of Klan abuses—even when the defendants on trial had not taken part in all of the incidents. In his closing argument, Chamberlain explained another crucial assumption in the prosecution's theory of the case. Because Mitchell and Whitesides were influential members of the community, their actions carried consequences beyond the limited number of raids in which they participated. They were not underlings merely carrying out orders, as Robert

Hayes Mitchell had argued. They were opinion leaders. These defendants, whom Chamberlain called "nobody's dupes," should be assigned "the full responsibility for acts done and purposes planned."[26]

Defense attorneys Reverdy Johnson and Henry Stanbery remained on hand to advise the defendants on strategy, but Whitesides and Mitchell had engaged local counsel. Colonel William Blackburn Wilson, a well-known attorney and ardent Upcountry Democrat, appeared on the doctor's behalf. The colonel argued that Whitesides should not be held accountable for actions he neither took part in nor countenanced. In fact, he had never joined the Klan or engaged in a conspiracy of any sort. To buttress this claim, Wilson called a witness, Kirkland L. Gunn, to explain that he had once given Dr. Whitesides the "secret grip," a sign from one Klansman to another, and the good doctor had not recognized it. Another defense witness recounted a conversation in which Dr. Whitesides expressed his opposition to the Klan. In rebuttal, the prosecution produced witnesses who said they saw Whitesides with a Klan disguise borrowing a saddle so he could ride with the group before at least one nocturnal excursion. Back and forth the allegations flew, each side introducing evidence to rebut the opposition's claims.[27]

John W. Mitchell's attorney, C. D. Melton, faced a more difficult chore than Wilson faced in defending Dr. Whitesides. A series of government witnesses had seen Mitchell participate in Klan activities on more than one occasion. Recognizing that an outright denial would strain credibility even in the eyes of sympathetic jurors, Melton's strategy was threefold. First, he portrayed John Mitchell as a peace-loving pillar of the community. To this end, the lawyer introduced character witnesses who recalled Mitchell as "kindly disposed towards the colored people." Next, he argued that the Ku Klux Klan was not an organization "designed or intended to interfere with African citizens as a class," much less to prevent freedmen from voting. He repeated the standard description of the KKK as a purely defensive group dedicated to protecting upstanding white families from the evil machinations of black militiamen and dark, unseen forces. Finally, he provided an alibi to account for Mitchell's whereabouts at the time of the Leech beating.

Mitchell could not have participated in the Charles Leech beating, friends and relatives swore, because Mitchell's elderly mother had been ill and her son, a good, Christian family man, had sat up with her throughout the night. Apparently with Colonel Wilson's consent, witnesses also placed Doctor Whitesides at the bedside during the ailing woman's nighttime struggle to reclaim her health. The alibi defense might have worked but for confusion in dates. Defense witnesses recalled the date of the bedside vigil as January 9, 1871, but testimony conflicted on the exact date of the Klan visit to Charles Leech's house, calling into question the accuracy of the alibi. Several prosecution witnesses remembered that the Leech incident occurred later in January. Ultimately, the testimony of a white Republican, William Wilson, pinpointed a late January date precisely. On the evening in question, Wilson's wife was confined to her bed after giving birth, and the new father recollected his child's birth date without doubt or hesitation.[28]

When all was said and done, Mitchell and Whitesides were convicted on two of the four counts, namely general conspiracy to obstruct the voting rights of black citizens and a special conspiracy to injure one freedman, Charles Leech, by preventing him from voting in the future. As gratifying as these convictions were for prosecutors, they again fell short of incorporating Bill of Rights protections through the Fourteenth Amendment. Still, Mitchell and Whitesides would be punished, and a prosecution victory was no small thing. With the momentum of two successful convictions behind them, Corbin and Chamberlain moved to the next case.[29]

In *United States v. John S. Millar*, the defendant, a local property owner of wealth and position, was indicted under the 1870 Enforcement Act on one count of conspiracy to prevent citizens of African descent from voting. As in the previous cases, trial testimony established the political nature of the KKK and the atrocities committed by its members, but this time prosecutors failed to tie the defendant to the group's activities apart from showing that he had attended two organizational meetings. In fact, some testimony suggested that Millar was among the few anti-Klan whites living in the Piedmont region. Even if he had participated in KKK activities, it was probably owing to the pressure brought to bear by his friends and neighbors. Assuming that the federal government's goal was to prosecute Klan leaders, as Amos T. Akerman had suggested, Millar should not have been tried. The jury found Millar guilty, but many commentators subsequently viewed the record and concluded that Millar's case was a poor one to try owing to his tenuous connection to the Klan.[30]

The fourth and final case brought to trial during the 1871 session of the circuit court was *United States v. Edward T. Avery*. The defendant was a prominent physician who lived in the Ebenezer community near Rock Hill. According to the evidence presented at the trial, Avery led a nighttime raid at the home of several freedmen, including Abram Brumfield and Samuel Sturgis. When Brumfield escaped, the Klan focused its wrath on Sturgis. They pounded him with their fists, kicked him senseless, and strung him to a tree in a "mock hanging" that did not kill him but served as a lesson of what might happen in the future. That same evening, the

KKK visited the home of a local black preacher, Isaac Postle, sometimes called "Isaac the Apostle" in acknowledgment of his well-known religious piety.

The Postle episode was another sordid affair that undermined the Klan's claim to be a noble organization defending the vulnerable and defenseless. When Postle and his wife saw the Klan approaching their house, the reverend hid beneath the floorboards. Harriet Postle, "some seven or eight months gone in travail," opened the door. She held a baby in her arms. The masked band demanded that the reverend step outside to answer for his offenses, but Mrs. Postle claimed he was not there. She recognized the defendant, Dr. Avery, as the man who knocked her down and pinned her baby to the floor with his foot. Another Klansman stepped forward and repeatedly kicked the pregnant woman. Not satisfied with the extent of her injuries, they yanked Mrs. Postle to her feet and, in her words, "beat my head against the side of the house till I had no sense hardly left." Someone tied a rope around her neck and threatened to hang her.

As with the Jim Williams beating and murder, the Klansmen lifted the floorboards and discovered their prey. Dragging the minister from the house, they berated him for stirring up trouble. The terrified man assured them he "never preached nothing but peace and harmony," but his protests fell on deaf ears. Throwing a rope around his neck, they hung him from a tree so that he could breathe only if he stood on his toes. Pulling the rope tight and relaxing it several times, they taunted him repeatedly, apparently delighted by his tearful pleas for mercy. The vigilantes could have killed him that night, but they did not. Postle was permitted to live.

Later in the year, as Major Merrill's men swept the countryside in search of Klan leaders, Dr. Avery was arrested and confined to the York County jail for his part in the Postle kidnapping and beatings. The doctor's wife—the same woman who supposedly faced down federal troops when they searched for her husband in the middle of the night, according to the Rock Hill newspaper, the *Lantern*—launched a campaign to secure his release. Accompanied by a white minister, the Reverend Robert E. Cooper, Mrs. Avery visited the Postle household. She claimed to have obtained "lawful evidence" that her husband had not participated in the events of that evening. Reverend Postle remained unconvinced, but the woman was undeterred and would not leave until he recanted. She threatened to charge Postle with perjury and have him incarcerated in the penitentiary. Buckling from the relentless pressure exerted by Mrs. Avery, Reverend Cooper, and two female servants from the Avery house, Postle reluctantly agreed to sign an affidavit exonerating Edward Avery.

Figure 7.4. In this famous drawing from the February 24, 1872, edition of *Harper's Weekly*, artist Frank Bellew depicted the kinds of crimes—in this case, a nighttime home invasion—perpetrated by the Klan. The scene is reminiscent of Klan episodes in South Carolina in 1870–1871.
The Library of Congress

Working through an intermediary—possibly Dr. Avery's attorney—the family had the affidavit presented to Major Merrill during his investigation. "I sent for Postle and questioned him in regard to it," Merrill later testified. "He repeated, substantially, the story he told here on the witness stand." Faced with conflicting evidence, Merrill might have dismissed Postle's case. Nonetheless, he had collected enough evidence against the KKK to recognize a not-so-subtle form of intimidation when he saw it. He also found at least one additional witness, John Rateree, who claimed that Dr. Avery had participated in the incident. Rather than dismiss Postle's account, the major forwarded the case to Corbin and Chamberlain. The prosecutors agreed with Major Merrill that intimidation and coercion had been employed against the black preacher. Mrs. Avery, Reverend Cooper, and the servants were later indicted by a grand jury, although their cases were never tried in court.[31]

Defense counsel presented the falsified affidavit at trial. Colonel Wilson, who was defending Dr. Avery after having represented Dr. Whitesides in *Mitchell and Whitesides*, was joined by co-counsel, Colonel F. W. McMaster of Columbia. The two attorneys produced the affidavit as evidence that Avery was not involved in the matter, and Postle had perjured himself. The judges were not persuaded.

With the collapse of the alibi, Avery's attorneys presented an expert witness to prove that the doctor's hand was so withered from a war wound he could not have tied a rope around Harriet Postle's neck. Although this defense seemed promising, other witnesses indicated that Dr. Avery had not tied the rope around her neck; therefore, the expert testimony did not answer the question of whether he was on the scene. Watching each day in the courtroom as his defense collapsed, Dr. Avery recognized that he probably would be convicted. Therefore, the weekend before closing arguments were slated to begin, he forfeited his $3,000 bond and fled from South Carolina. He eventually showed up in Canada with Dr. Rufus Bratton, his co-conspirator.

As closing arguments commenced in the courtroom on Monday morning, prosecutor David Corbin suddenly realized that the defendant was absent. He demanded to know where Avery had gone, but defense attorney McMaster refused to say. Judge Bond was livid; he promised to "lay a rule on Mr. McMaster to answer the question or show cause why he should not be thrown over the bar." Eventually, cooler heads prevailed and closing arguments continued.

Jurors were not convinced of Dr. Avery's innocence, especially given his absence at the conclusion of the case. After fifteen minutes of deliberations, the jury produced a guilty verdict. Sentencing was delayed until the defendant could be found and brought back to the court. When that did not happen, the case dragged on for several years until it was discontinued during a later term of court, along with similar KKK cases. In the meantime, McMaster was tried for contempt and could have been disbarred from practicing law. As with so many KKK trials, a decision was never reached on the contempt-of-court charge.[32]

The federal case against Edward Avery was the final decision rendered on the Ku Klux Klan outrages in the South Carolina Upcountry during the November 1871 term of court. The session ended on January 2, 1872. By early 1872, only fifty-four defendants had been sentenced for their part in the KKK reign of terror in South Carolina—five in trials and forty-nine by waiving the right to a jury trial and pleading guilty. For the April 1872 term of court, more than 400 defendants in 278 cases awaited prosecution. Corbin and Chamberlain did not express public reservations, but they recognized that something must be done to dispose of the backlog. Otherwise, the federal courts would be clogged for years to come.[33]

Although the overall results were disappointing, Attorney General Akerman publicly proclaimed satisfaction with the trials. They had served the purpose of exposing Klan outrages to the light of day and pierced the veil of secrecy. "As far as I can learn, the prosecuting lawyers have managed the business ably," he remarked. Later, he expressed pride in the belief "that I have borne some part in the exposure and destruction of that terrible conspiracy." Privately, however, the attorney general feared that Northerners were losing the will to pursue a tough Reconstruction policy. He warned Justice Department officials and prosecutors that, "as long as these bad men believe you are unable to protect yourselves, they will cherish the purpose of injuring you as soon as the hand of the Government shall be withdrawn."[34]

Ironically, in the hour of its triumph, the Grant administration relaxed its hold on the Southern states. The iron hand of the federal government, so feared and decried by Southerners, soon would be withdrawn. With the successful prosecution of the Ku Klux Klan in South Carolina and in other Southern states, weary Northerners argued it was time to move on to more pressing national issues. Opinion leaders increasingly questioned whether it was worth the time and treasure necessary to occupy the South. With each passing year, the horrors of the Civil War receded further into the mists of time. Citizens on both sides of the Mason-Dixon Line yearned to look ahead, not behind. They need not have worried—change was on the horizon.[35]

NOTES

1. Quoted in Kermit L. Hall, "Political Power and Constitutional Legitimacy: The South Carolina Ku Klux Klan Trials, 1871–1872," *Emory Law Journal* 33 (Fall 1984): 928. See also, Robert J. Kaczorowski, "Federal Enforcement of Civil Rights During the First Reconstruction," *Fordham Urban Law Journal* 23 (Fall 1995): 163–65; Michael Vorenberg, "Imagining a Different Reconstruction Constitution," *Civil War History* 51 (December 2005): 419–24; Wyn Craig Wade, *The Fiery Cross: The Ku Klux Klan in America* (New York and Oxford: Oxford University Press, 1987), 102–3; Lou Falkner Williams, *The Great South Carolina Ku Klux Klan Trials, 1871–1872* (Athens: University of Georgia Press, 1996), 50–57; Richard Zuczek, *State of Rebellion: Reconstruction in South Carolina* (Columbia, SC: University of South Carolina Press, 1996), 118–22.

2. Eric Foner, *Reconstruction: America's Unfinished Revolution, 1863–1877* (New York: Francis Parkman Prize Edition, History Book Club, 2005; originally published by HarperCollins, 1988), 457–59; Hall, "Political Power and Constitutional Legitimacy," 929; Kaczorowski, "Federal Enforcement of Civil Rights During the

First Reconstruction," 178–79; Francis B. Simkins and R. H. Woody, *South Carolina During Reconstruction* (Chapel Hill: The University of North Carolina Press, 1932), 464; Allen W. Trelease, *White Terror: The Ku Klux Klan Conspiracy and Southern Reconstruction* (Baton Rouge: Louisiana State University Press, 1971), 406–07; Williams, *The Great South Carolina Ku Klux Klan Trials*, 10–11, 55–56; Lou Falkner Williams, "The South Carolina Ku Klux Klan Trials and Enforcement of Federal Civil Rights, 1871–1872," *Civil War History* 39 (March 1993): 48–50.

3. *Barron v. Baltimore*, 7 Pet. 243 (1833); David Everitt, "1871 War on Terror," *American History* 38 (June 2003): 32–33; Hall, "Political Power and Constitutional Legitimacy," 928–30; Stanley F. Horn, *Invisible Empire: The Story of the Ku Klux Klan, 1866–1871* (Montclair, NJ: Patterson Smith, 1969), 240–41; Kaczorowski, "Federal Enforcement of Civil Rights During the First Reconstruction," 169–76; Francis B. Simkins and R. H. Woody, *South Carolina During Reconstruction* (Chapel Hill: The University of North Carolina Press, 1932), 463–64; Vorenberg, "Imagining a Different Reconstruction Constitution," 419–24; Williams, *The Great South Carolina Ku Klux Klan Trials*, 57–63.

4. Richard Paul Fuke, "Hugh Lennox Bond and Radical Republican Ideology," *The Journal of Southern History* 45 (November 1979): 569–71; Hall, "Political Power and Constitutional Legitimacy," 933–34; Kaczorowski, "Federal Enforcement of Civil Rights During the First Reconstruction," 173–74; Trelease, *White Terror*, 407; Williams, *The Great South Carolina Ku Klux Klan Trials*, 50–52.

5. Quoted in Kaczorowski, "Federal Enforcement of Civil Rights During the First Reconstruction," 173. See also, Fuke, "Hugh Lennox Bond and Radical Republican Ideology," 569–86; Hall, "Political Power and Constitutional Legitimacy," 934–35; Jerry L. West, *The Reconstruction Ku Klux Klan in York County, South Carolina, 1865–1877* (Jefferson, NC: McFarland & Company, Inc., 2002), 97–98; Williams, *The Great South Carolina Ku Klux Klan Trials*, 53.

6. Hall, "Political Power and Constitutional Legitimacy," 933–35; Horn, *Invisible Empire*, 240; Kaczorowski, "Federal Enforcement of Civil Rights During the First Reconstruction," 173–75; Simkins and Woody, *South Carolina During Reconstruction*, 464; Trelease, *White Terror*, 407; West, *The Reconstruction Ku Klux Klan in York County, South Carolina*, 97–98; Williams, *The Great South Carolina Ku Klux Klan Trials*, 53–54; Zuczek, *State of Rebellion*, 100.

7. Quoted in *Dred Scott v. Sanford*, 60 U.S. 393, 404 (1857). See also, Simkins and Woody, *South Carolina During Reconstruction*, 464; Trelease, *White Terror*, 407; Williams, *The Great South Carolina Ku Klux Klan Trials*, 54–55; Zuczek, *State of Rebellion*, 100.

8. Hall, "Political Power and Constitutional Legitimacy," 933–35; Trelease, *White Terror*, 407; William M. Wiecek, "The Great Writ and Reconstruction: The Habeas Corpus Act of 1867," *Journal of Southern History* 36 (November 1970): 540; Williams, *The Great South Carolina Ku Klux Klan Trials*, 54–55.

9. Quoted in David Miller DeWitt, *The Impeachment and Trial of Andrew Johnson, Seventeenth President of the United States: A History* (New York: The MacMillan

Company, 1903), 502. See also, Hall, "Political Power and Constitutional Legiti-macy," 936–37; Simkins and Woody, *South Carolina During Reconstruction*, 464; Williams, *The Great South Carolina Ku Klux Klan Trials*, 55; Zuczek, *State of Rebellion*, 100.

10. Quoted in Williams, *The Great South Carolina Ku Klux Klan Trials*, 57. See also, Everitt, "1871 War on Terror," 32; Robert Selph Henry, *The Story of Reconstruction* (New York: Konecky & Konecky, 1999), 450; Horn, *Invisible Empire*, 240; Louis F. Post, "A Carpetbagger in South Carolina," *Journal of Negro History* 10 (January 1925): 64–72.

11. Quoted in Hall, "Political Power and Constitutional Legitimacy," 937. See also, United States Congress, *Report of the Joint Select Committee to Inquire into the Condition of Affairs in the Late Insurrectionary States*, 42 Cong., 2 Sess., No. 22 (1872), Vol. III, 1615–17; Williams, *The Great South Carolina Ku Klux Klan Trials*, 57–59.

12. Hall, "Political Power and Constitutional Legitimacy," 937–39; Kaczorowski, "Federal Enforcement of Civil Rights During the First Reconstruction," 172; Williams, *The Great South Carolina Ku Klux Klan Trials*, 58–59.

13. Hall, "Political Power and Constitutional Legitimacy," 941–42; United States Congress, *Report of the Joint Select Committee*, Vol. III, 1631–43; Williams, *The Great South Carolina Ku Klux Klan Trials*, 60–63; Williams, "The South Carolina Ku Klux Klan Trials and Enforcement of Federal Civil Rights, 1871–1872," 51–54.

14. Kaczorowski, "Federal Enforcement of Civil Rights During the First Reconstruction," 174–76; Everette Swinney, "Enforcing the Fifteenth Amendment, 1870–1877," *Journal of Southern History* 28 (May 1962): 207; Wiecek, "The Great Writ and Reconstruction," 540.

15. *United States v. Crosby*, 25 F. Cas. 701 (C.C.D.S.C. 1871) (No. 14,893). See also, United States Congress, *Report of the Joint Select Committee*, Vol. III, 1745–46; West, *The Reconstruction Ku Klux Klan in York County, South Carolina*, 98.

16. Hall, "Political Power and Constitutional Legitimacy," 943; Williams, *The Great South Carolina Ku Klux Klan Trials*, 60–66; Williams, "The South Carolina Ku Klux Klan Trials and Enforcement of Federal Civil Rights, 1871–1872," 51–54.

17. Quoted in Hall, "Political Power and Constitutional Legitimacy," 945. See also, Michael Les Benedict, "Preserving the Constitution: The Conservative Basis of Radical Reconstruction," *The Journal of American History* 61 (June 1974): 65–90; Fuke, "Hugh Lennox Bond and Radical Republican Ideology," 577–86; Williams, *The Great South Carolina Ku Klux Klan Trials*, 71–74.

18. Everitt, "1871 War on Terror," 32–33; "Ku Klux Pardons," *Yorkville Enquirer*, Yorkville, SC (March 27, 1873); West, *The Reconstruction Ku Klux Klan in York County, South Carolina*, 137, 143; Williams, *The Great South Carolina Ku Klux Klan Trials*, 73–74.

19. *United States v. Avery*, 80 U.S. (13 Wall.) 251 (1871). See also, Trelease, *White Terror*, 353–54, 363–66, 372–74, 403–4; West, *The Reconstruction Ku Klux Klan in York County, South Carolina*, 40, 98–99; Williams, *The Great South Carolina Ku Klux Klan Trials*, 47, 74, 105; Zuczek, *State of Rebellion*, 102.

20. Hall, "Political Power and Constitutional Legitimacy," 947–48; Horn, *Invisible Empire*, 241–42; Williams, *The Great South Carolina Ku Klux Klan Trials*, 74–75.

21. Quoted in West, *The Reconstruction Ku Klux Klan in York County, South Carolina*, Appendix 1, 119. See also, Everitt, "1871 War on Terror," 32–33; *United States v. Mitchell*, 26 F. Cas. 1283 (C.C.D.S.C. 1871) (No. 15,790); Williams, *The Great South Carolina Ku Klux Klan Trials*, 77–78.

22. Quoted in West, *The Reconstruction Ku Klux Klan in York County, South Carolina*, appendix 1, 119. See also, Williams, *The Great South Carolina Ku Klux Klan Trials*, 79–80.

23. Quoted in Williams, *The Great South Carolina Ku Klux Klan Trials*, 80. See also, Everitt, "1871 War on Terror," 32–33; Horn, *Invisible Empire*, 240–41; West, *The Reconstruction Ku Klux Klan in York County, South Carolina*, 99; Zuczek, *State of Rebellion*, 101.

24. Quoted in Williams, *The Great South Carolina Ku Klux Klan Trials*, 81. See also, Everitt, "1871 War on Terror," 32–33; Trelease, *White Terror*, 407–08; Wade, *The Fiery Cross*, 102–03; West, *The Reconstruction Ku Klux Klan in York County, South Carolina*, 99.

25. Foner, *Reconstruction: America's Unfinished Revolution*, 458–59; Trelease, *White Terror*, 407–8; Williams, *The Great South Carolina Ku Klux Klan Trials*, 75–76.

26. United States Congress, *Report of the Joint Select Committee*, Vol. III, 1848; West, *The Reconstruction Ku Klux Klan in York County, South Carolina*, 99; Williams, *The Great South Carolina Ku Klux Klan Trials*, 86–87.

27. Horn, *Invisible Empire*, 240–41; West, *The Reconstruction Ku Klux Klan in York County, South Carolina*, 99; Williams, *The Great South Carolina Ku Klux Klan Trials*, 86–91.

28. Everitt, "1871 War on Terror," 32–33; Horn, *Invisible Empire*, 240–42; West, *The Reconstruction Ku Klux Klan in York County, South Carolina*, 99; Williams, *The Great South Carolina Ku Klux Klan Trials*, 90–91.

29. Everitt, "1871 War on Terror," 33; Kaczorowski, "Federal Enforcement of Civil Rights During the First Reconstruction," 179–82; Williams, *The Great South Carolina Ku Klux Klan Trials*, 91.

30. United States Circuit Court [4th Circuit], *Proceedings in the Ku Klux Klan Trials at Columbia, S.C., in the United States Circuit Court, November Term, 1871* (Columbia, SC: Republican Printing Company, State Printers, 1872), 608–38; West, *The Reconstruction Ku Klux Klan in York County, South Carolina*, 99; Williams, *The Great South Carolina Ku Klux Klan Trials*, 91–95.

31. United States Circuit Court [4th Circuit], *Proceedings in the Ku Klux Klan Trials at Columbia, S.C., in the United States Circuit Court, November Term, 1871*, 745; West, *The Reconstruction Ku Klux Klan in York County, South Carolina*, 99–100; Williams, *The Great South Carolina Ku Klux Klan Trials*, 95–100.

32. Horn, *Invisible Empire*, 241; Fred Langdon, "The Kidnapping of Dr. Rufus Bratton," *Journal of Negro History* 10 (July 1925): 332; Trelease, *White Terror*, 403; United States Circuit Court [4th Circuit], *Proceedings in the Ku Klux Klan Trials at*

Columbia, S.C., in the United States Circuit Court, November Term, 1871, 748–63; West, *The Reconstruction Ku Klux Klan in York County, South Carolina*, 100; Williams, *The Great South Carolina Ku Klux Klan Trials*, 96–100.

33. Henry, *The Story of Reconstruction*, 450; Kaczorowski, "Federal Enforcement of Civil Rights During the First Reconstruction," 176–77; Trelease, *White Terror*, 407–08; Wade, *The Fiery Cross*, 103.

34. Quoted in Williams, *The Great South Carolina Ku Klux Klan Trials*, 100. See also, Everitt, "1871 War on Terror," 33; Foner, *Reconstruction: America's Unfinished Revolution*, 458; Trelease, *White Terror*, 411; Wade, *The Fiery Cross*, 109; Zuczek, *State of Rebellion*, 102–03.

35. Kaczorowski, "Federal Enforcement of Civil Rights During the First Reconstruction," 181–83; Swinney, "Enforcing the Fifteenth Amendment, 1870–1877," 205–7; Wade, *The Fiery Cross*, 109–14; C. Vann Woodward, *The Strange Career of Jim Crow* (Oxford and New York: Oxford University Press, 1966), 22–44.

8

"THE CAUSES FROM WHICH
KU KLUXISM SPRUNG ARE
STILL POTENT FOR EVIL"

J. Rufus Bratton's case illustrates as well as anything the ambivalence of the federal government toward prosecuting the South Carolina Ku Klux Klan after the conclusion of the November 1871 term of court. Bratton was the Klan leader who led the raid on Jim Williams's home. If anyone in York County should have been punished for Klan transgressions, Bratton was the man. Recognizing he probably would be prosecuted, the doctor fled to his sister's house in Barnwell, South Carolina, as federal troops combed the countryside in search of defendants.

During most of the next year, Bratton lived under the assumed name "Simpson," and fled when he believed federal law enforcement officials were on his trail. From South Carolina, he traveled to Selma, Alabama, then to Memphis, Tennessee, before heading north into Canada. Settling into a house on Wellington Street in London, Ontario, "John Simpson" was assisted by a group of expatriates, including co-conspirator James W. Avery. Convinced he was beyond the reach of U.S. authorities, the fugitive settled into a quiet routine.

The routine was short-lived. On the afternoon of Tuesday, June 4, 1872, as Bratton strolled along a street in London, he spied three suspicious men watching him. He grew alarmed as they approached him on the street. To his astonishment, the doctor recognized one fellow, Isaac Bell Cornwell, an associate of South Carolina Governor Robert K. Scott. Cornwell's appearance in London could not be coincidental.

Before Bratton could react, Cornwell announced that he had secured an arrest warrant. Stalling for time, Bratton insisted that the warrant be read aloud. Cornwell would not be duped. He and another man pushed Bratton to the ground and used a chloroform-soaked rag to render the prisoner compliant, although not quite unconscious. Hustling him into a taxicab, they alighted for the train depot.

Disoriented but cognizant of his predicament, Bratton vehemently protested. The agents would not be dissuaded from their task. Pushing the captive onto a train, they headed across the border into the United States. An eyewitness who saw the men during the journey noted Bratton's "stupid, vacant look," probably caused by the chloroform. Arriving in Detroit, the agents met Joseph G. Hester, an officer ordered by the U.S. Secret Service to take custody of the escapee and arrange for his transportation to South Carolina.

"I am under Canadian law," a dazed and befuddled Bratton proclaimed. "I refuse to obey you. Neither your government, or you, sir, have a right to detain me here, and if you do, you will pay for it."

Dr. Bratton undoubtedly was captured in Ontario, but the details of the arrest are contested to this day. Some accounts indicate that the warrant, signed by President Grant, was issued for James W. Avery's arrest; therefore, Bratton was illegally abducted from Canadian soil. In this version, an international incident occurred when federal agents attempted to transport Bratton across the border on a defective warrant. Another version suggests that Bratton escaped while passing through Virginia and hid until Hester spotted him the next day at the train depot. The men exchanged pleasantries, at which time the federal agent again arrested the doctor, this time without incident.

However it happened, Bratton reappeared in Yorkville on June 10 to face charges in connection with the Jim Williams raid in March. Judge Bryan ordered the defendant released on a $12,000 bond, but it was not enough to ensure the doctor's presence at trial. As soon as he was released, Bratton fled back to Canada. The only court proceeding he attended that summer was a July 16 hearing to consider charges against Isaac Cornwell for kidnapping a Canadian resident. Cornwell was sentenced to prison, but Bratton escaped further confinement.

During the next four years, the good doctor played a waiting game. Federal agents dared not follow him into Canada and trigger an international incident, and he dared not return to the United States. In July 1872, his family joined him in Ontario. While the U.S. government slowly retreated from its Reconstruction policies during the 1870s, Bratton established a thriving Canadian medical practice. He returned to the United States after the president offered amnesty to former Klansmen in 1876. He lived for another two decades. Bratton was said to be the inspiration for Thomas Dixon Jr.'s 1905

Figure 8.1. Dr. J. Rufus Bratton, a prominent York County citizen and Klan leader, fled to Canada when federal troops intervened in South Carolina in 1871. His capture and return to York County became the stuff of legend.
The York County Historical Commission

novel, *The Clansman*, which glorified the KKK and served as a model for the resurrection of the group in 1915. Loosely based on *The Clansman,* D. W. Griffith's film *The Birth of a Nation* included a protagonist—a colonel, the morally righteous Ben Cameron who organized the KKK to save white Southerners from evil carpetbaggers and renegade blacks—that resembled Bratton, or the mythic figure he had become to some Southerners.[1]

The Bratton case illustrates the frustration that federal officials felt as they struggled with the question of how to handle the Ku Klux Klan after 1871. In one sense, the Klan was broken and never again would it rule a community or state with as much power as it had in the South Carolina Upcountry during 1870–1871. In another sense, few Klansmen were punished to a degree commensurate with their crimes. If Rufus Bratton could lead a vicious assault and murder of a freedman and escape the most serious consequences of his actions, the plan for reconstructing America by establishing a place for emancipated slaves was little more than an empty promise. In fact, owing to his enshrinement as a cult hero in the South, J. Rufus Bratton, the bitter, failed Civil War surgeon who blamed his misfortune on freedmen and Northern interlopers, had the last laugh. Lawlessness had become its own reward.

As the federal government retreated from Radical Republicans' promises to reformulate Southern society, the future of race relations appeared grim. In December 1871, Attorney General Akerman announced his resignation. It was never clear whether he quit to protest the Grant administration's refusal to pursue future Klan prosecutions with vigor or was forced out for political considerations apart from the Ku Klux Klan. A loyal cabinet minister, Akerman was deliberately vague in explaining his departure. "The reasons for this step I would not detail fully without saying what, perhaps, ought not to be said," he wrote to U.S. attorney David T. Corbin. Akerman assured an anxious Major Merrill that the new attorney general, George H. Williams, was "an able and experienced man" who enjoyed the administration's full support, which meant he would be "free from some of the hostilities that have obstructed me." Whatever the reasons for his swift exit from the administration, it soon became clear that he had been mistaken; his successor was not the man Akerman was and the Justice Department would no longer actively prosecute the KKK.

George H. Williams ostensibly continued his predecessor's policies, but his lack of commitment was readily apparent to all. The charitable view of Williams was that he was a staunch ally and political supporter of President Grant; thus, he was rewarded for his support with a prestigious cabinet position. He made no pretense of possessing a strong will or exceptional ability. A less kindly perspective set forth by his many detractors was that Williams was a "third-rate lawyer" and political hack, no more and no less than one of the "chief flatterers and hangers-on" that doomed the Grant administration in the judgment of history. This perspective suggests that he was worse than a mediocre obstructionist; he was an agent of the forces that undermined federal policies to such an extent that Reconstruction was dead in all but name before Grant vacated the Executive Mansion.

Williams's credentials initially promised that he would pursue a tough Reconstruction policy. A Republican senator from Oregon, he was a principal author of the Tenure of Office Act that had served as grounds for the Radical Republicans' impeachment of President Johnson. Later, Williams served on the Joint Committee of Fifteen on Reconstruction. His Radical Republican leanings made Williams's initial performance as attorney general mystifying. No sooner had he assumed the helm than he confronted the federal case styled *United States v. James W. Avery*. Arguing that the U.S. Supreme Court lacked jurisdiction to hear the case, Williams asked the Justices for direction in trying KKK cases in the South Carolina federal court. The high court agreed with the attorney general that it lacked jurisdiction; therefore, it remanded the case to the circuit court in March 1872, albeit without providing direction for trying the matter. Federal prosecutors David T. Corbin and Daniel H. Chamberlain wanted the Supreme Court to expand its jurisdiction; therefore, they found themselves in the curious position of opposing their boss's view of the proceedings. After working so closely with Amos T. Akerman to prosecute the Klan, Williams's obstructionism served as a stinging rebuke.[2]

Throughout the spring and summer of 1872, Major Merrill remained in York County and arrests continued, but at a substantially reduced level. Corbin and Chamberlain brought additional cases during the April 1872 term of court, but the new attorney general's apparent reluctance to support his prosecutors hampered their efforts at every turn. In *Ex Parte T. Jefferson Greer*, the first major case during the new term, the U.S. Supreme Court again was presented with the question of whether it exercised jurisdiction in a Klan case. The defendant contended that his petition for habeas corpus had been unconstitutionally denied, but a divided Supreme Court refused to grant the petition. Although the decision represented a victory for the prosecution—it upheld the arrests and prosecution of suspected Klansmen—the high court's failure to explain its reasoning left all parties unclear on how future cases should be tried. Corbin warned his superiors in Washington that the successful prosecution of a handful of Klansmen during the November 1871 term of court was not enough to prevent a future resurgence of the group. In Corbin's opinion, would-be white terrorists were waiting for the storm to blow over so they could "resume operations" before the next election.[3]

The prosecution team recognized that federal support for trying KKK cases was waning. To salvage what they could during the April 1872 term, Corbin and Chamberlain negotiated guilty pleas to lesser crimes whenever possible. They also selected cases where the facts were essentially uncontested or where the defendants' behavior was so egregious that justice demanded prosecution.

The murder and mutilation of Thomas Roundtree fit the bill. With the victim shot more than thirty times, his throat slit from ear to ear, and his corpse tossed into a nearby river, the case cried out for trial. The defendant, Elijah Sapaugh (sometimes spelled "Sepaugh" and "Sapoch"), was convicted of first-degree murder despite his absence from the murder scene. The case was later certified to the U.S. Supreme Court to decide the issue of federal jurisdiction for what was generally a state crime. The case languished for several years before Attorney General Williams directed federal prosecutors to enter a nolle prosequi, a formal entry on the record indicating that the government literally "will no further prosecute" the case. Although a nolle prosequi is not tantamount to exoneration, it removes the case from the court's docket and allows the defendant to negotiate a lesser penalty or go free. Williams explained that his decision was "not for the sake of Sapaugh, but for the sake of the public good." Thus the South Carolina Ku Klux Klan trials ended, in the words of one commentator, "not with a bang but a whimper."[4]

Additional retreats were in the offing. In September 1872, Williams responded favorably to a clemency request submitted by former Confederate vice president Alexander H. Stephens. Alarmed at the change of heart exhibited by the head of the Justice Department, Major Merrill sent a letter to Williams strongly recommending that the administration reject Stephens's request. "The causes from which Ku Kluxism sprung are still potent for evil," the major argued. "The blind, unreasoning, bigoted hostility to the results of the war is only smothered, not appeased or destroyed, and where there appears anything which can be construed into weakness or releasing of purpose in enforcing that protection the head of the snake may be instantly seen." Merrill's words fell on deaf ears. "When the President is satisfied that the danger from Ku Klux violence has ceased and that such unlawful associations have been abandoned," Williams wrote in his terse reply, "he will be ready to exercise executive clemency in all cases in the most liberal manner."[5]

Figure 8.2. George H. Williams, Amos T. Akerman's successor as attorney general in the Grant administration, did not share his predecessor's commitment to prosecuting the Klan or protecting the freedmen.
Picture History

George H. Williams was completely in step with his times. The period between 1877 and 1915—an era that Mark Twain called the "Gilded Age"—saw a wholesale retreat from Reconstruction. Northern whites grew weary of the North-South schism. Apathy set in. The world of commerce and industry beckoned. Rare indeed was the politician or political leader with the stomach for policing the South. When the new president ordered federal soldiers to stop guarding the statehouses in Louisiana and South Carolina in 1877, Southern political affairs—long characterized by former Confederates as a "local matter" properly administered through "home rule"—were left in the hands of men who had once championed the birth of a separate nation. Slavery was a dead institution and secession had been discredited on the battlefield but white supremacy and legal segregation would soon reign supreme.

Virtually every major leader in every branch of the federal government turned his back on the freedmen during the 1870s. With the death of the Radical Republicans in the 1860s and 1870s, a new generation of congressional leaders simply had no interest in stirring up the divisive, intractable issues of race and social relations raised by the Civil War. A series of weak, ineffectual presidents came and went, none expressing much interest in reviving federal Reconstruction policy. The Republican Party gradually turned its attention to economic affairs as a desire for industrialization took hold of the American landscape. What once had been the party of Lincoln became, by the turn of the century, the party of big business and unfettered free enterprise.[6]

The U.S. Supreme Court, an institution specifically designed by the Founders to be immune from direct political pressure, led the most disappointing retreat from Reconstruction. In a later age, the court would restore civil and political rights to disenfranchised peoples despite the general unpopularity of its decisions. During the last three decades of the nineteenth century, however, the judiciary joined the other branches of the federal government in retreating from the early promises of Reconstruction.

The trend was first visible in the 1873 *Slaughterhouse* cases. Four years earlier, Louisiana had enacted a law allowing the city of New Orleans to establish a corporation centralizing all slaughterhouse operations in one location. The stated purpose of the law was to prevent a public health hazard that resulted from butchers dumping carcasses and rotten meat into the streets. Protesting what they viewed as a legalized monopoly, twenty-five butchers filed suit. Five of their cases eventually won appeal to the U.S. Supreme Court. A central issue raised on appeal was whether the Due Process, Equal Protection, and Privileges and Immunities clauses of the Fourteenth Amendment protected the butchers' livelihood. In a narrowly tailored five-to-four decision, the high court ruled that the Privileges and Immunities Clause affected only "national citizenship," not state citizenship. As for the other clauses in the amendment, the court restricted them to situations involving former slaves—and, even then, it refused to afford protection from racial discrimination—thereby undercutting the practical utility of the Fourteenth Amendment and ensuring that it would not be a legal remedy for discriminatory state actions in most instances. The Supreme Court continued this restrictive interpretation of the Fourteenth Amendment in *United States v. Reese* and *United States v. Cruikshank* in 1876.[7]

If the high court had limited itself to eviscerating the Fourteenth Amendment, the result would have represented a staggering setback for the freedmen, but there was more to come. The judicial dismantling of Reconstruction had barely begun. A series of U.S. Supreme Court cases late in the century upheld the constitutionality of segregation and broadened state power to discriminate against citizens unencumbered by the U.S. Constitution. In *Hall v. de Cuir*, an 1878 case, the court held that a state could not prohibit segregation on a common carrier. Twelve years later, in *Louisville, New Orleans, and Texas Railway Company v. Mississippi*, the court ruled that a state could enact a statute requiring "equal, but separate, accommodation for the white and colored races." In the *Civil Rights Cases* of 1883, the Justices determined that the first two sections of the Civil Rights Act of 1875 were unconstitutional because they vested the federal government with too much authority over states. *Williams v. Mississippi*, an 1898 case, brought the imprimatur of the U.S. Constitution to the Mississippi Plan, a scheme hatched in 1875 to "redeem" the state of Mississippi from carpetbagger rule. The plan called for whites to "persuade" more than 10 percent of Republican voters to change their party affiliation when they arrived at the polls. The second plank in the strategy was to threaten blacks with violence if they tried to vote. In reviewing a legal challenge to this plan, the court concluded that actions undertaken by private persons to intimidate others were not akin to state action. "It cannot be said, therefore, that the denial of the equal protection of the laws arises primarily from the constitution and laws of Mississippi; nor is there any sufficient allegation of an evil and discriminating administration of them," the court concluded.[8]

The most infamous segregation case of the late nineteenth century was *Plessy v. Ferguson*, which began in 1890 when the state of Louisiana passed a law requiring railroads to provide "separate but equal" cars for blacks. Homer Plessy, a light-skinned Creole man who was one-eighth black, challenged the constitutionality of the statute after he purchased a first-class ticket on a Louisiana train and sat in the first-class section of the "white" car. When directed to move to the colored section, Plessy refused. He was arrested for violating the law. When the case entered the federal district court, Plessy argued that the statute had violated his Thirteenth Amendment rights as well as the Equal Protection Clause of the Fourteenth Amendment. The Supreme Court disagreed. Although clearly the Thirteenth Amendment abolished slavery, that amendment did not protect blacks from discriminatory state laws. In upholding Louisiana's authority to enforce a "separate but equal" policy, Justice Henry Billings Brown delivered the opinion of the court. "We consider the underlying fallacy of the plaintiff's argument to consist in the assumption that the enforced separation of the two races stamps the colored race with a badge of inferiority," he explained. "If this be so, it is not by reason of anything found in the act, but solely because the colored race chooses to put that construction upon it."

In a blistering dissent, Justice John Marshall Harlan, a former slave-owner-turned-civil-libertarian, argued against state-sanctioned "separate but equal" discrimination. "In my opinion, the judgment this day rendered will, in time, prove to be quite as pernicious as the decision made by this tribunal in the *Dred Scott* Case." Later in his dissent, Harlan argued, "The sure guaranty of the peace and security of each race is the clear, distinct, unconditional recognition by our governments, national and state, of every right that inheres in civil freedom, and of the equality before the law of all citizens of the United States, without regard to race." In time, Harlan's plea for racial tolerance would carry the day, but his lone dissent was written fifty-eight years too early. Until *Brown v. Board of Education* was handed down during a different era, Jim Crow would fret his hour upon the stage.[9]

Plessy was the culmination of the federal government's movement away from protecting newly emancipated slaves and their progeny after the early 1870s. The Fifteenth Amendment, the last of the Civil War Amendments, was passed in 1870 to ensure that all men twenty-one years of age or older could vote, but Southerners used numerous methods apart from the KKK to discourage black participation in the political process. Many white citizens who otherwise deplored the use of violence and believed KKK activities to be unlawful and illegitimate supported the creation of paramilitary organizations such as the White League of Louisiana and the Red Shirts of South Carolina. Compared with the Klan, these groups were much more sophisticated in their approach. They based their "philosophy" of government on the Mississippi Plan and similar legally protected, but unquestionably discriminatory, measures. Where the KKK illegally prevented blacks from taking part in the social and political life of their states and communities, soon the Mississippi Plan, poll taxes, and literacy tests accomplished the goal under the color of law.

Reconstruction ended in the 1870s as Republicans, the nominal champions of the freedmen, relinquished control to Democrats. As early as 1870, Democrats seized control of state governments in Virginia, North Carolina, and Georgia. Texas went Democratic in 1873, and Alabama and Arkansas followed suit the following year. Mississippi returned to white Southern control in 1875.[10]

The contentious 1876 presidential election placed the final nail in the coffin of federal Reconstruction of the Southern states. Not only did the election mark the centennial year of the nation's existence but it caught the United States in search of a new identity. By 1876, whites had captured control of state legislatures in every Southern state save Louisiana, Florida, and South Carolina, which remained nominally under federal control with troops—numbering approximately 2,800—still guarding the Louisiana and South Carolina statehouses and patrolling the streets of some cities.

The nation was poised on the cusp a new age. A quarter of a million factories employed 2.5 million workers in 1876, manufacturing flour, refined sugar, rolled cigars, liquors, textiles, and farm equipment. Steel production, the bedrock of industrial growth, increased from 19,643 tons in 1867 to 533,191 tons in 1876, an astonishing 2,700 percent increase. Almost 170,000 immigrants entered the country that latter year. Even in light of these developments, which greatly challenged the country's infrastructure, 65 percent of children aged five to seventeen attended school, albeit sporadically. The literacy rate was 80 percent for whites and 20 percent for blacks.[11]

It was an age without extensive media coverage, at least by twenty-first-century standards, although 1,000 daily newspapers with a combined coverage of 3.6 million readers brought news, albeit filtered through rose-colored lenses, to their readers. Candidates' careers flourished or foundered by the partisan swords of powerful newsmen. Against this backdrop, Democrat Samuel J. Tilden squared off against Republican Rutherford B. Hayes in the presidential contest.

The former was a well-known reform governor of New York, having destroyed New York City's infamous political machine, the Tweed Ring, as well as the upstate Canal Ring. In a career that began during Andrew Jackson's presidency and spanned almost the rest of the century, Tilden was revered by many and favored to win over his lesser-known rival, the governor of Ohio. Nicknamed "Whispering Sammy" for his soft-spoken approach to oratory and "The Great Forecloser" for his sober approach to handling business affairs, he seemed the antithesis of the hard-drinking, blustery, bombastic orators generally popular on the stump in rural communities. His staid, even-keeled approach to campaigning and governance was a soothing, calm voice in a sea of histrionics and demagoguery.

Not that his rival was a silver-tongued orator. Rutherford B. Hayes was a Harvard-educated lawyer, former U.S. congressman, Ohio governor, and Union veteran. He had enjoyed little national exposure before 1876 but he was known to have disliked former president Andrew Johnson and favored the punitive Reconstruction policies championed by the Radical Republicans. His opinions were hardly set in stone. The historian Henry Adams described Hayes as "a third-rate nonentity whose only recommendation is that he is obnoxious to no one." In 1875, when Hayes won reelection as Ohio governor, he professed his support for the scandal-plagued Grant administration despite its many troubles. As talk of Hayes's presidential prospects increased during the ensuing year, however, the candidate-to-be distanced himself from the incumbent president. His high-minded, Radical-sounding rhetoric softened, sounding far more pliable than it had in days past. "I doubt the ultra measures relating to the South," Hayes declared in a statement seemingly repudiating his previous public stance.[12]

Hayes's statement placed him in the middle of a Republican Party schism between the Stalwarts, led by New York Senator Roscoe Conkling, who supported a third term in office for President Grant, and the Half-Breeds, led by Maine Congressman James G. Blaine, who opposed the Stalwarts. Hayes's waffling was a blessing for his presidential aspirations; he became the compromise candidate when Grant refused to seek a third term. In the meantime, the intraparty fighting between Conkling and Blaine ensured that neither man would capture the Republican nomination without effectively dividing the party and guaranteeing the election of a Democrat in the November general election. During the Republican convention in Cincinnati in June 1876, Hayes was nominated on the seventh ballot along with Congressman William A. Wheeler of New York as his vice-presidential running mate.[13]

Facing a Democratic Party that had long been out of power was both a blessing and a curse. On one hand, Republicans enjoyed an advantage as the party in power because they could control the mechanisms of government to keep Democrats more or less in line. Patronage appointments proved to be especially effective at overcoming the division between Stalwarts and Half-Breeds. On the other hand, the Democrats were so anxious to recapture the Executive Mansion after an extended period in the wilderness that the party faithful worked together as a team in a manner seldom seen in the contentious realm of party politics.

To counter the Democrats' relative unity, Republican strategists resolved to employ the 1871 Federal Elections Act, a law that regulated the registration of immigrants. Traditionally, Democratic machine bosses had persuaded new immigrants to vote Democratic through various means, legal and otherwise. This virtual monopoly on immigrant votes at a time when foreigners arrived in droves each year ensured the ascendancy of the Democratic Party, particularly in large cities. The Federal Elections Act was designed to correct the fraudulent registration of immigrant voters that ran rampant in the wake of increased immigration. Fortunately for Republicans, Tilden's reputation as a crusader for good, honest government meant that he could hardly object to the use of a statute enacted specifically to reduce corruption in federal elections. By imposing stringent requirements on the method for registering immigrants to vote in the 1876 election, Republicans precluded a large number of new voters from casting ballots for the Democratic Party, especially in the urban North.

Republican efforts to secure an advantage at the polls extended beyond using strictly legalistic maneuvers. In an early example of negative campaigning, the party launched an organized effort to vilify Tilden as a man with a less-than-reputable character. In light of the governor's squeaky clean image at the beginning of the contest, it was no easy task to tarnish the man's reputation. At all levels of the party, the Republicans attacked the chore with relish, questioning Tilden's Civil War record, casting suspicion on the source of his personal wealth and his failure to pay an adequate amount of income taxes, and his connection with railroad interests. Although the strategy was not entirely effective, it did yield some dividends. Unaccustomed to defending his character, Tilden refused to dignify the charges with a response, which implied that the allegations might be valid. Even when voters did not suspect Tilden of corruption, the candidate's haughty demeanor was off-putting. He appeared aloof and arrogant even to his most faithful supporters.[14]

For their part, Democrats highlighted the corruption often found in Southern carpetbagger governments as well as the numerous scandals that had engulfed the Grant administration. Although he occasionally came off as too aristocratic to descend into the political muck, Tilden possessed fine qualities for a candidate of that era. He was a natural organizer who understood the workings of party politics; his lengthy network of political operatives stretched back almost four decades. He also understood the use of publicity, and he effectively advertised his candidacy in pro-Democratic newspapers. Tilden's strategy proved to be one of the earliest and most savvy uses of paid political advertising in American history.

Tilden also showed himself to be a shrewd fundraiser. His name, syn-onymous with good government and honesty for many Americans, was al-most magical in securing campaign contributions. The Great Forecloser was not personally interested in raising money—in fact, he contributed a relatively small amount of his own considerable fortune—but his campaign financiers used the candidate's strong reputation to good advantage in ap-proaching potential donors.[15]

The election held on November 7, 1876, was one of the closest in American history, but Tilden appeared to have won. When he retired for the evening, Rutherford B. Hayes felt certain he had lost the presidency. Tilden had carried New York, New Jersey, Connecticut, Indiana, and the entire South, giving him a plurality of about 250,000 popular votes and, it appeared, 203 electoral votes. Only 185 electoral votes were needed for vic-tory. Hayes had carried his home state of Ohio, which had been in jeop-ardy early on election night, but he had little cause for celebration.[16]

In one of the most intriguing episodes in American history, Hayes's candidacy was snatched from the jaws of defeat by a bizarre set of circum-stances and machinations. The events culminating in Hayes's eventual vic-tory began when General Daniel Sickles stopped at the Republican National Committee Headquarters on his way home from the theater. The one-legged Sickles was a bona fide character. While serving as a Democratic con-gressman and protégé of President James Buchanan during the 1850s, he learned that his wife was locked in a torrid affair with the son of Francis Scott Key, author of the "Star-Spangled Banner." Sickles shot and killed the young man in Lafayette Square, directly across the street from the Executive Mansion. He was acquitted of the crime by reason of temporary insanity, the first time such a defense had been employed successfully in an American court of law. In 1863, Sickles disobeyed orders while fighting at Gettysburg. As a result, he lost a leg and, incredibly, gained a Medal of Honor for his im-prudence. Always an opportunist, Sickles embraced the Radical Republican cause after the war, served as the military commander of South Carolina, and convinced President Grant to appoint him the American minister to Spain. His well-known tryst with Isabella II, Spain's deposed queen, earned him the nickname of the "Yankee King of Spain" and led to numerous jokes about the genuine meaning of the phrase "foreign affairs."[17]

When this larger-than-life character arrived at Republican headquar-ters late on election night, he sifted through arriving dispatches and realized that all hope was not lost. Hayes could win the election if he carried the Western states of California, Nevada, and Oregon. Recognizing that sev-eral Southern states could swing into the Republican camp as well, he telegraphed Republican leaders in South Carolina, Louisiana, Florida, and Oregon: "With your state sure for Hayes, he is elected. Hold your state."[18]

At 3:00 a.m., Daniel H. Chamberlain, the former prosecutor in the KKK trials who had become governor of South Carolina and was himself in the midst of a bitterly contested, and ultimately unsuccessful, gubernatorial campaign, responded to Sickles's telegram. "All right," he wrote, "South Carolina is for Hayes. Need more troops. Communication with the interior cut off by mobs." Similar positive responses trickled in from Louisiana, Florida, and Oregon.[19]

Another cadre of Republican characters dropped by party headquarters to help engineer the come-from-behind strategy. Campaign manager extraordinaire William E. Chandler joined Sickles in telegraphing state Republican operatives to ask for support in closely contested states. John C. Reid, Republican editor of the *New York Times* and a survivor of the Confederate Libby Prison in Richmond, also appeared and agreed to do whatever he could to swing the election for Hayes. In the next edition of the *Times*, he wrote that a Democratic victory was "uncertain." In his opinion, the Republicans could win if Florida, with its four electoral votes, sided with the Grand Old Party. In an inspired move, Chandler and Reid scurried over to Republican National Committee chairman Zachariah Chandler's house. A well-known aficionado of bottled spirits, the chairman was sleeping off a drink-induced stupor. Dazed and confused, he blinked up at his associates as they regaled him with tales of inconclusive election returns. After a few minutes, he was overwhelmed. "Do what you think is necessary," he said as he fell back into bed.[20]

The men took his words to heart. Throughout the night, wires hummed with telegrams shooting back and forth among party leaders in states where the results were close. In the morning, the outcome remained unclear. Tilden apparently maintained a slight edge in the popular vote, but neither candidate could boast of having secured 185 electoral votes. Tilden clearly had 184 votes and Hayes had 165 votes. Both sides claimed three contested states—Florida, Louisiana, and South Carolina. To complicate matters, an Oregon elector was found to be ineligible because he was serving as a postmaster in Lafayette, Oregon. Under the U.S. Constitution, an elector is prohibited from holding public office at the same time he serves as an elector.[21]

Stunned by the uncertain outcome, both Tilden and Hayes refused to enter the political fray, a position common for presidential candidates of the era. Each man relied on party leaders to work out the details that would lead to victory. For Hayes, surrounded by sophisticated and unscrupulous men such as Daniel Sickles, the two Chandlers, and John C. Reid, his apparent aloofness probably did not harm his cause. Tilden's refusal to fight for the presidency was another matter. He was so anxious to appear high-minded that he did not push his advisors to counteract Republican maneuvers. In an inexplicable move, he issued a bizarre public statement that he would be satisfied with the results of the voting "whether elected or not." Accustomed as he was to legalistic decision making, Tilden apparently believed it was beneath his dignity to rally public opinion to his cause. "Oh, Tilden won't do anything," one Democratic newspaper reported. "He's as cold as a damn clam."[22]

The U.S. Constitution provides that electoral votes should be counted in the presence of both houses of Congress, yet the political parties represented in each chamber could not agree on which electors should be recognized and which votes should be counted. When the electoral votes were tallied on December 6, 1876, the election was still very much in dispute, with each side claiming the necessary votes to win the presidency. No end of the controversy was in sight.

In January 1877, realizing that the stalemate had to cease, prominent Republicans and Democrats resolved to appoint an independent electoral commission to decide how the disputed votes would be counted. The commission was composed of seven Democrats, seven Republicans, and one independent. At the last minute, the commission's independent member, U.S. Supreme Court Justice David Davis, unexpectedly retired. He was replaced by a fellow Justice, Republican Joseph P. Bradley.[23]

The commission began counting votes on February 1, 1877. The arduous process dragged on for a month. On March 2, three days before a new chief executive was to be sworn into office, the commission announced the results. Not surprisingly, commission members voted along party lines. The eight Republicans voted for Hayes and the seven Democrats cast their ballots for Tilden. In the end, the commission concluded that Hayes had garnered 50.14 percent of the popular vote to carry twenty-one states and exactly 185 electoral votes, the precise number needed to claim the presidency. Tilden was found to have won 49.86 percent of the popular vote. He carried seventeen states and 184 electoral votes, one shy of the number required for victory.[24]

The presidential election of 1876 has been deconstructed and studied endlessly since the results were announced. Historians are divided on the reasons for Hayes's triumph aside from partisan support on the electoral commission. His success in the disputed states of South Carolina, Louisiana, and Florida might have been attributable to continued Republican occupation of

Figure 8.3. **This cartoon was published in *Frank Leslie's Illustrated Newspaper* in January 1877, while the winner of the 1876 presidential election was undecided. The imaginary scene depicts a Southern soldier offering Republican candidate Rutherford B. Hayes election returns from South Carolina, Louisiana, and Florida on the end of a bayonet. Here, Hayes refuses to accept the returns but in reality he accepted them and became president.**
Picture History

those states; however, Republicans did not fare as well in other Southern state elections. This apparent anomaly has led some observers to speculate on the terms of a "Southern deal." Hayes's detractors labeled it the "Corrupt Bargain."

Whatever it is called, the deal is theorized to have been a pledge by Hayes, or his election managers, that if the electoral commission membership were to include a sufficient number of Republicans to guarantee Hayes's ascension into the Executive Mansion, Republicans would order federal troops to stop guarding the statehouses in Louisiana and South Carolina. The terms of the Corrupt Bargain are murky. Hayes is known to have met with Colonel William H. Roberts, managing editor of the *New Orleans Times*, on December 1, 1876. Roberts said he represented the views of prominent Southern leaders, including L. Q. C. Lamar, Wade Hampton, John B. Gordon, and others who wished to know the candidate's views. Roberts later recalled that he told Hayes, "If we felt that you were friendly to us, we would not make that desperate personal fight to keep you out that we certainly will make if you are not friendly." Hayes was predictably circumspect in reporting the gist of his conversation with Roberts, remarking only that "in case of my election there will be further conferences, and I hope for good results."[25]

Another occasion at which a Corrupt Bargain might have been struck involved a meeting among several members of the Electoral Commission on February 26, 1877, at the Wormley House, a hotel owned by a wealthy black man, James Wormley, in Washington, D.C. Five Ohio Republicans met with three Louisiana Democrats. James A. Garfield, an Ohio congressman and member of the commission, was among the attendees, but he departed not long after the discussions commenced because he said he was uncomfortable pledging Hayes's support for an agreement without leaving room for additional negotiations. In Garfield's absence, the Wormley Agreements were reached. Republicans agreed to withdraw their support for carpetbagger governments in the Southern states provided that blacks and other Republicans in Louisiana were afforded "proper protection," whatever that might mean.[26]

Historians are unable to say definitively that a bargain existed or whether, if it did, Hayes agreed to abandon or reverse all federal Reconstruction policies. Republicans thought so at the time. They also believed that the Democratic members of the electoral commission would push for a filibuster and thereby delay the March 5 inauguration of a new president if Hayes's claim were denied. Whatever calculations were involved, the Democrats capitulated. Without a filibuster in the offing, Rutherford B. Hayes was inaugurated as the nineteenth President of the United States on March 5, 1877.

Whether it was the result of a deal or because of an expected shift in emphasis with a new president in office, Hayes announced a "new Southern policy" within a month of taking office. The administration removed federal troops from the South Carolina statehouse on April 10, 1877. Exactly two weeks later, the last U.S. troops stationed in any Southern state marched from the city of New Orleans. Twelve years of troubled federal Reconstruction of the Southern states had officially ended.[27]

South Carolina experienced its own electoral drama in the 1876 election apart from the presidential contest. After successfully prosecuting the Klan, Daniel H. Chamberlain moved from the attorney general's office to the governor's mansion when he handily won the 1874 election. He faced a far more formidable opponent when he stood for reelection two years later. Former Confederate general and influential planter Wade Hampton had agreed to throw his hat into the gubernatorial arena, and he represented the Democrats' best hope to recapture the state executive branch.

Anxious to "redeem" state government from the Republican carpet-baggers who had become ensconced in power during the years since the war, Democrats mobilized whites from all areas of the state and among every social class. Decked out in distinctive red shirts that became a recognizable uniform of sorts, Hampton's supporters generally were members of the rifle and saber clubs that formed during the 1870s. The clubs were social organizations that also served as extralegal policemen patrolling white neighborhoods to ensure that black militia groups did not stir up trouble. Although not as militant or violent as the Klan had been in its heyday, the clubs nonetheless promised to employ violence, if necessary. Aside from their readiness for armed confrontation, the Red Shirts also served as a genuine grassroots lobbying force that promised a good turnout on Election Day. For the first time since the war, Democrats had a strong chance to take control of South Carolina government.[28]

Tensions between Republicans and Democrats became clear a month before Election Day. On October 15, 1876, just outside the small town of Cainhoy, thirty miles from Charleston, Republicans met for a rally at a small brick church. Much to their consternation, a crowd of some two hundred Democrats turned out. Both sides were guarded by armed militia groups but cooler heads enjoined the parties to lay down their arms. The men agreed to stack their weapons in nearby buildings while they attended the rally. All seemed to go well until two fellows exchanged angry words; thereafter, events escalated as each side feared the other was intent on slaughter. Gunfire erupted when Republicans and Democrats alike ran for their weapons, and heavily armed blacks managed to push white Democrats to the river. Later, the whites returned with reinforcements. The "Cainhoy riot" was one of several violent disturbances that occurred as a prelude to the elections. Fearful of lawlessness in the Palmetto State, President Grant put the War Department on alert and threatened to send federal troops to restore order. For the first time since the 1871 Ku Klux Klan arrests, U.S. soldiers were poised to ensure domestic tranquility through the use of force.[29]

The November gubernatorial election was extremely close. The Board of Canvassers, which included five Republicans, counted the returns and found that Hampton received 92,261 votes and Chamberlain received 91,127. Had the tabulations ended there, clearly Hampton would have been the victor; however, the board was not satisfied with the election returns in Edgefield and Laurens Counties. Because the Democrats had received more votes than the total number of registered voters in those counties, the board excluded the results. This modification changed the election from a 1,134 victory for Hampton to a 3,145 victory for Chamberlain. Incensed, the

Democratic Party brought a lawsuit in the state supreme court. The court ruled that the state legislature was the final arbiter of the dispute.

In 1876, the South Carolina legislature was embroiled in its own dispute about which party held a majority. Republicans tried to prevent entry by anyone claiming a seat in the legislature until that person—especially candidates from Edgefield and Laurens Counties—could produce a certificate of authenticity issued by the Board of Canvassers. In protest, Democrats withdrew from the state House of Representatives and established their own alternative state house. The dueling legislatures struggled for supremacy until early in 1877, when Chamberlain and the Republicans realized their position was untenable and opted to end the embarrassing "Mexican style of government" by capitulating. Through it all, Wade Hampton urged calm, preached nonviolence, and acted the part of a statesman in the eyes of many South Carolinians. Had the federal government been willing to aid Chamberlain in providing troops and preventing the election results in the disputed counties from being counted, the Republicans might have retained power. As it was, the federal retreat from Reconstruction was nearly complete, and no federal official had the will to intervene. Moreover, when Rutherford B. Hayes apparently agreed to the Corrupt Bargain, Governor Chamberlain's raison d'être ceased to exist. He had held the state for the Republicans but the Republicans would not hold the state for him.[30]

As the controversial presidential and South Carolina gubernatorial elections vividly illustrated, by the mid-1870s, federal Reconstruction policies had lost whatever marginal benefits they once had promised. Reconstruction had become less a method of reincorporating the states of the former Southern Confederacy into the Union than a method of punishing a way of life and attitudes unpopular north of the Mason-Dixon Line. The presidential election of 1876 was important not so much because of Hayes's new Southern policy, which was inevitable, but because it marked a dividing line between the slower-paced, economically isolated world of the nineteenth century and the fast-paced, economically expansionist world of the twentieth century. By 1877, antebellum America seemed so far away in time and sentiment it was almost impossible to believe that the Civil War had erupted only sixteen years earlier.

Reconstruction left the South unrecognizable to its inhabitants. The abandonment of agricultural slave labor would have been enough to cripple the region for generations, but that was not the only loss inflicted on the vanquished Confederates. The destruction of Southern homes, industrial capacity, transportation facilities, and economic institutions decimated the region for decades to follow. One quarter of the South's men of military age had been killed—approximately 260,000 people. During the 1860s, the value of Northern wealth increased by a staggering 50 percent, while the South lost 60 percent of its wealth during the same period. In 1860, the average per capita income of Southerners, even when accounting for slave labor, was two-thirds of the average per capita income of a Northern citizen. After the war, Southerners earned about two-fifths of what a Northern wage earner brought home. This disparity would stretch well into the coming century.[31]

With the end of Reconstruction, Southern whites hammered out a new economic and social arrangement to control blacks. The effects were immediately apparent within the halls of state governments throughout the South. During Reconstruction, approximately 15 percent of the officeholders in the region were black—a larger percentage than at any time until the 1990s—but after 1877 blacks occupied less than 1 percent of elected offices in the former Confederate States of America. Although they were no longer slaves, people of color were relegated to the bottom of the social ladder as segregation statutes sprang up in one state after another.[32]

The Ku Klux Klan had ceased to exist as an active organization before President Hayes implemented his Southern strategy. With Democrats firmly in control of their states, whites had no need of extralegal mechanisms to accomplish under cover of night what they could accomplish far more effectively under color of law. Although it no longer existed, the idea of the Klan persisted, assuming a nostalgic sheen that insulated it from clear-headed scrutiny.

From time to time after the mid-1870s, masked vigilante groups sprang up in the tradition of the KKK, although none captured the public imagination the way the Ku Kluxers had captured it during Reconstruction. The Whitecaps, a group that began in Indiana in the 1880s and spread to parts of the Midwest and South, threatened to resurrect the Reconstruction-era KKK at the end of the century, but around 1900 the group withered away. Booth Tarkington's *The Gentleman from Indiana*, a muckraking exposé of the band, played a part in the group's destruction when it heaped scorn on the Whitecaps and severely undermined its cachet.[33]

In a sense, the Ku Klux Klan went underground, waiting to be reborn. The group's founders and practitioners died off during or before the World War I era, but books and pamphlets continued to extol the virtues of masked heroes who rescued imperiled whites from immoral, traitorous scalawags; wicked, corrupt Republican carpetbaggers; and armed, liquored-up black radicals that ran rampant after the ignominious end of the War Between the States. With the influx of immigrants during the Gilded Age, the uncertainties of an era where rich robber barons grew richer while poor, rural farmers grew poorer, and the myriad changes in American life as revolutions in industry, transportation, and communications profoundly transformed the world, populist sentiment grew and flourished. Deep within the heart of many a Southerner, existing side by side with this developing populist sentiment, a quiet resentment germinated. Not only in the South but in many small communities in the Midwest, men and women sensed that life was becoming more complicated and large forces were at work, driven by hidden elites that made the rules and enforced them but felt no compulsion to abide by them.

Race was still a key distinguishing factor in determining social status, but ethnicity and class became more important than ever. A fellow who harbored a deep resentment at his day-to-day travails and economic hardships need only look around to see new immigrants—often they were foreigners with difficult-to-pronounce names speaking incomprehensible, guttural languages and practicing strange, inexplicable religions. Such a fellow felt his populist outrage grow and his carefully cultivated resentment seethe. In the face of swift, unrelenting change, a fellow might find himself choking with a longing for something to come along and offer him a better life. If a better life could not be had, an outlet for expressing his rage would suffice.[34]

Following the publication of a popular book in 1905 and the appearance of a subsequent movie version, coupled with a sensationalized murder case featuring an evil Jew who preyed on a virginal young girl, disaffected whites found a romantic symbol from the past that perfectly expressed their discontent. They looked to the dark days of Reconstruction for inspiration. That symbol—a symbol of white supremacy that had served an earlier generation of alienated Southerners with a promise of power and control over threats to their way of life—was the Ku Klux Klan. One chapter in the story of the "great organization" had closed; a new one would soon open.[35]

NOTES

1. "The Abduction of Dr. Bratton," *Yorkville Enquirer*, Yorkville, SC (August 1, 1872); "The Arrest of Dr. J. R. Bratton," *Yorkville Enquirer*, Yorkville, SC (June 20, 1872); "The Case of Dr. J. R. Bratton," *Yorkville Enquirer*, Yorkville, SC (June 27, 1872); Stanley F. Horn, *Invisible Empire: The Story of the Ku Klux Klan, 1866–1871* (Montclair, NJ: Patterson Smith, 1969), 239–40; Fred Langdon, "The Kidnapping of Dr. Rufus Bratton," *Journal of Negro History* 10 (July 1925): 330–32; Louis F. Post,

"A Carpetbagger in South Carolina," *Journal of Negro History* 10 (January 1925): 61–62; Francis B. Simkins, "The Ku Klux Klan in South Carolina," *Journal of Negro History* 12 (October 1927): 645; Allen W. Trelease, *White Terror: The Ku Klux Klan Conspiracy and Southern Reconstruction* (Baton Rouge: Louisiana State University Press, 1971), 404; Jerry L. West, *The Reconstruction Ku Klux Klan in York County, South Carolina, 1865–1877* (Jefferson, NC: McFarland & Company, Inc., 2002), appendix 3, 126–30; Richard Zuczek, "The Federal Government's Attack on the Ku Klux Klan: A Reassessment," *South Carolina Historical Magazine* 97 (January 1, 1996): 57–58; Richard Zuczek, *State of Rebellion: Reconstruction in South Carolina* (Columbia, SC: University of South Carolina Press, 1996), 119–20.

2. David Everitt, "1871 War on Terror," *American History* 38 (June 2003): 33; Eric Foner, *Reconstruction: America's Unfinished Revolution, 1863–1877* (New York: Francis Parkman Prize Edition, History Book Club, 2005; originally published by HarperCollins, 1988), 458; Robert J. Kaczorowski, "Federal Enforcement of Civil Rights During the First Reconstruction," *Fordham Urban Law Journal* 23 (Fall 1995): 182; Trelease, *White Terror*, 411; Wyn Craig Wade, *The Fiery Cross: The Ku Klux Klan in America* (New York and Oxford: Oxford University Press, 1987), 109; Lou Falkner Williams, *The Great South Carolina Ku Klux Klan Trials, 1871–1872* (Athens: University of Georgia Press, 1996), 101–2; Zuczek, *State of Rebellion*, 102–3.

3. Everitt, "1871 War on Terror," 33; Kermit L. Hall, "Political Power and Constitutional Legitimacy: The South Carolina Ku Klux Klan Trials, 1871–1872," *Emory Law Journal* 33 (Fall 1984): 950–51; Kaczorowski, "Federal Enforcement of Civil Rights During the First Reconstruction," 180–83; Post, "A Carpetbagger in South Carolina," 64–72; Wade, *The Fiery Cross*, 103–4; West, *The Reconstruction Ku Klux Klan in York County, South Carolina*, 101–8; Williams, *The Great South Carolina Ku Klux Klan Trials*, 102–6; Zuczek, "The Federal Government's Attack on the Ku Klux Klan: A Reassessment," 60–62; Zuczek, *State of Rebellion*, 102–8.

4. The commentator is Williams, *The Great South Carolina Ku Klux Klan Trials*, 111. See also, United States Congress, *Report of the Joint Select Committee to Inquire into the Condition of Affairs in the Late Insurrectionary States*, 42 Cong., 2 Sess., No. 22 (1872), Vol. V, 1472; West, *The Reconstruction Ku Klux Klan in York County, South Carolina*, appendix 5, 134–36; Zuczek, *State of Rebellion*, 120–22.

5. Everitt, "1871 War on Terror," 33; Kaczorowski, "Federal Enforcement of Civil Rights During the First Reconstruction," 182; Everette Swinney, "Enforcing the Fifteenth Amendment, 1870–1877," *Journal of Southern History* 28 (May 1962): 205–6; Trelease, *White Terror*, 411–12; Williams, *The Great South Carolina Ku Klux Klan Trials*, 107–111; Zuczek, *State of Rebellion*, 121.

6. Foner, *Reconstruction: America's Unfinished Revolution*, 442–59; Wade, *The Fiery Cross*, 112–13; Williams, *The Great South Carolina Ku Klux Klan Trials*, 113–114, 126–30; Zuczek, *State of Rebellion*, 107–8.

7. *The Slaughterhouse Cases*, 83 U.S. (16 Wall.) 36 (1873); *United States v. Reese*, 92 U.S. 214 (1876); *United States v. Cruikshank*, 92 U.S. 542 (1876). See also, Richard L. Aynes, "Freedom: Constitutional Law: Constricting the Law of Freedom: Justice

Miller, the Fourteenth Amendment, and the Slaughter–House Cases," *Chicago–Kent Law Review* 70 (1994): 632–37; Michael P. O'Connor, "Time Out of Mind: Our Collective Amnesia About the History of the Privileges and Immunities Clause," *Kentucky Law Journal* 93 (2004/2005): 700–5; Wade, *The Fiery Cross*, 113; Williams, *The Great South Carolina Ku Klux Klan Trials*, 131–42; C. Vann Woodward, *The Strange Career of Jim Crow*, 2d. ed. (New York and Oxford: Oxford University Press, 1966), 70–72.

8. Quoted in *Williams v. Mississippi*, 170 U.S. 213, 222 (1898). See also, The *Civil Rights Cases*, 109 U.S. 3 (1883); Foner, *Reconstruction: America's Unfinished Revolution*, 559–63; *Hall v. de Cuir*, 95 U.S. 485 (1878); Robert Selph Henry, *The Story of Reconstruction* (New York: Konecky & Konecky, 1999), 544–53; *Louisville, New Orleans, and Texas Railway Company v. Mississippi*, 133 U.S. 587 (1890); Williams, *The Great South Carolina Ku Klux Klan Trials*, 142–44; Woodward, *The Strange Career of Jim Crow*, 70–71.

9. Justice Brown is quoted in *Plessy v. Ferguson*, 163 U.S. 537, 551 (1896). Justice Harlan is quoted at 163 U.S. 559 and 560. See also, N. Lee Cooper, "President's Message—The Harlan Standard: Former Associate Justice Can Teach Us the Value of Reasoned Dissent," *ABA Journal* 83 (June 1997): 8; Cheryl I. Harris, "Symposium: Race Jurisprudence and the Supreme Court: Where Do We Go From Here? In The Shadow of *Plessy*," *University of Pennsylvania Journal of Constitutional Law* 7 (February 2005): 889–901; Frederic Rodgers, "'Our Constitution is Color Blind': Justice John Marshall Harlan and the *Plessy v. Ferguson* Dissent," *American Bar Association Judges' Journal* 43 (Spring 2004): 15; Wade, *The Fiery Cross*, 113; Woodward, *The Strange Career of Jim Crow*, 54, 71.

10. Dee Brown, *The Year of the Century: 1876* (New York: Charles Scribner's Sons, 1966), 199–201; Foner, *Reconstruction: America's Unfinished Revolution*, 588–601; Henry, *The Story of Reconstruction*, 401.

11. Brown, *The Year of the Century: 1876*, 199–200; Ari Hoogenboom, *The Presidency of Rutherford B. Hayes* (Lawrence: University Press of Kansas, 1988), 2–3.

12. Foner, *Reconstruction: America's Unfinished Revolution*, 575–77; Henry, *The Story of Reconstruction* 554–55; Hoogenboom, *The Presidency of Rutherford B. Hayes*, 11; Lewis L. Gould, *Grand Old Party: A History of the Republicans* (New York; Random House, 2003), 71–73; Roy Morris Jr., *Fraud of the Century: Rutherford B. Hayes, Samuel Tilden, and the Stolen Election of 1876* (New York: Simon & Schuster, 2003), 57–68, 84–108; William H. Rehnquist, *Centennial Crisis: The Disputed Election of 1876* (New York: Alfred A. Knopf, 2004), 33–51, 58–79; Wynell Schamel, Lee Ann Potter, and Katherine Snodgrass, "Documents Related to the Disputed General Election of 1876," *Social Education* 64 (September 2000), 286–87; Jules Witcover, *Party of the People: A History of the Democrats* (New York: Random House, 2003), 245–46; Rowland L. Young, "The Year They Stole the White House," *American Bar Association Journal* 62 (November 1976): 1459–60.

13. Foner, *Reconstruction: America's Unfinished Revolution*, 485–88; Gould, *Grand Old Party*, 72–73; Henry, *The Story of Reconstruction*, 554; Hoogenboom, *The Presi-*

dency of Rutherford B. Hayes, 11–21; Joseph Nathan Kane, *Facts About the Presidents* (New York: Charter Communications, 1976), 213; Witcover, *Party of the People*, 245–46; Young, "The Year They Stole the White House," 1459.

14. Alexander Clarence Flick, *Samuel Jones Tilden: A Study in Political Sagacity* (New York: Dodd, Mead & Company, 1939), 308–15; Foner, *Reconstruction: America's Unfinished Revolution*, 553–58; Hoogenboom, *The Presidency of Rutherford B. Hayes*, 22–24; Schamel, Potter, and Snodgrass, "Documents Related to the Disputed General Election of 1876," 286–87; Witcover, *Party of the People*, 246–47; Kerwin C. Swint, *Mudslingers: The Top 25 Negative Political Campaigns of All Time: Countdown from No. 25 to No. 1* (Westport, CT: Praeger, 2005), 79–86; Young, "The Year They Stole the White House," 1459.

15. Flick, *Samuel Jones Tilden: A Study in Political Sagacity*, 303–04; Schamel, Potter, and Snodgrass, "Documents Related to the Disputed General Election of 1876," 287; Witcover, *Party of the People*, 246–47.

16. Steven G. Calabresi and Christopher S. Yoo, "The Unitary Executive During the Second Half-Century," *Harvard Journal of Law & Public Policy* 26 (Summer 2003): 769; Foner, *Reconstruction: America's Unfinished Revolution*, 575; Gould, *Grand Old Party*, 75; Henry, *The Story of Reconstruction*, 571–72; Hoogenboom, *The Presidency of Rutherford B. Hayes*, 25; John Copeland Nagle, "How Not to Count Votes," *Columbia Law Review* 104 (October 2004): 1732–63; Witcover, *Party of the People*, 247; Young, "The Year They Stole the White House," 1460–61.

17. Foner, *Reconstruction: America's Unfinished Revolution*, 575; Hoogenboom, *The Presidency of Rutherford B. Hayes*, 25; Morris, *Fraud of the Century*, 10–11.

18. Quoted in Keith Ian Polakoff, *The Politics of Inertia: The Election of 1876 and the End of Reconstruction* (Baton Rouge: Louisiana State University Press, 1973), 202. See also, Foner, *Reconstruction: America's Unfinished Revolution*, 575; Gould, *Grand Old Party*, 74–75; Rehnquist, *Centennial Crisis*, 97.

19. Quoted in Hoogenboom, *The Presidency of Rutherford B. Hayes*, 26. See also, Ronald F. King, "Counting the Votes: South Carolina's Stolen Election of 1876," *Journal of Interdisciplinary History* 32 (Autumn 2001): 169–91; Polakoff, *The Politics of Inertia*, 202; Zuczek, *State of Rebellion*, 165–74.

20. Quoted in Hoogenboom, *The Presidency of Rutherford B. Hayes*, 26. See also, Foner, *Reconstruction: America's Unfinished Revolution*, 575; Polakoff, *The Politics of Inertia*, 202–03; Schamel, Potter, and Snodgrass, "Documents Related to the Disputed General Election of 1876," 287; Swint, *Mudslingers*, 82–83; Witcover, *Party of the People*, 247; Young, "The Year They Stole the White House," 1460.

21. Foner, *Reconstruction: America's Unfinished Revolution*, 575; Kane, *Facts About the Presidents*, 217; Polakoff, *The Politics of Inertia*, 225–27; Swint, *Mudslingers*, 82–83; Witcover, *Party of the People*, 247–48; Young, "The Year They Stole the White House," 1460.

22. Quoted in Flick, *Samuel Jones Tilden: A Study in Political Sagacity*, 351. See also, Harry Barnard, *Rutherford B. Hayes and His America* (Indianapolis: Bobbs-Merrill Company, Inc., 1954), 357; Brown, *The Year of the Century: 1876*, 117–18;

Foner, *Reconstruction: America's Unfinished Revolution*, 576–77; Young, "The Year They Stole the White House," 1461.

23. Calabresi and Yoo, "The Unitary Executive During the Second Half-Century," 769; Foner, *Reconstruction:America's Unfinished Revolution*, 576–82; Henry, *The Story of Reconstruction*, 581–82; Kane, *Facts About the Presidents*, 215; Swint, *Mudslingers*, 84; Witcover, *Party of the People*, 248–49; Young, "The Year They Stole the White House," 1460–61.

24. Calabresi and Yoo, "The Unitary Executive During the Second Half-Century," 769; Foner, *Reconstruction: America's Unfinished Revolution*, 581–82; Gould, *Grand Old Party*, 74–75; Kane, *Facts About the Presidents*, 216; Schamel, Potter, and Snodgrass, "Documents Related to the Disputed General Election of 1876," 291; Swint, *Mudslingers*, 84–85; Witcover, *Party of the People*, 249–50; Young, "The Year They Stole the White House," 1461.

25. Quoted in C. Vann Woodward, *Reunion and Reaction: The Compromise of 1877 and the End of Reconstruction* (Boston: Little, Brown, and Company, 1951), 25. See also, Calabresi and Yoo, "The Unitary Executive During the Second Half-Century," 769; Foner, *Reconstruction: America's Unfinished Revolution*, 576–81; Young, "The Year They Stole the White House," 1460–61.

26. Calabresi and Yoo, "The Unitary Executive During the Second Half-Century," 769; Foner, *Reconstruction: America's Unfinished Revolution*, 580–81; Hoogenboom, *The Presidency of Rutherford B. Hayes*, 46–47; Witcover, *Party of the People*, 250–51.

27. William Blair, "The Use of Military Force to Protect the Gains of Reconstruction," *Civil War History* 51 (December 2005): 388, 396; Foner, *Reconstruction: America's Unfinished Revolution*, 582; Gould, *Grand Old Party*, 75–76; Henry, *The Story of Reconstruction*, 591–92; Swint, *Mudslingers*, 84–86; Witcover, *Party of the People*, 251–52; Young, "The Year They Stole the White House," 1461.

28. Henry, *The Story of Reconstruction*, 573–79; King, "Counting the Votes," 169–70; Edward G. Longacre, *Gentleman and Soldier: The Extraordinary Life of General Wade Hampton* (Nashville, TN: Rutledge Hill Press, 2003), 262–64; Zuczek, *State of Rebellion*, 170, 206–7, 210.

29. King, "Counting the Votes," 170; Longacre, *Gentleman and Soldier*, 263–64; Zuczek, *State of Rebellion*, 177–80.

30. Foner, *Reconstruction: America's Unfinished Revolution*, 570–75; Henry, *The Story of Reconstruction*, 573–78; King, "Counting the Votes," 169–72; Longacre, *Gentleman and Soldier*, 265–67; Zuczek, *State of Rebellion*, 188–201.

31. Foner, *Reconstruction: America's Unfinished Revolution*, 602–12; James M. McPherson, *Abraham Lincoln and the Second American Revolution* (New York and Oxford; Oxford University Press, 1991), 11–12; Wade, *The Fiery Cross*, 112–16.

32. Michael Les Benedict, "Preserving the Constitution: The Conservative Basis of Radical Reconstruction," *The Journal of American History* 61 (June 1974): 89–90; Foner, *Reconstruction: America's Unfinished Revolution*, 602–05; McPherson, *Abraham Lincoln and the Second American Revolution*, 19; Swinney, "Enforcing the Fif-

teenth Amendment, 1870–1877," 205–6; Woodward, *The Strange Career of Jim Crow*, 12–29; Zuczek, *State of Rebellion*, 206–10.

33. Blair, "The Use of Military Force to Protect the Gains of Reconstruction," 400–2; Everitt, "1871 War on Terror," 33; Trelease, *White Terror*, 420; Wade, *The Fiery Cross*, 114–15; Woodward, *The Strange Career of Jim Crow*, 85–86.

34. Kenneth T. Jackson, *The Ku Klux Klan in the City, 1915–1930* (Chicago: Ivan R. Dee, 1967), 3–4; J. Michael Martinez, "Traditionalist Perspectives on Confederate Symbols," in *Confederate Symbols in the Contemporary South*, J. Michael Martinez, William D. Richardson, and Ron McNinch-Su, eds. (Gainesville: University Press of Florida, 2000), 258; James Ridgeway, *Blood in the Face: The Ku Klux Klan, Aryan Nations, Nazi Skinheads, and the Rise of a New White Culture*, 2d. ed. (New York: Thunder's Mouth Press, 1995), 52; Trelease, *White Terror*, 417–22; Wade, *The Fiery Cross*, 115–16.

35. Nancy Bishop Dessommes, "Hollywood in Hoods: The Portrayal of the Ku Klux Klan in Popular Film," *Journal of Popular Culture* 32 (Spring 1999): 15–17; Leonard Dinnerstein, *The Leo Frank Case* (Birmingham, AL: Notable Trials Library, 1991), 1–7; Nancy MacLean, "The Leo Frank Case Reconsidered: Gender and Sexual Politics in the Making of Reactionary Populism," *The Journal of American History* 78 (December 1991): 938–40, 947; Martinez, "Traditionalist Perspectives on Confederate Symbols," 258–61; Rory McVeigh, "Structural Incentives for Conservative Mobilization: Power Devaluation and the Rise of the Ku Klux Klan, 1915–1925," *Social Forces* 77 (June 1999): 1464–66; Steve Oney, *And the Dead Shall Rise: The Murder of Mary Phagan and the Lynching of Leo Frank* (New York: Vintage Books, 2003), 605–7; Wade, *The Fiery Cross*, 119–66.

9

"HE BECAME SO OFFENSIVE A PARTISAN THAT THE PAPERS OF THAT SECTION APPLIED TO HIM THE MOST OPPROBRIOUS EPITHETS"

Major Lewis Merrill was stationed in Yorkville from March 1871 until June 1873. During the last eighteen months that he served in South Carolina, he watched as the new attorney general, George H. Williams, and the U.S. Department of Justice backed away from the commitment to prosecuting the Ku Klux Klan. The major grew despondent. He and his men continued to investigate Klan atrocities and arrest suspects, but their efforts seemed pointless if the defendants were not arraigned and tried in federal court.[1]

In May 1872, he applied for a leave of absence. The War Department considered his request for nine months before referring the matter to the post surgeon for a recommendation. On February 20, 1873, the Yorkville army surgeon concluded that Merrill enjoyed "very little time for rest or mental recreation" and, as a result, "was suffering from general prostration of the nervous system incident to long and laborious mental labor in the discharge of the duties assigned him." Following an initial examination, the surgeon forwarded Merrill's request to the army surgeon in Columbia, Dr. Frantz, who agreed that a leave of absence should be granted. Dr. Frantz wrote, "He is suffering from exhaustion of brain power, in my opinion, from the history of the case, consequent upon close and protracted mental application to duties incident to his official position at Yorkville, S.C."

On June 4, 1873, Merrill received a one-year leave of absence along with a note from George H. Williams. "Please accept my thanks for the efficient manner in which you have discharged the duties imposed upon you by the Department [of Justice]," the attorney general wrote in a perfunctory acknowledgment of the major's service. Merrill later received effusive praise from his direct superior, General Alfred Terry, as well as similar accolades from high-ranking War Department officials. In a controversial move, the South Carolina General Assembly showed its appreciation by voting to provide him with a $20,000 financial reward.[2]

The legislature's payment to Merrill galled white Southerners incensed at federal interference with state rights and home rule. An episode involving York County probate judge Samuel B. Hall stands out as an example of the antipathy felt by Yorkville residents toward the major. While campaigning for political office in August 1872, Hall denounced Merrill to a crowd of five hundred amassed near the courthouse steps. Described as "a native of York with a good classical education, married, a father, and politically ambitious," Hall had joined the Radical Republicans, in his own words, "to make money out of it." The plan worked; he was elevated into the position of probate judge on the strength of his Republican ties as well as his earlier decision not to serve in the Confederate States Army. Once in office, Hall proved that his professed goal of making money from his Republican Party affiliation was no idle boast. He allegedly used his position as a judge to extort money from persons conducting business before the probate court. Discovering evidence of possible malfeasance, Merrill had exposed Hall's schemes. Infuriated with the major's charges of financial impropriety lodged against him as well as the state legislature's decision to compensate a career army officer for performing his duty, the judge realized that an effective strategy compelled him to meet Merrill's charges with a few of his own.

Calling out to the sympathetic throng assembled in front of the York County courthouse, Hall said the major was guilty of "the most infamous lie that was ever told on the streets of Yorkville, even in the State House at Columbia." He explained that Merrill had orchestrated the KKK arrests through bribery and bullying tactics. Merrill, "by the use of money and having men swear lies, thought he could go to work to have the Writ of Habeas Corpus suspended." In a subsequent booklet, "A Shell in Radical Camp," the judge developed this thesis at length. Aside from questioning the financial "reward" that Merrill received from the South Carolina General Assembly for his work fighting the Klan, he impugned the major's Civil War record, intimating that the officer was a well-known coward.

Judge Hall was later convicted of "official misconduct" for the financial improprieties Merrill had identified. He served a year in the county jail and was ordered to pay a $1000 fine. Despite his humiliating circumstances and discredited accusations, Hall's charges caught the attention of Democratic Senator James A. Bayard Jr. of Delaware, scion of a famous political family. Bayard's father had played a small but vital part in U.S. history. During the election of 1800, when Thomas Jefferson tied Aaron Burr in the Electoral College, the election was thrown into the U.S. House of Representatives. Apparently following the advice of Alexander Hamilton, the elder Bayard persuaded his Federalist colleagues in the House to abstain from voting, which allowed Jefferson to win the election and altered the course of early American history. Now, the younger Bayard recognized an opportunity to play a pivotal role in congressional history, albeit in a much less celebrated fashion than his father.

Bayard introduced a resolution into the U.S. Senate calling for a congressional investigation into Hall's allegations against Merrill. Merrill understood that Senator Bayard was a Democrat playing a political game because the major had served Republican political interests by exposing the KKK; nonetheless, the charges were an affront to Merrill's wounded pride. Faced with another potential scandal only a few years after the Lauffer case, the major barely kept his anger in check when he filed his official report. The document dripped with sarcasm and vituperation. After railing against his political enemies and explaining that Hall's charges were false and without foundation, the aggrieved officer ended with an apology of sorts. "If therefore I have exceeded the coldness of diction which is becoming to an Official paper, I hope it will be credited to no intention to be disrespectful, but to the fact that I am put on my defense against a stab in the back." Because Bayard's ploy was pure political theater and his resolution was based on fabrications supplied by an unreliable source, nothing came of it. It was not the first or last time that Merrill's foes would investigate his performance, nor would it be the last indignity he suffered at the hands of Congress. In 1876, he would again face a congressional investigation, this time a second inquiry into the Lauffer incident. As he had done previously, he would challenge his opponents to prove their case. Again, they would fail to do so.[3]

After he left South Carolina in 1873, Merrill spent fourteen months on sick leave before resuming his duties. In August and September 1874, he was stationed at Fort Rice in the Dakota Territory, although his assignment was short-lived. When a KKK-style vigilante group called the White League disrupted Louisiana state government in 1874, the major and his men were dispatched to restore law and order. As a veteran of the South Carolina Klan wars, Merrill was well suited to investigate another secret society formed to restore Southern home rule and oppose the interests of the freedmen.[4]

The White League was not formally associated with the Ku Klux Klan, but the two groups shared similar characteristics. Individuals calling

Figure 9.1.   As this 1874 Thomas Nast drawing in *Harper's Weekly* illustrates, the activities of vigilante groups such as the White League and the Ku Klux Klan made the lives of the freedmen "worse than slavery."
The Library of Congress

themselves the "White League" may have been active as early as 1873, but their activities are a matter of dispute. From its first undisputed appearance in Opelousas, Louisiana, in April 1874, the White League was seen as a successor to several earlier secret societies, including the Society of the White Camelia (sometimes linked to the Knights of the White Camellia), the Chalmette Club, and especially the Crescent City Democratic Club, which formed from the Chalmette Club. General Frederick N. Ogden and F. R. Southmayd founded the White League. Unlike Klansmen who preferred to work under masks and darkness, White Leaguers brazenly championed white supremacy, confident that they spoke for a majority of white Louisianans. In an early manifesto, published in several state newspapers in

July 1874, acting under the banner of the "Crescent City White League," the group listed its goals, which included "restoring an honest and intelligent government to the State of Louisiana." The only effective method of accomplishing this objective was to undermine Reconstruction governments, which included blacks in several high offices. According to the manifesto, "Where the white rules, the negro is peaceful and happy; where the black rules, the negro is starved and oppressed." Blacks were so "maddened by the hatred and conceit of race" that "it has become our duty to save them and to save ourselves from the fatal consequences of their stupid extravagance and reckless vanity by arraying ourselves in the name of white civilization, resuming that just and legitimate superiority in the administration of our state affairs to which we are entitled by superior responsibility, superior numbers, and superior intelligence."[5]

As the White League spread to the Upper Red River District of Louisiana during a series of increasingly violent confrontations with state authorities, soldiers of the Seventh U.S. Cavalry were assigned to the region. Stationed in Shreveport for fifteen months beginning in October 1874, Merrill found that his task was far more complicated than it had been in South Carolina. Where the Ku Klux Klan had been a loosely organized, decentralized series of dens united only by the general purpose of resisting carpetbagger rule and oppressing blacks, the White League was more centralized. Based on a military-style hierarchy, its members exhibited the discipline and a penchant for coordinated action that was lacking with most Klan dens. Moreover, because the White League had no need to operate beneath masks, Southern leaders acted with breathtaking audacity. Part of the federal government's strategy for combating the KKK had been to expose members of the "Invisible Empire" on the premise that sunlight is the best disinfectant. The White League operated in the open, unimpeded by public condemnation; hence, publicizing the identity of League members proved to be unsuccessful in Louisiana. Absent the strong support of an attorney general such as Amos T. Akerman or another high-ranking official within the Grant administration, Merrill realized that he could not pursue his investigation with the alacrity that had brought good results in the South Carolina Upcountry.

A notable clash between U.S. soldiers and the White League demonstrated federal impotence in Louisiana. During a routine patrol with a U.S. marshal, Lieutenant B. H. Hodgson, one of Merrill's leading aides, and a dozen U.S. soldiers were surprised when a local sheriff at the head of a two-hundred-man posse appeared from the woods and arrested them on the trumped up charge of cutting telegraph wires. The prisoners were detained at the little town of Vienna. When he learned of the incident, Merrill repeatedly wired his superiors to ask for reinforcements, but six days passed before he could send troops to Vienna to ensure the safety of his men. Without orders allowing him to interfere with civil proceedings, Merrill was forced to stand by helplessly. He eventually hired a civilian lawyer to represent Hodgson against criminal charges in a state court. As if this indignity were not enough, the lawyer provided such poor, lackluster representation that Merrill felt compelled to intervene. He and the lawyer exchanged recriminations that did nothing to aid in the release of his men. Eventually, civilian authorities agreed to drop the charges against Hodgson and his men. By that time, the white ruling class had illustrated the point: They, not federal soldiers, would rule the Red River District.

Louisiana state officials were not the only forces arrayed against Merrill and his men. The local press constantly derided the soldiers in a barrage of stories that were as vitriolic as they were relentless. Recognizing that he would never receive orders to round up suspects for trial in federal court as he had when he combated the KKK in South Carolina, the major grew increasingly frustrated with the negative publicity. In the wake of an especially virulent series of newspaper articles, he reported, "So long as freedom of the press means license to lie and slander at pleasure every officer whose discharge of duty offends one, or frequently both political parties, there would seem to be no remedy for the officer, and nothing for him to do but possess his soul in patience, and wait for a change of station to some frontier post, where the savages, whose feelings he must hurt, have no newspapers through which to assail him."[6]

The major did not have to wait long for a new assignment, although he did not immediately return to the frontier. In February 1876, he received orders from the adjutant general to report for duty "in connection with the International Exhibition of 1876, under the direction of the President, U.S. Centennial Commission." The commission president, Joseph Roswell Hawley, was a career politician and journalist who previously had served as governor of Connecticut, a U.S. congressman, and an influential newspaper editor. Later in life, he would represent Connecticut in the U.S. Senate for four terms. A Union veteran, this plain-spoken, North Carolina-born, Connecticut-bred lawyer served as president of the United States Centennial Commission from 1873 to 1876.

Although he never explained how he arranged the transfer, Merrill apparently used family or professional connections to land a comfortable position far from the frontier outposts and scenes of guerilla warfare where he usually served. On February 18, 1876, Hawley wrote to the secretary of

war, William Belknap, informing him that he required the services of a career military man to greet foreign officers and ensure their safety and security during the Exhibition. In Hawley's view, it "would be very agreeable
to myself and useful to the Commission if some officer of the army were
at liberty to devote himself to our assistance" serving as "a member of my
staff." The commission president had a specific officer in mind. "Major
Lewis Merrill of the Cavalry, Brevet Brigadier General, would be very glad
to assist in these matters." To ensure that Secretary Belknap understood
Merrill's unique qualifications, Hawley listed the attributes that made this
particular officer so desirable for duty at the Exhibition. "He is a Pennsylvanian, a graduate of the Academy, and much interested in the Exhibition.
Could he be permitted to stay here, say, six months?"[7]

The Centennial International Exhibition of 1876—officially titled the
"International Exhibition of Arts, Manufactures and Products of Soil and
Mine"—was the first world's fair held in the United States. The event
opened in Philadelphia during the spring of 1876, and celebrated the one
hundredth anniversary of the signing of the Declaration of Independence.
For ten million visitors, the fair was a carnival featuring a wide array of new
consumer products and industrial gadgets, including Hires Root Beer,
Heinz Ketchup, the Remington Typographic Machine—later called, simply, a "typewriter"—and Alexander Graham Bell's promising new invention, which he called a "telephone." Major Merrill's service from March until November 1876 was a welcomed respite from his usual duties and it
proved to be a fortuitous interlude.[8]

Merrill's position working with Hawley not only removed him from
the intractable problem of dealing with the White League in Louisiana but,
as an added benefit, he did not accompany the Seventh U.S. Cavalry to the
Great Plains. While Merrill was still assigned to the Exhibition, his colleagues, including his estranged commander, Lieutenant Colonel George A.
Custer, galloped toward a date with history. On June 25, 1876, more than
six hundred U.S. soldiers, including a core group of veterans from the Seventh U.S. Cavalry, rode under Custer's command to engage three thousand
Indians in battle near the banks of the Little Bighorn River in Montana
Territory. Custer and his troops were grossly unnumbered. Scores of the
men with whom Lewis Merrill had served for more than seven years were
slaughtered on a hot, dry, dusty afternoon in an incident that captured the
imagination of Americans for generations to come.[9]

A more prosaic fate awaited Lewis Merrill. At the conclusion of his
duty at the International Exhibition, he returned to the frontier, but with
the exception of playing a small part in the pursuit of Chief Joseph in 1877,

the glamour and excitement of his life in uniform, to the extent that it was ever glamorous and exciting, was over. For the next decade, he served in various frontier posts in the Dakota Territory. Several times during the early 1880s, he guarded the extension of the Northern Pacific Railroad. Probably his most noteworthy experience during the last ten years of his military career occurred at Canyon Creek, near the newly established Yellowstone National Park.

The Nez Perce Indians, led by Chief Joseph, fought with the U.S. Army in a series of engagements in 1876 and 1877. As the Nez Perce marched through the new national park with soldiers in pursuit, the Indian band harassed a new set of Americans—tourists—that derived pleasure from communing with nature. On several occasions, young tribal warriors captured foolhardy tourists and roughed them up. Although the incidents were exaggerated as the tales were retold, generally the encounters between whites and Indians were annoying but not deadly. In one memorable instance, however, Nez Perce warriors carried the assault too far and two white men died. It was only a matter of time before the U.S. Army exacted a heavy toll for these violent episodes.

Responsibility for apprehending the Nez Perce and preventing further disturbances fell to Samuel D. Sturgis, the general officer who commanded the Seventh Cavalry in 1877. He and Lewis Merrill had shared similar experiences in the army. Like Merrill, Sturgis had suffered through his experiences with the late, cantankerous Lieutenant Colonel Custer. Fortunately for Sturgis, he was not Custer's subordinate. An 1846 graduate of the U.S. Military Academy at West Point, Sturgis had served with the dragoons in the war with Mexico. Captured before the Battle of Buena Vista, he languished in a Mexican prison until war's end. Before the Civil War, he served throughout the West in campaigns against Apaches, Comanches, and Kiowas. Sturgis fought valiantly in 1861–1862 at Wilson's Creek, Antietam, and Fredericksburg. The only stain on his record occurred when he was bested by the legendary Confederate cavalryman Nathan Bedford Forrest—the man who would do so much to legitimize the Ku Klux Klan after the war—at the Battle of Brice's Cross Roads, Mississippi, on June 10, 1864. Humiliated but not quite scandalized, Sturgis sat out the rest of the war "awaiting orders."

In 1869, he assumed command of the Seventh U.S. Cavalry. Sturgis was not only dismayed when his men were killed at the Little Bighorn; he was devastated when he learned that his own son, Lieutenant James G. Sturgis, a recent West Point graduate, was among the fallen. Now, a year after the massacre, the Seventh consisted of two battalions of three companies each, and Sturgis had orders to pursue marauding Indians and prevent further civilian bloodshed. He fulfilled his orders with relish, no doubt owing in part to his personal anguish. Among the men under his command was Major Lewis Merrill, who headed a battalion consisting of companies F, I, and L.[10]

The Seventh had been chasing the Nez Perce for three months when Sturgis received intelligence that the tribe had been spotted crossing the Yellowstone River near the present-day city of Billings, Montana. Although his men were suffering extreme fatigue from heavy marching with reduced rations, the general ordered them to act on the information and corner the Indians. Four companies of the Seventh, supported by the First U.S. Cavalry, trotted after their prey. Because they were so noisy and weighed down with two howitzers mounted on pack mules, the troops could not hope to surprise the Nez Perce.

When the Indians saw the soldiers approaching, they sent their young warriors to create a diversion while women and children fled to safety. Afterward, the Nez Perce retreated into a narrow wash with banks ten to twenty feet high. Known as Canyon Creek, it was an almost ideal defensive position. The tribe could hide behind scrub brush that grew from the steep ravines and fire down at the oncoming enemy. Caught with no cover, soldiers would be hard-pressed to return fire.

Unaware of the potential trap, General Sturgis ordered Major Merrill to initiate combat. With two companies under his command, the major moved across a series of ridges. To his surprise, Indian sharpshooters launched a deadly volley of shots. Desperate to avoid the bullets raining down into the valley, Merrill's troops took refuge behind a ridgeline. They were trapped until reinforcements could be moved into place.

Realizing that his plans were in jeopardy, Sturgis ordered Captain Frederick Benteen, a survivor of the massacre at the Little Bighorn, to lead reserve troops and cut off the Indians' escape route at the opposite end of the canyon. Unfortunately for Benteen, the Nez Perce had anticipated his move and he met withering resistance. No longer pinned down by Indian sharpshooters, Merrill tried to come to Benteen's aid but the exhausted men of the Seventh could not move quickly enough to prevent the enemy from escaping. When Merrill finally arrived, Benteen attempted to pursue the fleeing Indians but their sharpshooters again proved to be equal to their task. By the time federal troops secured the ridgeline, the Nez Perce had disappeared and "not an Indian was in sight."

Sturgis's soldiers continued to pursue the Nez Perce and eventually triumphed. For his part, Lewis Merrill had performed his duty competently, but without the fanfare or heroics required to capture the public imagination. To the limited extent that the engagement was reported, it proved to be a boon for Captain Benteen, whose bravery and coolness under fire were praised by most eyewitnesses. Merrill's performance was dismissed, at best, as delayed and fatigued; at worst, it was judged lackluster and uninspired. His dreams of glory and approbation went unfulfilled. Later, as part of the effort to rehabilitate Merrill's reputation in retirement, he was once again granted the rank of (brevet) brigadier general for "conspicuous gallantry," this time for the heroism he displayed at Canyon Creek on September 13, 1877. That judgment was rendered thirteen years after the fact, however; eyewitness accounts and military reports failed to record a high opinion of his actions at the time.[11]

Merrill's health and finances began a long, slow decline as his assignment on the Great Plains stretched into the 1880s. The bullet wound he had suffered during the Battle of Little Rock in 1863 continued to plague him, as did an ailment later identified as Brights Disease, or nephritis, a chronic inflammation of the kidneys resulting in an inability to excrete salt and other wastes. Brights Disease is manifested by extreme back pain and vomiting. As if this affliction were not enough to waylay the major, in 1882 Merrill applied for another medical leave of absence after army doctors observed a "tumor of obscure origin and character." According to the post surgeon, the tumor was "of considerable size, deep seated, situated on the left side of the abdomen, in front and on a line with anterior Iliac spine." The major was absent on sick leave from November 1882 until February 1883. He returned to service for three months before he left on sick leave for an additional three years.

Merrill's military record during the 1880s contains letters from creditors demanding payment for goods and services he had purchased, and threatening legal action if he did not settle his accounts immediately. In response, an increasingly frustrated Merrill disputed the amounts in question and offered long-winded explanations for why he had not tendered payment, although on some occasions he agreed that monies were due and owing. When he could not offer a reasonable explanation for why the account was overdue, the major pleaded for additional time to establish a payment schedule. He would have been in a better position to meet his financial obligations, he wrote to one creditor, had he enjoyed better health and had he advanced in rank throughout his military career.[12]

By 1885, it was clear that he would never be well enough to resume his position as an active member of the U.S. military. After an army retiring board determined that he was eligible to be placed on a list of retired officers owing to "a disability incident to the effects of an injury sustained in the

Figure 9.2. Lewis Merrill's health declined steadily over the years, forcing him to retire on disability in 1886. He is shown here proudly displaying his medals toward the end of his life.
The U.S. Army Military History Institute and the Civil War Library & Museum, MOLLUS

line of duty at the Battle of Little Rock," Merrill announced his intention to leave the army. He was only fifty years old but he had lived a hard life in the saddle, his health was poor, and he looked far older than the calendar indicated. All that remained was the matter of a promotion and the accompanying pay increase.

It was not uncommon for a career military officer to wait until he was promoted to a higher rank based on his seniority and years of service before he formally retired. Except for periods when he was absent on sick leave, Lewis Merrill had spent thirty years in the U.S. Army. He expected to advance to the rank of lieutenant colonel when an opening became available. Thus, when Colonel John P. Hatch of the Second U.S. Cavalry retired from active service on January 9, 1886, his retirement created a vacancy. His immediate subordinate, Lieutenant Colonel N. B. Switzer, was slated to advance into Hatch's old position. Merrill expected a promotion into Switzer's former rank as lieutenant colonel. Early in 1886, President Grover Cleveland formally placed Merrill on the Retired List, as expected, and the promotion seemed to be a foregone conclusion.[13]

Merrill did not realize that the animosity he had engendered when he opposed the White League in Louisiana would come back to haunt him but it did. Among the many community leaders he had alienated was the well-connected Blanchard clan. In 1874 and 1875, Newton Crain Blanchard, then a young lawyer in his middle twenties setting up a practice in Shreveport, had watched as federal troops audaciously meddled in Louisiana politics and government affairs. Just commencing his storied career, Blanchard had not been well positioned to oppose Major Merrill and the Seventh Cavalry in the 1870s. Now, more than a decade later, Blanchard was five years into his thirteen-year tenure as a member of the U.S. House of Representatives. He would later serve as a U.S. Senator, state Supreme Court justice, and governor of Louisiana. He was politically well connected and a man who harbored a grudge against the federal troops that dared to humiliate the great State of Louisiana.

Before Merrill's seemingly routine promotion was sent to the U.S. Senate for pro forma ratification, Congressman Blanchard decided to block the confirmation. The "irrepressible and indefatigable Congressman of the Red River District," as the *New York Times* labeled him, convinced President Grover Cleveland to withdraw the nomination and announce a new policy. Henceforth, President Cleveland agreed, an army officer found to be incapacitated would not be promoted to a higher rank upon retirement.

Even the *New York Times*, hardly a supporter of Republican causes, reported that Blanchard was motivated by revenge. The *Times* observed that

Figure 9.3. Congressman (later, U.S. Senator, state Supreme Court justice, and governor) Newton Blanchard of Louisiana, pictured here, convinced President Grover Cleveland not to promote Merrill to the permanent rank of lieutenant colonel when the career army officer retired from active duty.

Merrill "made himself very obnoxious to the Democrats of the Northern portion of the State by the arrests he made for election offenses under warrants issued by Deputy United States Marshals. He became so offensive a partisan that the papers of that section applied to him the most opprobrious epithets." Congressman Blanchard's influence on the president was remarkable because the Louisianan was a junior House member, albeit their mutual affiliation with the Democratic Party was beneficial. "Mr. Blanchard deserves all the more credit since he has induced the President to ignore all precedents heretofore established in such cases, for it has been the custom to land the worn-out veterans as high in rank as possible on the retired list," the *Times* concluded.[14]

Merrill immediately recognized Blanchard's strategy. Bringing his own political influence to bear, the major asked former colleagues to write to Cleveland on his behalf. From his Wall Street law office, former South Carolina governor and KKK prosecutor Daniel H. Chamberlain opened his letter with an apology to the president. "I am most reluctant to claim a moment of your time, and only do so in order to discharge an obligation to one who deserves it of me," he wrote on February 26, 1886. "Major Merrill has incurred the hostility of some Southern Senators and Representatives, but I am sure—and I knew the circumstances well—he only meant to do his duty at the South." Chamberlain hastened to add that although he was not accusing the president of bowing to political pressure from Southern Democrats, he asked that Cleveland "carefully examine this case and see that no injustice has been done."[15]

Similarly, on February 22, 1886, Wayne Mac Veagh, formerly U.S. attorney general under President Chester A. Arthur, wrote to Congressman Samuel J. Randall, a Pennsylvania Democrat and former Speaker of the House, imploring him to speak with the president. Referring to Merrill, Veagh explained that, "It looks as if he was really being punished long after the event, and when the passions to which his actions gave rise ought to have subsided, and what is still worse for perhaps having simply obeyed in good faith the orders of his superior officers." Veagh argued that Cleveland probably had been unduly influenced by advisors unfamiliar with the nature and extent of Merrill's service. "I cannot help thinking that if in your next talk with the President you call his attention to the matter, he might see it in a different light from that in which it has heretofore been presented to him."[16]

No amount of lobbying would persuade President Cleveland to reconsider his decision. In a handwritten letter he sent to Major Merrill dated July 16, 1886, the president explained his position. After reviewing the new policy and the retiring board's decision that Merrill was disabled, he got to the heart of the matter. "I cannot see in all this anything irregular; and considering all the facts of the case I cannot see that any injustice has been done to you." Without referring to Congressman Blanchard, Southern opposition to Merrill's promotion, or the natural Democratic disinclination to assist a man who had done much to aid the Republican Party, President Cleveland rested his decision on legal grounds. In so doing, he ignored the political machinations that caused a new policy to be developed. "If I should send your name to the Senate for this promotion, it would be in the teeth of the statute prohibiting such promotions from the retired list." Cleveland lectured Merrill on the need to follow accepted laws and protocol, even citing a similar unfortunate episode involving a retired naval officer. "I am, in view of all the facts, constrained to decline your application to change the present situation of your case," he concluded.[17]

Having appealed directly to the president and lost, Merrill could do nothing but spend the next four years as a retired major. Still, he was not beaten; he had one trick left up his sleeve. After President Cleveland was defeated for reelection in 1888, but before he returned to the Executive Mansion in 1893, the major contacted his friend Joseph Roswell Hawley, whom he had served during the Centennial International Exhibition of 1876. Now a U.S. Senator, Hawley agreed to assist in the cause. On January 20, 1890, during the Fifty-first Congress, First Session, Senator Hawley introduced Senate Bill 2157, a measure to promote Lewis Merrill to the permanent rank of lieutenant-colonel of cavalry. A year later, the bill passed the Senate and President Benjamin Harrison, a Republican, signed the commission. Merrill's long-awaited promotion was secure.[18]

He spent his twilight years living quietly in his home state of Pennsylvania, enjoying his family, and participating in community affairs. According to his descendants, Merrill especially enjoyed researching his family's genealogy and spent many happy hours tracing his lineage. He and his wife, the former Anna Rhoda Houston, raised three children during their life together, although she died in November 1882, more than thirteen years before her husband. Their only son, John Houston Merrill, became a prominent Philadelphia lawyer.

After many years of poor health, Lewis Merrill died unexpectedly on February 27, 1896, in the Presbyterian Hospital in Philadelphia. He was sixty-one years old. The cause of death was listed as Brights Disease, the same kidney ailment he had wrestled with for twenty years. Merrill left behind no monuments apart from his simple headstone in Arlington National Cemetery and his thirty-year legacy of military service.

Figure 9.4. Lewis Merrill was buried in Arlington National Cemetery after his death in 1896. His highest military rank—(brevet) brigadier general—and his home state affiliation are displayed on the headstone.
The author

During his long career, Merrill was proud of his many accomplishments but nothing caused him greater pride than reflecting on the years when he fought against the Invisible Empire of the Old South. In his own small way, Merrill helped to usher in the New South. It was a long time coming, but the new era owed much to men like Lewis Merrill for exposing the lies and hypocrisy of terrorist groups such as the Ku Klux Klan.[19]

NOTES

1. George W. Cullum, *Biographical Register of the Officers and Graduates of the U.S. Military Academy at West Point, N.Y. From its Establishment, in 1802, to 1890 with the Early History of the United States Military Academy* (Boston and New York: Houghton, Mifflin and Company, and Cambridge, MA: The Riverside Press, 1891), 624–25; United States Military Academy, *Twenty-Seventh Annual Reunion of the Association of Graduates of the United States Military Academy, at West Point, New York, June 11, 1896* (Saginaw, MI: Seemann & Peters, 1896), 136–37.

2. Merrill Military Files, M.103.C.B.1863 (Record Group 94, National Archives & Records Administration, hereinafter RG 94); United States Military Academy, *Twenty-Seventh Annual Reunion of the Association of Graduates of the United States Military Academy*, 137.

3. Barry C. Johnson, *Custer, Reno, Merrill and the Lauffer Case: Some Warfare in "The Fighting Seventh"* (London: The Pilot Printing & Publicity Service on Behalf of the English Westerners' Society, 1971), 11; "Lewis Merrill Dead," *Yorkville Enquirer*, Yorkville, SC (March 4, 1896); Merrill Military Files, RG 94; Louise Pettus, "Samuel B. Hall & Maj. Lewis Merrill," *The Quarterly* (Rock Hill, SC: York County Genealogical and Historical Society, 1997), n.p.; James E. Sefton, *The United States Army and Reconstruction, 1865–1877* (Westport, CT: Greenwood Press, 1967), 226.

4. William Blair, "The Use of Military Force to Protect the Gains of Reconstruction," *Civil War History* 51 (December 2005): 396; Cullum, *Biographical Register of the Officers and Graduates of the U.S. Military Academy at West Point, N.Y.*, 625; Merrill Military Files, RG 94.

5. Blair, "The Use of Military Force to Protect the Gains of Reconstruction," 396–97; "Everything Points to a Democratic Victory This Fall," *Harper's Weekly* (October 31, 1874): 901; John Kendall, *History of New Orleans* (Chicago and New York: The Lewis Publishing Company, 1922), 359–60; Sefton, *The United States Army and Reconstruction, 1865–1877*, 226–27; "Worse Than Slavery," *Harper's Weekly* (October 24, 1874): 878.

6. Quoted in Sefton, *The United States Army and Reconstruction, 1865–1877*, 228. See also, Cullum, *Biographical Register of the Officers and Graduates of the U.S. Military Academy at West Point, N.Y.*, 625; Merrill Military Files, RG 94.

7. Joseph Roswell Hawley to William W. Belknap, February 18, 1876, in Merrill Military Files, M.103.C.B.1863 (Record Group 94, National Archives &

Records Administration). See also, Cullum, *Biographical Register of the Officers and Graduates of the U.S. Military Academy at West Point, N.Y.*, 625; Johnson, *Custer, Reno, Merrill and the Lauffer Case*, 2; Merrill Military Files, RG 94.

8. Edward C. Bruce, *The Century, Its Fruits and Its Festival; Being a History and Description of the Centennial Exhibition, with a Preliminary Outline of Modern Progress* (Philadelphia: J. B. Lippincott & Company, 1877), 1–8; Robert Shenk Fletcher, *The Centennial Exhibition of 1876: What We Saw and How We Saw It* (Philadelphia: S. T. Souder & Company, 1876), 3–25; Johnson, *Custer, Reno, Merrill and the Lauffer Case*, 2; Merrill Military Files, RG 94.

9. Stephen E. Ambrose, *Crazy Horse and Custer: The Parallel Lives of Two American Warriors* (New York: Anchor Books, 1996), 435–47; Cullum, *Biographical Register of the Officers and Graduates of the U.S. Military Academy at West Point, N.Y.*, 625; Clyde A. Milner II, "National Initiatives," in *The Oxford History of the American West*, Clyde A. Milner II, Carol A. O'Connor, and Martha A. Sandweiss, eds. (New York and Oxford: Oxford University Press, 1994), 182; Neil C. Mangum, "The Little Bighorn Campaign," *Blue & Gray* 23 (Campaign 2006): 6–27, 42–50.

10. Cullum, *Biographical Register of the Officers and Graduates of the U.S. Military Academy at West Point, N.Y.*, 278–80; Jerome A. Greene, *Nez Perce, Summer 1877: The U.S. Army and the Nee-Me-Poo Crisis* (Helena: Montana Historical Society Press, 2000), 206–07; Kenneth Hammer, *Biographies of the Seventh Cavalry, June 25th 1876* (Fort Collins, CO: Old Army Press, 1972), 5.

11. Greene, *Nez Perce, Summer 1877*, 215–30; Merrill Military Files, RG 94.

12. Cullum, *Biographical Register of the Officers and Graduates of the U.S. Military Academy at West Point, N.Y.*, 625; Merrill Military Files, RG 94; United States Military Academy, *Twenty-Seventh Annual Reunion of the Association of Graduates of the United States Military Academy*, 136–37.

13. Lewis Merrill to Grover Cleveland, June 19, 1886, in Merrill Military Files, M.103.C.B.1863 (Record Group 94, National Archives & Records Administration). See also, Merrill Military Files, RG 94; United States Military Academy, *Twenty-Seventh Annual Reunion of the Association of Graduates of the United States Military Academy*, 136–37.

14. Quoted in "Major Merrill's Southern Foes," *The New York Times*, New York, NY (February 18, 1886). See also, *Biographical Directory of the United States Congress*, bioguide.congress.gov/scripts/biodisplay.pl?index=B000541 (accessed April 24, 2006); Johnson, *Custer, Reno, Merrill and the Lauffer Case*, 11–13; Merrill Military Files, RG 94; "Sick Man in the Army," *The New York Times*, New York, NY (May 12, 1886); United States Military Academy, *Twenty-Seventh Annual Reunion of the Association of Graduates of the United States Military Academy*, 136–37.

15. Daniel H. Chamberlain to Grover Cleveland, February 26, 1886, in Merrill Military Files, M.103.C.B.1863 (Record Group 94, National Archives & Records Administration).

16. Wayne Mac Veagh to Samuel J. Randall, February 22, 1886, in Merrill Military Files, M.103.C.B.1863 (Record Group 94, National Archives & Records Administration).

17. Grover Cleveland to Lewis Merrill, July 16, 1886, in Merrill Military Files, M.103.C.B.1863 (Record Group 94, National Archives & Records Administration).

18. Merrill Military Files, RG 94; United States Military Academy, *Twenty-Seventh Annual Reunion of the Association of Graduates of the United States Military Academy*, 136–37.

19. "Lewis Merrill Dead"; "Major Merrill's Southern Foes"; "A Merrill Memorial," www.merrill.org/genealogy/mm/index.html (accessed April 12, 2006); Merrill Military Files, RG 94; "Sick Man in the Army"; United States Military Academy, *Twenty-Seventh Annual Reunion of the Association of Graduates of the United States Military Academy*, 136–37.

Epilogue

"IT IS LIKE WRITING HISTORY WITH LIGHTNING"

Lewis Merrill and his generation of political and military leaders slipped into their graves secure in the knowledge that the Ku Klux Klan was dead and forgotten, a curious relic of the past best left buried in the pages of history. In one sense, they were correct—they had exposed the secrets of the Reconstruction-era KKK to the gleaming light of posterity and thereby hastened its demise—but they seriously underestimated the resiliency of the group's mythology and the message of hope the Klan communicated to disaffected whites. As a result of congressional anti-Klan legislation and federal court prosecutions during the 1870s, the KKK died away as an active organization, but the *idea* of the Klan resonated in many Southern hearts and minds.

Decades passed and a new century dawned. All the while, public memory of the Klan changed. The image of buffoons carrying on like immature teenagers cavorting beneath sheets or brutal, cowardly racists circumventing the U.S. Constitution evolved for some Southerners into a nostalgic view of noble Klansmen championing the cause of good, hardworking, Christian, white families.

The resurrection of the KKK commenced in 1905 when a writer named Thomas Dixon Jr. published a novel, *The Clansman*, romanticizing the KKK's heroism in defending white Southerners against the ignominious efforts of scalawags, carpetbaggers, drunken Union soldiers, and immoral freedmen who wished only to desecrate the South and her cherished traditions. A lawyer who had turned his back on the bar to become a Baptist preacher, Dixon felt the call to arms in 1901 when he saw a stage version of *Uncle Tom's Cabin*. Furious at such transparent Northern propaganda

241

designed to distort Southern history, he penned a series of books correcting defects in the historical record. Later, he explained, "My object is to teach the North, the young North, what it has never known—the awful suffering of the white man during the dreadful Reconstruction period." In the pages of *The Leopard's Spots: A Romance of the White Man's Burden, 1865–1900* and *The Clansman*, he launched his career as a polemicist.

A book saturated with racism on virtually every page, *The Clansman* was Dixon's most popular work. His view of blacks was hostile and insulting; he wrote of "a thick-lipped, flat nosed, spindle-shanked Negro, exuding his nauseous animal odor." This sentence was but one of many such descriptions. For his loyal readers, Dixon's views on race were far from extraordinary; he described what many whites already believed. What captivated the audience was not the denigration of the Negro. Instead, the mawkishly histrionic, ridiculously contrived plot lines appealed to whites who nursed a lingering resentment over Reconstruction. Tom Dixon wrote of a noble Southland where oppressed white families rose above the indignities of Reconstruction to defeat the immoral, tyrannical Powers That Be. The author was hardly a master of the pen, but he understood the mood prevalent among many whites, North and South.[1]

Four decades after the end of chattel slavery, race remained an important factor in day-to-day American life. The U.S. Supreme Court had legitimized legal segregation in a series of opinions culminating in *Plessy v. Ferguson*. President Woodrow Wilson later adopted policies providing for discrimination in federal executive branch agencies. With de jure segregation firmly ensconced in Southern states and Northern racial tensions on the rise as blacks increasingly migrated to Northern cities, the era was well suited for novels and plays that revived interest in the pro-Southern view of Reconstruction. Ex-Confederate soldiers still walked the earth and they recounted their experiences in magazines such as *Confederate Veteran* and in numerous novels, history books, plays, pamphlets, and sermons. The Lost Cause mythology that developed after the Civil War intimated that the South may have been vanquished on the battlefield but Southerners' love of family and place, coupled with their willingness to defend Southern honor, endured. Dixie was a region where "old times there are not forgotten."[2]

Mythical Hollywood, the land of motion pictures and celluloid dreams, was still in its infancy when *The Clansman* appeared, but within a few years a multimillion industry had sprung up. Moviemakers were hungry for stories offering recognizable symbols and visually arresting imagery. No one was hungrier than David Wark Griffith, the son of an unreconstructed Confederate veteran. D. W. Griffith, as he was identified in his film

Figure E.1. D. W. Griffith's unabashedly racist 1915 motion picture, *The Birth of a Nation*, glorified the Ku Klux Klan and helped to revive the group during the twentieth century. In this scene, the heroic Klan punishes an evil Negro, Gus, for having caused the death of an innocent white woman.
Photofest

credits, was an ambitious motion picture director making a name for himself following his 1908 debut. A Kentucky native, he had grown up hearing stories about the mythic South of the antebellum years. He knew in his heart the injustices that Reconstruction-era state governments had perpetrated against white Southerners.

When a friend introduced him to *The Clansman*, Griffith instantly appreciated the cinematic possibilities of the novel. Here was a story he longed to tell. Dixon's whitewashed soap opera had everything he was looking for—a compelling story with a well-delineated beginning, middle, and end, clearly defined heroes (Klansmen) and villains (carpetbaggers and freedmen), as well as a large cast of exciting, visually stunning characters. The timing was propitious, for the period from 1911 to 1915 represented the fiftieth anniversary of the Civil War and interest in the conflict was increasing.[3]

Griffith's technically breathtaking but factually inaccurate motion picture was shot from July to November 1914. Both Dixon and Griffith altered the facts to suit their needs—a practice that became de rigueur in Holly-wood—but they did so to emphasize the inherent drama of the tale. In an odd twist of logic, major black characters in the film were played by whites wearing blackface makeup because black actors were regarded as incapable of convincingly portraying black characters. The only black actors who ap-peared in the film were bit players seen running in groups, leading horses to food and water, or performing the menial chores thought to be within their innate abilities.

When the motion picture, renamed *The Birth of a Nation*, premiered early in 1915, critics proclaimed it an instant classic. Audiences flocked to theaters to see the first full-length feature film ever released, a three-hour extravaganza that followed the fate of two families—one Southern, one Northern—through the Civil War and into the trials and tribulations of Reconstruction. Here was a familiar story told from the Southern perspec-tive using new conventions and pioneering motion picture techniques—cross-cutting and editing to heighten tension, close-up camera work to cap-ture actors' facial expressions and reactions, and cameras tracking the action shots as though the viewer were on horseback together with the riders. Whatever else it accomplished, *The Birth of a Nation* showed the exciting artistry that could be achieved when a gifted filmmaker directed the action.

The first half of the film traces the war years as Southerners fall vic-tim to the greater industrial might of the North. Abraham Lincoln appears as a big-hearted, well-meaning stooge, too happily moronic to be fully en-gaged in fighting the war and too weak to govern. After Lincoln's assassi-nation at Ford's Theatre, depicted more or less faithfully in the film, Radi-cal Republicans seize power and impose their evil machinations on the prostrated South. Thus begin the dark days of Reconstruction.

The second half of the film presents striking images of noble, brave Klansmen righting the many wrongs imposed on Southerners by the cor-rupt leaders of an obdurate federal government. In one memorable scene, a bestial, out-of-control freedman, Gus, terrorizes a white woman—lovely, innocent Flora Cameron, the virginal daughter of a good, Christian, Southern white family struggling to live under an oppressive carpetbagger regime—causing her to tumble from a cliff and die rather than be ravished by a brutish black man. Ben Cameron, the film's protagonist (a figure loosely based on J. Rufus Bratton, the Yorkville doctor who fled to Canada to avoid prosecution for Jim Williams's murder), swears that her death will be avenged by all that is holy and righteous in the world. The morally pure Cameron cannot rely on the civil authorities because they are infested with evil carpetbaggers and power-hungry scalawags, assisted by marauding freedmen. Tormented by the sad state of affairs, Cameron spies a group of white children playing a game where they hide beneath sheets and pretend to be ghosts. Inspired, Cameron knows what he must do to avenge his sister's death. With truth, justice, and Christian virtue on his side, "the Little Colonel" joins with other noble Southern white men to form the Ku Klux Klan.

After they are adorned in full Klan regalia and mounted in the saddle, the masked forces of goodness track down the wily Gus, the embodiment of darkness and evil, and hold a quick, vigilante-style trial. The nasty Negro, with his shifty eyes, coal-black skin, and scruffy attire, is unquestionably guilty. Without undue delay, the Klansmen lynch the offender and dump his body on the doorstep of the leading mulatto carpetbagger, Silas Lynch, protégé of Congressman Austin Stoneman, a greedy, animalistic Radical Republican loosely modeled on Pennsylvania Congressman Thaddeus Stevens. The audience can tell that Congressman Stoneman is evil, for several times in the motion picture he cavorts about with his Negro servant, an allusion to Stevens's real-life relationship with his black housekeeper.

Later in the film, at the climatic moment when the evil carpetbaggers and wild-eyed freedmen are poised to overwhelm the besieged, noble whites, the Klan rides in to save the day. Foes are vanquished, the Camerons are reunited, and the corrupt, illegitimate Reconstruction government of the dastardly Silas Lynch is driven into exile. As the scene fades, a smiling figure bearing an uncanny resemblance to popular conceptions of Jesus Christ looks down from the sky in apparent satisfaction that white Southerners have regained control over their lives and all is right with the world.[4]

Although it took numerous liberties with the historical record and could hardly be credited with adopting a subtle, nuanced approach to the subject, *The Birth of a Nation* was a powerful film. It triggered different reactions depending on the political sensibilities of the audience. One overwhelmingly positive reaction came from the upper echelon of the federal government. In January 1915, Tom Dixon wrote to a fellow Johns Hopkins alumnus who had ascended to lofty heights, President Woodrow Wilson. Wary of jobseekers, Wilson reluctantly received Dixon at the Executive Mansion on February 3, 1915. He was immediately relieved to learn that his old college friend was not seeking federal employment; he only wanted Wilson to watch a motion picture. The president readily agreed. On February 18, 1915, Dixon arrived in the East Room along with D. W. Griffith and members of the crew. They set up a projector and showed the film to President Wilson, his daughters, and several cabinet officers. It was the inaugural screening of a motion picture in the Executive Mansion.

The first Southerner to serve as president since the Civil War, Wilson shared Dixon's and Griffith's antipathy for Reconstruction. He could be expected to respond favorably. Nonetheless, his enthusiastic reaction was more than Dixon and Griffith could have imagined. As the film ended and the lights came up, the president, obviously moved, shook hands with the author, director, and the crew. The film's creators anxiously awaited the verdict. Wilson famously gushed, "It is like writing history with lightning, and my only regret is that it is all so terribly true." His remark presaged the sentiments of many white filmgoers.[5]

Other audiences were not as enamored of the work. Representatives of the National Association for the Advancement of Colored People (NAACP) objected that *The Birth of a Nation* perpetuated demeaning stereotypes. The film suggested that blacks were either happy, contented simpletons who reveled in their native inferiority and were out to please "ol' massa" in the Stepin Fetchit mold or they were brutal renegades who did not know their place and were little more than wild animals that must be controlled or put down as if they were mad dogs foaming at the mouth. Through a lobbying campaign before the National Board of Censorship and in a series of public protests, NAACP representatives called on all Americans, black and white, to avoid seeing the movie. NAACP members were arrested on several occasions when they attempted to enter the "Whites Only" section of theaters showing the film. They scored a notable success when Boston mayor James Curley objected to the content, although he allowed the movie to be shown in the city after several offensive scenes were deleted. A similar protest required additional revisions before the film could be shown in New York. The state of Kansas prohibited the film from playing at theaters until 1923.[6]

Despite its popularity, *The Birth of a Nation* probably would not have led to a KKK revival by itself. The film set the stage and captured the mood of many whites, but arguably the single most important event that led to the resurrection of the Klan as an active organization occurred a few years before *The Birth of a Nation* appeared. On April 26—Confederate Memorial Day—1913, Mary Phagan, a thirteen-year-old employee of the National Pencil Factory in Atlanta, was brutally murdered, and her body was deposited in sawdust and shavings in the factory basement. A night watchman found her the following day. A day after the body was discovered, bloodstains "identified positively as the dead girl's" were recovered in a workroom near the office of Mary Phagan's employer, Leo M. Frank, the man eventually convicted of her murder.

Frank was well suited to play the villain. He was Jewish, well educated, Northern-bred, seemingly cool and aloof, a thin, bespectacled, and slightly effeminate figure. The evidence against him was circumstantial, at best, and hinged on the testimony of a black ne'er-do-well, Jim Conley. Although no conclusive proof exists, it appears likely that Conley was the culprit. In testifying against Leo Frank, Conley saved his own skin.[7]

The carnival-like atmosphere of the trial exposed a strong, previously unrecognized current of anti-Semitism in the South. Not surprisingly, Frank was convicted and sentenced to death. His case became a cause cele-bre, the American equivalent of the Dreyfus affair, an infamous case involving trumped-up espionage charges filed against a Jew serving in the French Army in 1894. Dreyfus was cleared of the offense but the affair symbolized the rampant anti-Semitism that infected Europe during the nineteenth century. Leo Frank seemed destined to follow in Dreyfus's footsteps from conviction toward eventual redemption when, unexpectedly, retiring Georgia governor John Slaton, in an act of supreme political courage, commuted the sentence to life imprisonment.[8]

Although many people around the country were convinced that Frank was innocent and would be exonerated, a large number of Georgians disagreed. A vocal minority menacingly called for a mob to take matters into its own hands. If the governor insisted on interfering with the judicial process, extralegal forces must avenge Mary Phagan's murder.

Among the notable Georgia opinion leaders crying out for "vigilante justice," none was as relentless as the charismatic Tom Watson, a sensationalistic newspaper editor and former congressman labeled a "reactionary populist." A zealous pro-Southern ideologue in the tradition of unreconstructed Confederates, Watson raised demagoguery to an art form. In the pages of his two widely read publications, *Watson's Magazine* and the *Weekly Jeffersonian*, he bitterly denounced the "jewpervert" that had destroyed an innocent white girl. Watson's newspaper columns repeatedly referred to Frank as "this filthy perverted Jew of New York," stirring up the latent racism and anti-Semitism lurking beneath Atlanta's mannerly façade. Always eager to traffic in salacious innuendo, Watson contended that it was obvious a Jew had slaughtered poor little Mary Phagan because Jews were known to have "a ravenous appetite for the forbidden fruit." He incessantly called for a mob to "let the Governor and the Prison Commission hear from the people."

Watson's call was answered by a group of prominent citizens from the Atlanta suburb of Marietta, Mary Phagan's hometown. During the summer of 1915, community leaders convened to discuss plans for executing the original death sentence. Owing in no small measure to Watson's incendiary rhetoric, the mob became enraged at the governor's leniency toward Frank

and believed that the group was empowered by forces higher than state government to intervene and set matters straight. Nonetheless, the conspirators
realized they must not actively take part in violent acts and thereby risk
prosecution.

On August 16, 1915, a smaller group of twenty-five men recruited by
the original conspirators to serve as field agents abducted Frank from the
prison farm in Milledgeville and drove him 175 miles to Marietta. They
called themselves the "Knights of Mary Phagan," a sobriquet similar to the
"Knights of the Ku Klux Klan." When a few squeamish fellows lost heart,
the more zealous mob leaders threw a rope around Frank's neck, led him
into a grove, placed handcuffs around his wrists and a rope around his legs,
and lynched him from a tree. The man's neck did not immediately snap
when the table was kicked from beneath his legs. Leo Frank slowly stran-
gled; his limbs flailed and his body twitched until, finally, after thirty minutes, he was still.

Fearful of the repercussions should they be apprehended, the Knights
of Mary Phagan fled with the coming sunrise but their deed already was
known throughout Marietta. As word spread across the state that Frank's
body was hanging from a tree on the outskirts of Mary Phagan's hometown, cars stuffed to overflowing with curious spectators converged on the
site. With each passing minute, a growing crowd of rural Georgians gawked
at the grisly scene. It was a festive occasion similar to a state fair or a stump
meeting for campaigning politicians. Local men and boys proudly posed for
photographs standing next to the body, which still swung from the hang-
man's noose, while others tore pieces of fabric from Frank's shirt or peaked
beneath his clothing at his blood-engorged genitalia.

With the arrival of ever more onlookers, the mood darkened. Marietta's base element, attracted by bloodlust and itching for violence, chanted
and called for more activity. The frenzy of the populace increased until a
local judge—himself a participant in the lynching—insisted that Frank's
corpse be removed and transported to a mortuary. As Frank was cut loose,
a throng of impassioned citizens rushed forward in a rage; at least one inflamed man repeatedly kicked at the body, grinding the dead man's face into
the dust. The group hurled a torrent of epithets at Frank in particular and
at Jews in general. It was an ugly scene, frightening even to citizens who
believed that Leo Frank had gotten his just desserts. Later, photographs and
authenticated pieces of the rope were sold as souvenirs in the streets of Marietta and Atlanta.[9]

The reaction to *The Birth of a Nation* and the Leo Frank murder case
suggested that an undercurrent of hate and fear was present in America,

Figure E.2. **Postcards showing the 1915 lynching of Leo Frank, a Jewish business-man accused of killing a young white girl, were popular in and near Atlanta, Georgia. The anti-Semitism aroused by the Frank case was a leading factor in the resurrection of the Ku Klux Klan.**

Georgia Division of Archives and History, Office of the Secretary of State particularly in rural areas. Immigration was on the rise. A world war raged in Europe. The automobile and new advances in technology were decreasing the size of the globe, threatening to undermine traditional kinship relations that had long defined the lives of rural Americans. The unease attendant to these concurrent events convinced a thirty-five-year-old former Methodist minister, William Joseph "Doc" Simmons, that the time was right to form a new organization based on an old idea.

Born in Alabama in 1880, Simmons grew up on a farm under the tutelage of his father, a country doctor. When he was older, Simmons claimed he had studied medicine at Johns Hopkins Medical School, although the school could locate no record of his attendance. A veteran of the Spanish-American War, Simmons became a Methodist minister and rode the circuit in Alabama and Florida. He spent his idle hours orating on that good old-time religion and imbibing large quantities of his favorite liquid refreshment, Kentucky bourbon. He claimed that while watching the sky one evening he saw a vision of ghost riders galloping across the stars, a celestial sign that he was destined to revive a noble, patriotic organization.

The messianic Simmons had harbored ambitions to advance in the ministry but when he was suspended for inattention to his duties, he became little more than a drifter. Wherever he roamed, he could not resist "teaching history" to anyone who would listen. He also joined numerous fraternal clubs where he could rub elbows with the boys and dream of a glorious, as-yet-to-be-determined future. His greatest success before 1915 was as the Atlanta-area organizer for the Woodmen of the World, a fraternal society stressing patriotism, civic pride, volunteerism, and financial solvency.[10]

While recuperating from an injury sustained when he was struck by an automobile on an Atlanta street early in 1915, Simmons read *The Clansman* as well as the original Reconstruction-era Ku Klux Klan Prescript from 1867. He knew *The Birth of a Nation* was based on Dixon's novel. He had followed the dramatic developments in the Leo Frank affair. Simmons was not drawn so much to the Frank case itself as he was to the spirit of vigilantism it represented; he was determined to use the momentum of the Knights of Mary Phagan for his own ends. To the superstitious ex-preacher, the confluence of events was no accident. They were a sign that he was destined to revive the ultimate fraternal organization, the Ku Klux Klan.

In the tradition of the original Pulaski Six, Simmons shrouded his organization in secrecy. He even created a shorthand language to confound outsiders. Using the prefix "KL" attached to words, he envisioned having a "klonversation" with fellow Klansmen. They would swear allegiance to a holy book known as the "Kloran." He created mysterious acronyms as well. AYAK stood for "Are you a Klansman"? The appropriate response was AKIA, short for "a Klansman I am."[11]

Simmons's silly fantasies might never have progressed beyond the planning stage had Leo Frank not been lynched during the summer of 1915. Press coverage about the mob's actions was mostly favorable in Georgia, largely thanks to Tom Watson's brand of populism. Interest in protecting the "Southern way of life" from outside forces—blacks, Jews, Catholics, Northerners, and modern technology—increased markedly through the summer and autumn of the year. Building on this rising sentiment, on October 26, 1915, Simmons and several Knights of Mary Phagan filed an application with the state of Georgia to create a "purely benevolent and eleemosynary" fraternal order. The Knights of the Ku Klux Klan had been reborn.

All that was missing was a dramatic inaugural event, which they soon found. On Thanksgiving night 1915, Simmons was among sixteen men who climbed Stone Mountain, a granite outcropping near Atlanta. Standing under an American flag, they read passages from the Bible and swore allegiance to Simmons's new group, the Invisible Empire, Knights of the Ku Klux Klan. In an important new development reflecting their affinity for Christian church rituals, the Klansmen burned a sixteen-foot wooden cross. The fire was "visible throughout the city" of Atlanta, sixteen miles away.

The modern KKK rose from the ashes of Reconstruction during that memorable night on Stone Mountain. The new organization would not confine itself to keeping blacks in line, as the original KKK had done. Any racial or ethnic group or "foreigner" threatening the status quo would be dealt with by whatever means were required to neutralize the threat. The Klan's glory days were yet to come but come they would. Before the KKK again fell on hard times, many leading citizens—including President Warren G. Harding as well as a host of candidates to elective office, state governors, state and local judges, and members of Congress—would swear allegiance to the goals and objectives of the revitalized Invisible Empire.[12]

The appeal of the Ku Klux Klan waxes and wanes but it never dies. The group's tenets persist because the Klan offers a message of hope for malcontents who believe that nonwhites undermine the traditional way of life—a way of life that appears to be slipping away in the modern era. For a time during the 1870s, Lewis Merrill and the federal government prevented the Klan from spreading beyond the states of the vanquished Southern Confederacy. It would be left to a later generation to bear the burden of suppressing the Ku Klux Klan in the twentieth century.

Figure E.3. In 1915, after *The Birth of a Nation* appeared and Leo Frank was hanged by an angry mob for supposedly murdering a young white girl, William Joseph "Doc" Simmons created a new Ku Klux Klan atop Stone Mountain, Georgia.
The Special Collections Department, Robert W. Woodruff Library, Emory University

NOTES

1. Quoted in Eric Niderost, "The Birth of a Nation," *American History* 40 (October 2005): 64. See also, David M. Chalmers, *Hooded Americanism: The History of the Ku Klux Klan*, 3d ed. (Durham, NC: Duke University Press, 1987), 2, 23–24; Nancy Bishop Dessommes, "Hollywood in Hoods: The Portrayal of the Ku Klux Klan in Popular Film," *Journal of Popular Culture* 32 (Spring 1999): 16; Glen Feldman, *Politics, Society, and the Klan in Alabama, 1915–1949* (Tuscaloosa and London: The University of Alabama Press, 1999), 12; Kenneth T. Jackson, *The Ku Klux Klan in the City, 1915–1930* (Chicago: Ivan R. Dee, 1967), 3–4; J. Michael Martinez, "Traditionalist Perspectives on Confederate Symbols," in *Confederate Symbols in the Contemporary South*, J. Michael Martinez, William D. Richardson, and Ron McNinch-Su, eds. (Gainesville: University Press of Florida, 2000), 258; Anthony Slide, *American Racist: The Life and Films of Thomas Dixon* (Lexington: University Press of Kentucky, 2004), 4; Allen W. Trelease, *White Terror: The Ku Klux Klan Conspiracy and Southern Reconstruction* (Baton Rouge: Louisiana State University Press, 1971), 421; Wyn Craig Wade, *The Fiery Cross: The Ku Klux Klan in America* (New York and Oxford: Oxford University Press, 1987), 122–24.

2. Feldman, *Politics, Society, and the Klan in Alabama*, 11–12; Gaines M. Foster, *Ghosts of the Confederacy: Defeat, the Lost Cause, and the Emergence of the New South* (New York: Oxford University Press, 1987), 46, 128–29; J. Michael Martinez and Robert M. Harris, "Graves, Worms, and Epitaphs: Confederate Monuments in the Southern Landscape," in *Confederate Symbols in the Contemporary South*, J. Michael Martinez, William D. Richardson, and Ron McNinch-Su, eds. (Gainesville: University Press of Florida, 2000), 141–47; Niderost, "The Birth of a Nation," 62–64; Wade, *The Fiery Cross*, 122–23; Charles Reagan Wilson, "The Religion of the Lost Cause: Ritual and Organization of the Southern Civil Religion: 1865–1920," *Journal of Southern History* 46 (May 1980): 226–34.

3. Chalmers, *Hooded Americanism*, 25–26; Feldman, *Politics, Society, and the Klan in Alabama*, 12; Niderost, "The Birth of a Nation," 62; Maxim Simcovitch, "The Impact of Griffith's *Birth of a Nation* on the Modern Ku Klux Klan," *Journal of Popular Film* 1 (1972): 45–48; Trelease, *White Terror*, 421; Wade, *The Fiery Cross*, 124–26.

4. Chalmers, *Hooded Americanism*, 24–26; Dessommes, "Hollywood in Hoods," 16; Nancy MacLean, *Behind the Mask of Chivalry: The Making of the Second Ku Klux Klan* (New York and Oxford: Oxford University Press, 1994), 12–13; Rory McVeigh, "Structural Incentives for Conservative Mobilization: Power Devaluation and the Rise of the Ku Klux Klan, 1915–1925," *Social Forces* 77 (June 1999): 1464; Niderost, "The Birth of a Nation," 62; Wade, *The Fiery Cross*, 123–25; Jerry L. West, *The Reconstruction Ku Klux Klan in York County, South Carolina, 1865–1877* (Jefferson, NC: McFarland & Company, Inc., 2002), appendix 3, 130.

5. Quoted in Wade, *The Fiery Cross*, 126. See also, Chalmers, *Hooded Americanism*, 26–27; Jackson, *The Ku Klux Klan in the City*, 3–4; Martinez, "Traditionalist Perspectives on Confederate Symbols," 258; Niderost, "The Birth of a Nation," 66;

James Ridgeway, *Blood in the Face: The Ku Klux Klan, Aryan Nations, Nazi Skinheads, and the Rise of a New White Culture*, 2d. ed. (New York: Thunder's Mouth Press, 1995), 52, 53; Simcovitch, "The Impact of Griffith's *Birth of a Nation* on the Modern Ku Klux Klan," 47–48.

6. Dessommes, "Hollywood in Hoods," 16; Niderost, "The Birth of a Nation," 66–67, 78, 80; Simcovitch, "The Impact of Griffith's *Birth of a Nation* on the Modern Ku Klux Klan," 45–48; Wade, *The Fiery Cross*, 131–39.

7. Leonard Dinnerstein, *The Leo Frank Case* (Birmingham, AL: The Notable Trials Library, 1991), 1–9, 19–28, 55–57; MacLean, *Behind the Mask of Chivalry*, 12; Nancy MacLean, "The Leo Frank Case Reconsidered: Gender and Sexual Politics in the Making of Reactionary Populism," *The Journal of American History* (December 1991): 917–18; Martinez, "Traditionalist Perspectives on Confederate Symbols," 259–60; Steve Oney, *And the Dead Shall Rise: The Murder of Mary Phagan and the Lynching of Leo Frank* (New York: Vintage Books, 2004), 18–33, 61–70; Wade, *The Fiery Cross*, 143–44.

8. Jean-Denis Bredin, *The Affair: The Case of Alfred Dreyfus* (New York: George Braziller, 1983), 505–45; Dinnerstein, *The Leo Frank Case*, 62–76; Martinez, "Traditionalist Perspectives on Confederate Symbols," 259–60; Oney, *And the Dead Shall Rise*, 469–512; Wade, *The Fiery Cross*, 143.

9. Chalmers, *Hooded Americanism*, 71; Dinnerstein, *The Leo Frank Case*, 139–47; MacLean, *Behind the Mask of Chivalry*, 12; MacLean, "The Leo Frank Case Reconsidered," 938, 940; Martinez, "Traditionalist Perspectives on Confederate Symbols," 260; Oney, *And the Dead Shall Rise*, 561–72; Wade, *The Fiery Cross*, 144.

10. Charles C. Alexander, "Kleagles and Cash: The Ku Klux Klan As a Business Organization, 1915–1930," *Business History Review* 39 (Autumn 1965): 349–50; Chalmers, *Hooded Americanism*, 28–38, 225; Feldman, *Politics, Society, and the Klan in Alabama*, 12–13; Charles O. Jackson, "William J. Simmons: A Career in Ku Kluxism," *Georgia Historical Quarterly* 50 (1966): 351–53; MacLean, *Behind the Mask of Chivalry*, 4–6, 12; Martinez, "Traditionalist Perspectives on Confederate Symbols," 258–59; McVeigh, "Structural Incentives for Conservative Mobilization," 1464; Michael Newton and Judy Ann Newton, *The Ku Klux Klan: An Encyclopedia* (New York: Garland Press, 1991), 51; Niderost, "The Birth of a Nation," 80; Ridgeway, *Blood in the Face*, 52; William Joseph Simmons, *America's Menace, Or the Enemy Within* (Atlanta: Patriotic Books, 1926), 60–65; Wade, *The Fiery Cross*, 140–48.

11. Chalmers, *Hooded Americanism*, 29–31; Jackson, "William J. Simmons: A Career in Ku Kluxism," 351–53; MacLean, *Behind the Mask of Chivalry*, 4–5; Ridgeway, *Blood in the Face*, 52; Simmons, *America's Menace*, 63–65; Wade, *The Fiery Cross*, 142–44.

12. Alexander, "Kleagles and Cash," 349–50; Chalmers, *Hooded Americanism*, 30; Feldman, *Politics, Society, and the Klan in Alabama*, 12–13; Jackson, *The Ku Klux Klan in the City*, 4; MacLean, *Behind the Mask of Chivalry*, 4–5; Martinez, "Traditionalist Perspectives on Confederate Symbols," 258; Newton and Newton, *The Ku Klux Klan: An Encyclopedia*, 51; Niderost, "The Birth of a Nation," 80; Wade, *The Fiery Cross*, 144–47.

BIBLIOGRAPHICAL ESSAY

Much has been written about the Ku Klux Klan. Probably the two most readily accessible and readable histories of the group are Allen W. Trelease, *White Terror: The Ku Klux Klan Conspiracy and Southern Reconstruction* (Baton Rouge: Louisiana State University Press, 1971), and Wyn Craig Wade, *The Fiery Cross: The Ku Klux Klan in America* (New York and Oxford: Oxford University Press, 1987). Trelease thoroughly documents Klan abuses in the Southern states, including South Carolina, during the Reconstruction era. Lewis Merrill appears briefly in the work, mostly in a single chapter on the South Carolina Klan. Unlike Trelease, who only focuses on the original Klan, Wade explores the history of the KKK from its inception in 1866 until the time the book was published in 1987. In an early chapter, Wade discusses Merrill's role in combating the Reconstruction-era group.

Several other excellent histories of the group exist, although they generally focus on the post-1915 Klan. In my view, the three most authoritative books on KKK history are: David M. Chalmers, *Hooded Americanism: The History of the Ku Klux Klan*, 3d ed. (Durham, NC: Duke University Press, 1987); Kenneth T. Jackson, *The Ku Klux Klan in the City, 1915–1930* (Chicago: Ivan R. Dee, 1967); and Nancy MacLean, *Behind the Mask of Chivalry: The Making of the Second Ku Klux Klan* (New York and Oxford: Oxford University Press, 1994). An excellent discussion of racist groups from a broader perspective—although the Klan is prominently featured—can be found in James Ridgeway, *Blood in the Face: The Ku Klux Klan, Aryan Nations, Nazi Skinheads, and the Rise of a New White Culture*, 2d ed. (New York: Thunder's Mouth Press, 1995).

A representative sampling of academic articles on the Klan includes: Charles C. Alexander, "Kleagles and Cash: The Ku Klux Klan as a Business Organization, 1915–1930," *Business History Review* 39 (Autumn 1965): 348–67; David Everitt, "1871 War on Terror," *American History* 38 (June 2003): 26–33; Edward John Harcourt, "Who Were the Pale Faces? New Perspectives on the Tennessee Ku Klux," *Civil War History* 51 (March 2005): 23–66; V. C. Jones, "The Rise and Fall of the Ku Klux Klan," *Civil War Times Illustrated* 2 (February 1964): 12–17; Enoch L. Mitchell, "The Role of General George Washington Gordon in the Ku-Klux Klan," *Western Tennessee Historical Society Papers* 1 (1947): 73–80; and Elaine Frantz Parsons, "Midnight Ramblers: Costume and Performance in the Reconstruction-Era Ku Klux Klan," *The Journal of American History* 92 (December 2005): 811–36.

The Reconstruction-era Klan has been the subject of numerous polemics. It is impossible to list them all, but some of the more useful sources include: Susan L. Davis, *Authentic History: Ku Klux Klan, 1865–1877* (New York: American Library Service, 1924) (pro-KKK); John Patterson Green, *Recollections of the Inhabitants, Localities, Superstitions, and Ku Klux Outrages of the Carolina, By a 'Carpetbagger' Who Was Born and Lived There* (Cleveland, Ohio: Author, 1880) (anti-KKK); Stanley F. Horn, *Invisible Empire: The Story of the Ku Klux Klan, 1866–1871* (Montclair, NJ: Patterson Smith, 1969) (pro-KKK); J. C. Lester and D. L. Wilson, *Ku Klux Klan: Its Origin, Growth, and Disbursement* (New York: Da Capo Press, 1973; originally published in Nashville, TN: Wheeler, Osborn & Duckworth Manufacturing Company, 1884) (pro-KKK); W. T. Richardson, *Historic Pulaski: Birthplace of the Ku Klux Klan; Scene of Execution of Sam Davis* (Pulaski, TN: Author, 1913) (pro-KKK); Mr. and Mrs. W. B. Romine, *A Story of the Original Ku Klux Klan* (Pulaski, TN: The Pulaski Citizen, 1934) (pro-KKK); Mrs. S. E. F. Rose, *The Ku Klux Klan or Invisible Empire* (New Orleans, LA: L. Graham Co., Ltd., 1914) (pro-KKK); Everette Swinney, *Suppressing the Ku Klux Klan: The Enforcement of the Reconstruction Amendments, 1870–1877* (New York: Garland, 1987) (generally balanced, but slightly anti-KKK); and Albion W. Tourgee, *The Invisible Empire: Part I—A New, Illustrated, and Enlarged Edition of a Fool's Errand, By One of the Fools; The Famous Historical Romance of Life in the South Since the War; Part II—A Concise Review of Recent Events, Showing the Elements on Which the Tale is Based, with Many Thrilling Personal Narratives and Other Startling Facts and Considerations, Including an Account of the Rise, Extent, Purpose, Methods, and Deeds of the Mysterious Ku-Klux Klan; All Fully Authenticated* (New York: Fords, Howard & Hulbert, 1879) (a well-known anti-KKK novel).

As for material on Klan activities in South Carolina during the 1870s, the historian Richard Zuczek has written two fine works. The first, an article, is titled: "The Federal Government's Attack on the Ku Klux Klan: A Reassessment," *South Carolina Historical Magazine* 97 (January 1, 1996): 47–64. The second work is a book that expands on the article: *State of Rebellion: Reconstruction in South Carolina* (Columbia: University of South Carolina Press, 1996).

Lou Falkner Williams's masterful account of the South Carolina KKK trials is required reading for anyone who hopes to understand the federal government's prosecutorial efforts in the 1870s. See Lou Falkner Williams, *The Great South Carolina Ku Klux Klan Trials, 1871–1872* (Athens: University of Georgia Press, 1996). Three academic articles on the KKK trials are useful as well: Kermit L. Hall, "Political Power and Constitutional Legitimacy: The South Carolina Ku Klux Klan Trials, 1871–1872," *Emory Law Journal* 33 (Fall 1984): 921–51; Robert J. Kaczorowski, "Federal Enforcement of Civil Rights During the First Reconstruction," *Fordham Urban Law Journal* 23 (Fall 1995): 155–86; and Lou Falkner Williams, "The South Carolina Ku Klux Klan Trials and Enforcement of Federal Civil Rights, 1871–1872," *Civil War History* 39 (March 1993): 47–66.

Other works that discuss conditions in South Carolina during Reconstruction and focus, to a greater or lesser extent, on Ku Klux Klan activities include: Martin Abbott, *The Freedmen's Bureau in South Carolina, 1865–1872* (Chapel Hill: The University of North Carolina Press, 1967); Lacy K. Ford, "Rednecks and Merchants: Economic Development and Social Tensions in the South Carolina Upcountry, 1865–1900," *Journal of American History* 71 (September 1984): 294–318; Asa H. Gordon, *Sketches of Negro Life and History in South Carolina*, 2d ed. (Columbia: University of South Carolina Press, 1929); John Porter Hollis, *The Early Period of Reconstruction in South Carolina* (Baltimore, MD: The Johns Hopkins Press, 1905); Thomas Holt, *Black Over White: Negro Political Leadership in South Carolina During Reconstruction* (Urbana: University of Illinois Press, 1977); Louis F. Post, "A Carpetbagger in South Carolina," *Journal of Negro History* 10 (January 1925): 10–79; Julie Saville, *The Work of Reconstruction: From Slave to Wage Laborer in South Carolina, 1860–1870* (Cambridge, UK: Cambridge University Press, 1994); Herbert Shapiro, "The Ku Klux Klan During Reconstruction: The South Carolina Episode," *Journal of Negro History* 49 (January 1964): 34–55; Francis B. Simkins, "The Ku Klux Klan in South Carolina," *Journal of Negro History* 12 (October 1927): 606–47; Francis Butler Simkins and R. H. Woody, *South Carolina During Reconstruction* (Chapel Hill: The University of North Carolina Press, 1932); J. C. A. Stagg, "The

Problem of Klan Violence: The South Carolina Up-Country, 1868–1871," *Journal of American Studies* 8 (December 1974): 303–18; Edward L. Wells, *Hampton and Reconstruction* (Columbia, SC: The State Company, 1907); Joel Williamson, *After Slavery: The Negro in South Carolina During Reconstruction, 1861–1877* (Chapel Hill: The University of North Carolina Press, 1965); and R. H. Woody, "The South Carolina Election of 1870," *The North Carolina Historical Review* 8 (April 1931): 168–86.

　　The literature on Reconstruction in general is voluminous, although arguably the most accessible work is Eric Foner, *Reconstruction: America's Unfinished Revolution, 1863–1877* (New York: Francis Parkman Prize Edition, History Book Club, 2005; originally published by HarperCollins, 1988). Other major works include: James S. Allen, *Reconstruction: The Battle for Democracy, 1865–1876* (New York: International Publishers, 1937); Myra Lockett Avary, *Dixie After the War: An Exposition on the Social Conditions Existing in the South, During the Twelve Years Succeeding the Fall of Richmond* (New York: Doubleday, Page & Company, 1906); Richard Nelson Current, ed., *Reconstruction [1865–1877]* (Englewood Cliffs, NJ: Prentice-Hall, 1965) and *Those Terrible Carpetbaggers* (New York: Oxford University Press, 1988); David H. Donald, *The Politics of Reconstruction, 1863–1867* (Baton Rouge: Louisiana State University Press, 1965); John Hope Franklin, *Reconstruction After the Civil War* (Chicago, IL: The University of Chicago Press, 1961); Robert Selph Henry, *The Story of Reconstruction* (New York: Konecky & Konecky, 1999); Martin E. Mantell, *Johnson, Grant, and the Politics of Reconstruction* (New York and London: Columbia University Press, 1973); James E. Sefton, *The United States Army and Reconstruction, 1865–1877* (Westport, Conn.: Greenwood Press, 1967); Hans L. Trefousse, *Reconstruction: America's First Effort at Racial Democracy* (New York: Van Nostrand Reinhold Company, 1971); and Harvey Wish, ed., *Reconstruction in the South, 1865-1877: First-Hand Accounts of the American Southland After the Civil War, By Northerners and Southerners* (New York: Farrar, Strauss and Giroux, 1965). A good source on the period immediately following the failure of Reconstruction is C. Vann Woodward, *The Strange Career of Jim Crow*, 2d ed. (New York and Oxford: Oxford University Press, 1966).

　　Sources specifically chronicling Lewis Merrill's activities in York County, South Carolina, in 1871–1873 are few and far between, and most are exceedingly difficult to come by for the casual reader. The most accessible and authoritative sources are: Douglas Summers Brown, *A City Without Cobwebs: A History of Rock Hill, South Carolina* (Columbia: University of South Carolina Press, 1953); George W. Cullum, *Biographical Register of the Officers and Graduates of the U.S. Military Academy at West Point, N.Y. From its*

Establishment, in 1802, to 1890 with the Early History of the United States Military Academy (Boston and New York: Houghton, Mifflin and Company, and Cambridge, MA: The Riverside Press, 1891); United States Circuit Court [4th Circuit], *Proceedings in the Ku Klux Klan Trials at Columbia, S.C., in the United States Circuit Court, November Term, 1871* (Columbia, SC: Republican Printing Company, State Printers, 1872); United States Congress, *Report of the Joint Select Committee to Inquire into the Condition of Affairs in the Late Insurrectionary States*, 42 Cong., 2 Sess., Senate Report No. 41 (1872), especially Vols. III and V; United States Military Academy, *Twenty-Seventh Annual Reunion of the Association of Graduates of the United States Military Academy, at West Point, New York, June 11, 1896* (Saginaw, MI: Seemann & Peters, 1896); and the York County Historical Commission, "History of York County," in *Historical Properties of York County, South Carolina* (Rock Hill, SC: York County Historical Commission, 1995). These sources can be supplemented with various articles from the local newspaper, *The Yorkville Enquirer*, from 1871–1873. The court proceedings and the congressional report are especially valuable because they include transcripts of Merrill's testimony on the Klan. Probably the most detailed and perspicacious analysis of Merrill's activities in York County found in a secondary source is Jerry L. West, *The Reconstruction Ku Klux Klan in York County, South Carolina, 1865–1877* (Jefferson, NC: McFarland & Company, Inc., 2002).

Detailed background information on Major Merrill also can be difficult to locate. His military records and correspondence files are housed within the National Archives & Records Administration, and can be found at Merrill Military Files, M.103.C.B.1863 (Record Group 94). A good source on Merrill's Civil War experiences is Samuel Baird, *With Merrill's Cavalry: The Civil War Experiences of Samuel Baird, Second Missouri Cavalry, U.S.A.*, with notes and an introduction by Charles Annegan (San Marcos, CA: The Book Habit, 1981). As for Merrill's postwar experiences, especially details about the Lauffer controversy, the best source for information is Barry C. Johnson, *Custer, Reno, Merrill and the Lauffer Case: Some Warfare in "The Fighting Seventh"* (London: The Pilot Printing & Publicity Service on Behalf of the English Westerners' Society, 1971). Aside from these works, Merrill's role in exposing the Klan usually merits three or four pages in the comprehensive histories of the KKK referenced earlier.

Anyone who delves into the literature on the Ku Klux Klan and Reconstruction is well-advised to proceed with caution. Many sources are notoriously biased, and accuracy is not always assured. In the struggle for public memory of the tumultuous 1860s and 1870s, Klansmen were not the only participants to hide their motives and intentions behind masks.

INDEX

References to photographs are in *italics*.

261

200; and Ulysses S. Grant, 51–52

Rainey, Amzi, 174–76

Rainey, James. *See* Williams, Jim

Rainey, Samuel, 1

Randall, Samuel J., 234

Randolph, Benjamin F., 25

Rateree, John, 185

Rawlinson's Hotel, 142, 174

Reconstruction, xii, 67, 214, 245, 246;
congressional, 13, 111; end of, xi,
156, 187, 194, 200–3, 210, 212–13;
and the Grant administration,
62–73, 156, 187; and the Johnson
administration, 34–54; and the
Lincoln administration, 31–34;
origins of, 25–26, 31–47, 52–54,
244; presidential, 13, 34–54;
Southern resistance to, 16, 54,
64–65, 108–9, 114–15, 135,
139–40, 164, 225, 241–42

Reconstruction Act of 1867 (First), 45

Reconstruction Act of 1867 (Second),
45–46

Red Shirts, 211. *See also* Hampton,
Wade

Redcaps, 14

Reed, Richard B., 7–9, 12

Reid, John C., 207–8

Republican Party, 20, 24–25, 36, 43,
64, 66, 70–71, 86–87, 111–13, 115,
117–19, 122–23, 126, 141–42, 152,
156, 163–64, 166, 171, 174, 181,
183, 200–1, 204–13, 222–23, 232,
235

Riley, Stephney, 118

Robber barons, 214

Roberts, William H., 209–10

Romine, Mr. and Mrs. William B.,
9–10, 15–16, 21, 23

Rose, Edward, 122

Rose, Mrs. S. E. F., 7, 20–21, 23

Rose's Hotel, 2

Roundtree, Harriet, 74

Roundtree, Thomas, 74, 146, 198

Sapoch, Abraham, 117

Sapaugh, Elijah, 198

scalawags, ix, 10, 16, 46, 54, 117, 156,
241, 243

Schwerner, Mickey, ix

Schofield, John, 50

Scott, John, 72, 144

Scott, Robert K., 25, 67, 113–17, 119,
120, 121, 194; asks Grant
administration for assistance, 25, 68,
72–73, 119, 124, 126, 147; meets
with "best citizens" of York
County, 124, 126

Second Amendment, 177

Second Missouri Volunteer Cavalry
Regiment, 89–90, 92–93

Second U.S. Cavalry, 232

Seventh U.S. Cavalry, 4–5, 75–76,
95–96, 100, 126–27, 136, 139,
145, 225, 227–30, 232. *See also*
Custer, George Armstrong; Merrill,
Lewis

Seymour, Horatio, 52, 61

sharecropping, 109–11

Shellabarger, Samuel, 69

Sherman, William T., 1, 48, 75, 101,
126

Sickles, Daniel, 167, 206–8

Simkins, Francis, 123

Simmons, William Joseph "Doc," x,
250–51, *252*

Sixth Massachusetts Regiment, 166

Slaton, John, 247

Slaughterhouse cases, 200–1

slavery, 1, 32, 39, 41, 52, 107, 110,
112, 134, 200, 212–13

Smith, Andrew J., 75

Sneed, W., 118

Snyder, William H., 142

ABOUT THE AUTHOR

J. Michael Martinez currently works as a corporate attorney and also teaches political science as a part-time faculty member at Kennesaw State University in Kennesaw, Georgia. A member of the bar in Georgia and South Carolina, Martinez earned a B.A. in philosophy and political science from Furman University, a law degree from Emory University, an M.P.A. from the University of Georgia, an M.S. in public policy from the Georgia Institute of Technology, and a Ph.D. in political science from Georgia State University. In addition to publishing more than a dozen articles in academic journals and popular history magazines, he has coedited and contributed chapters to three academic texts: *Ethics and Character: The Pursuit of Democratic Virtues* (1998); *Confederate Symbols in the Contemporary South* (2000); and *The Leviathan's Choice: Capital Punishment in the Twenty-First Century* (2002). His most recent book, *Life and Death in Civil War Prisons* (2004), traces the parallel lives of two Civil War prisoners. Martinez lives in Monroe, Georgia, with his wife and family.